IMAGES
of Sports

BASEBALL IN TAMPA BAY

IMAGES
of Sports

BASEBALL IN
TAMPA BAY

A.M. de Quesada Jr.

ARCADIA
PUBLISHING

ISBN 978-0-7385-0058-4

Published by Arcadia Publishing
Charleston, South Carolina

Printed in the United States of America

Library of Congress Catalog Card Number: 99067078

For all general information contact Arcadia Publishing at:
Telephone 843-853-2070
Fax 843-853-0044
E-mail sales@arcadiapublishing.com
For customer service and orders:
Toll-Free 1-888-313-2665

Visit us on the Internet at www.arcadiapublishing.com

A Dedication to Mr. Baseball

At the beginning, this project was intended to be a joint effort between Vincent Luisi and myself. In the very early stages of this project, however, Vinnie, as his friends and I call him, suffered from a heart attack and had to pull away from any strenuous projects, including this one. Since he would have loved to finish this project on a topic so dear to him, I am dedicating this book to Vinnie, who continued to lend advice—not because of any commitments, but because of his love for the game. Best of health for the future from your old friend.

Contents

ACKNOWLEDGMENTS

I would like to thank the following individuals and institutions for their assistance in the making of this book: Andrew Espolita; Al Lopez; Angie and Patrick Mantiega, *La Gaceta*; the National Baseball Library, Cooperstown, New York; the Baseball Hall of Fame, Cooperstown, New York; the Florida State Archives; Paul Dosal, El Circulo Cubano de Tampa; El Museo del Circulo Cubano; Don Spivey, the Pinellas County Historical Museum; Vincent Luisi, director, the Dunedin Historical Museum; Ron G. Hickox, the Veterans Memorial Museum; Special Collections, University of South Florida; the Oldsmar Cultural Affairs Department and the Oldsmar Public Library; Special Collections Room, Lakeland Public Library; and the Tampa-Hillsborough County Public Library System. The following baseball clubs (minor and major leagues) have also enthusiastically contributed material for this book: the Dunedin Blue Jays; the Tampa Yankees; Bill Veeck, the Tampa Bay Devil Rays; the St. Petersburg Devil Rays; and the Clearwater Phillies. Without the help of all mentioned, this book would not have been possible.

INTRODUCTION

Baseball is as much a part of the American fabric as the flag itself. Tampa Bay's interest in the sport spans from baseball's early beginnings to the city winning a major league franchise in the last decade of the 20th century. Tampa Bay has hosted more major league spring training games than any other region in the continental United States.

The sport began to take root in Florida in the years following the Civil War. Returning Union and Confederate veterans brought back the game learned during the lulls between battles and periods of boredom. Baseball clubs began to be formed, and traveling exhibitions were taken from town to town. In time, towns began organizing teams to compete against neighboring communities. Tampa formed a team when the first short-lived Florida State League began in 1892. By the time of the Spanish-American War, baseball had become a natural part of the American culture. Soldiers who boarded the ships from Tampa to invade Cuba took the game with them and introduced it to the Cubans during their occupation of the island. Eventually, with America's gunboat diplomacy in the early part of the 20th century, baseball was spread to America's far-flung colonies.

The first spring training game held in the Tampa Bay area was between the Chicago Cubs and the Cuban Athletics, an amateur Cuban championship team, in front of a crowd of 6,000 at Plant Field on February 26, 1913. The Cubs triumphed over the Cubans by a score of 4-2. It wasn't until March 26, 1914, that the first game between two major league teams was held in Tampa Bay. The Grapefruit League was established in Florida to provide teams with a five-week schedule of exhibition games. The Chicago Cubs played against the St. Louis Browns at Plant Field, and the Cubs won, 3-2, over the Browns.

The Chicago Cubs moved their spring training from New Orleans to Tampa in 1913, and the following year the St. Louis Browns came to St. Petersburg to set up their spring training operation. Tampa soon became the spring training home for six major league clubs: the Chicago Cubs, 1913–1916; the Boston Red Sox, 1919; the Washington Senators, 1920–1929; the Detroit Tigers, 1930; the Cincinnati Reds, 1931–1942 and 1946–1987; the Chicago White Sox, 1954–1959; and the New York Yankees, 1996–present. St. Petersburg boasted eight clubs that made the city their spring home: the St. Louis Browns, 1914; the Philadelphia Phillies, 1915–1918; the Boston Braves, 1922–1937; the New York Yankees, 1925–1942, 1946–1950, and 1952–1961; the St. Louis Cardinals, 1938–1942 and 1946–1997; the New York Giants, 1951; the New York Mets, 1962–1987; and the Baltimore Orioles, 1993–1995.

Both St. Petersburg and Tampa formed local teams for Florida State when the minor league was created in 1919. In St. Petersburg there were the Saints, 1920–1927; the Cardinals, 1966–1996; the Pelicans, 1989–1990; and the Devil Rays, 1996–present. Tampa had the Smokers, 1919–1927; the Tarpons, 1957–1988; and the Yankees, 1990–present. The Smokers had also played in the Southeastern League as the Tampa Krewes in 1928 and from 1929 to 1930. The Smokers team was later recreated to play in the Florida International League from 1946 to 1954, when the team was finally disbanded.

Tampa Bay's dream for a team of its own came true in 1995, when, at a meeting of baseball owners in West Palm Beach, the Tampa Bay Devil Rays and the Arizona Diamondbacks were voted in as the 13th and 14th expansion teams in major league history. By the following month, the new team had worked out a deal with the city of St. Petersburg for the lease of the Thunderdome, later to be known as the Tropicana Field. At the inaugural game in Tropicana Field on March 31, 1998, the first pitch was thrown by Wilson Alvarez of the Tampa Bay Devil Rays to Brian Hunter of the Detroit Tigers. The final score was Tigers 11, Devil Rays 6.

The collection of images found in this book span a century of the sport in the Tampa Bay area. Not only do the photographs show early teams but also focus on those who pioneered the sport in the area. From children to women, African Americans to Latinos, baseball crosses over every barrier and unites all. Baseball is more than just a game, it is our American heritage.

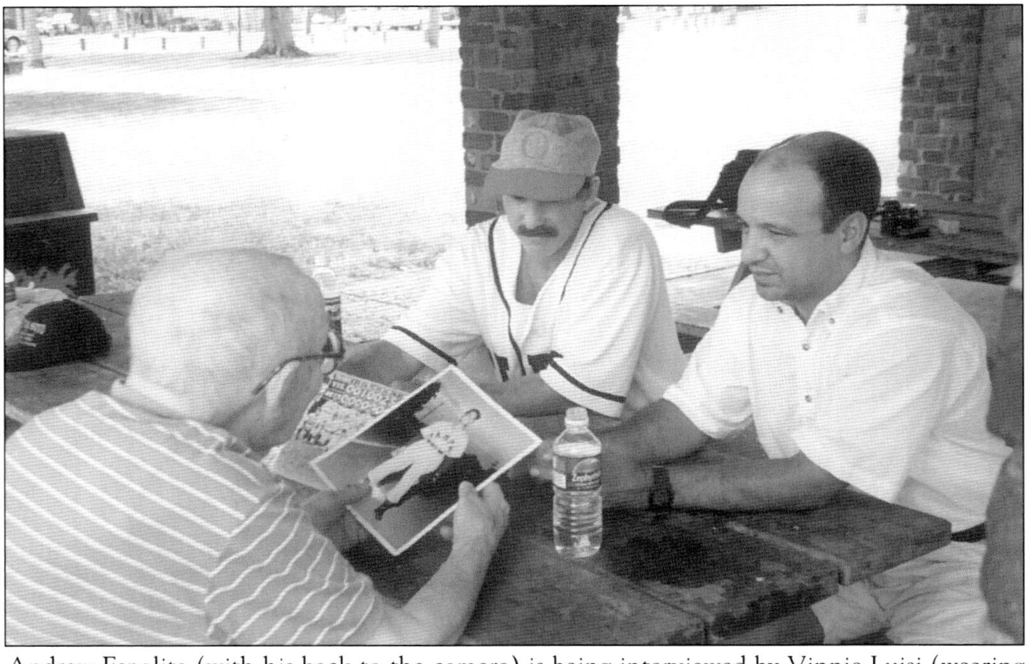

Andrew Espolita (with his back to the camera) is being interviewed by Vinnie Luisi (wearing cap), Paul Dosal, and Alejandro de Quesada (taking photograph) in MacFarlane Park, West Tampa, on June 22, 1998. Espolita began playing baseball in 1913 and led a very productive life, most of it around the game. Photographs from Espolita's albums are scattered throughout this work.

One

FROM TOWN BALL TO CITY LEAGUE

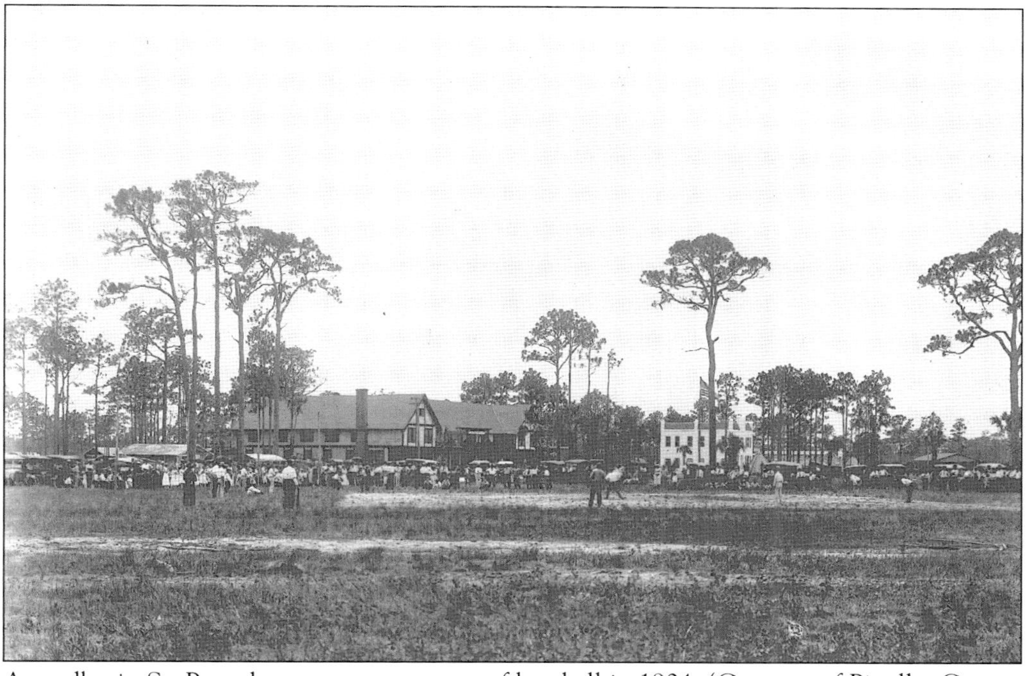

A sandlot in St. Petersburg caters to a game of baseball in 1904. (Courtesy of Pinellas County Historical Museum.)

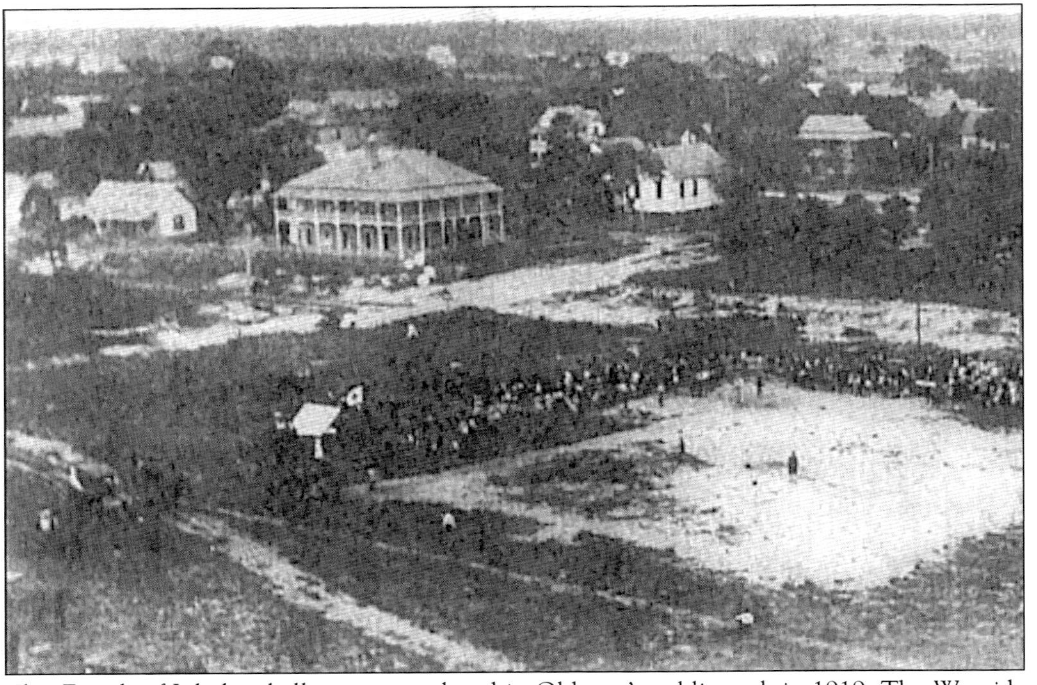

This Fourth of July baseball game was played in Oldsmar's public park in 1919. The Wayside Inn is in the background. (Courtesy of Tampa-Hillsborough County Public Library System.)

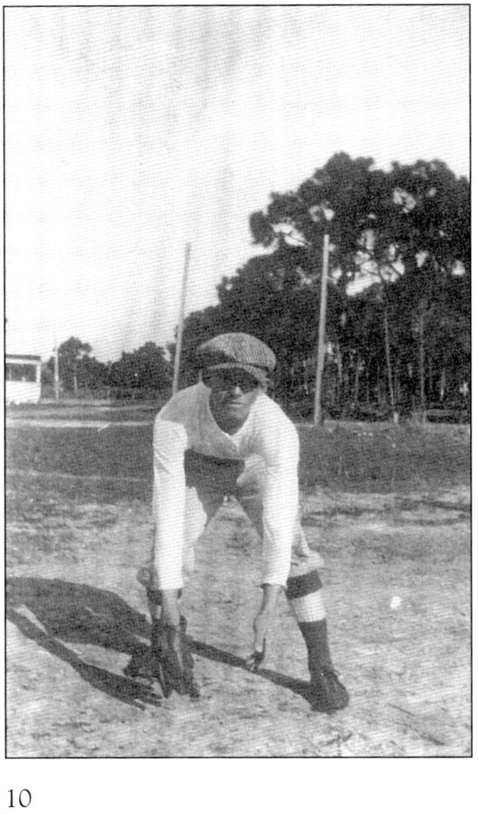

Prior to the construction of Dunedin's Grant Field in the 1930s, young boys used a sandlot baseball field near the present-day location of Morton-Plant Mease Hospital. Here, a Dunedin youngster takes ground field practice before a game begins in the 1920s. (Courtesy of Dunedin Historical Museum.)

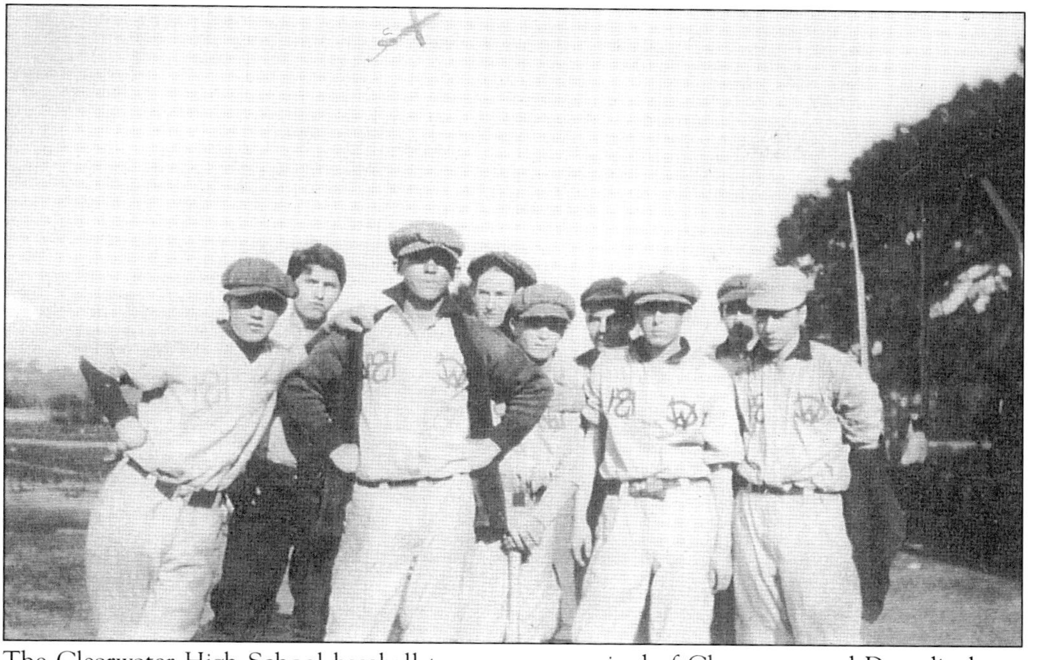

The Clearwater High School baseball team was comprised of Clearwater and Dunedin boys. Due to the fact that Dunedin did not have a high school until the 1960s, many of the young boys of Dunedin played in Clearwater uniforms. Notice that the negative for this print was reversed, showing the "CW" backwards, *c.* 1920s. (Courtesy of Dunedin Historical Museum.)

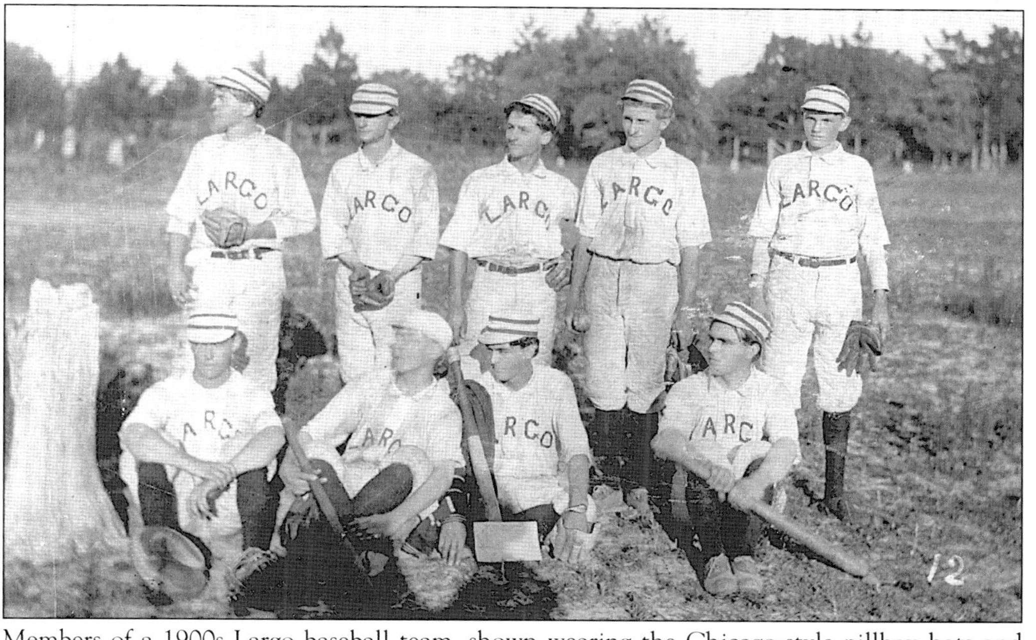

Members of a 1900s Largo baseball team, shown wearing the Chicago-style pillbox hats and collared shirts, pose in a winning stance after a successful game against another local team. Notice that the center player in the bottom row displays the winning score card. (Courtesy of Pinellas County Historical Museum.)

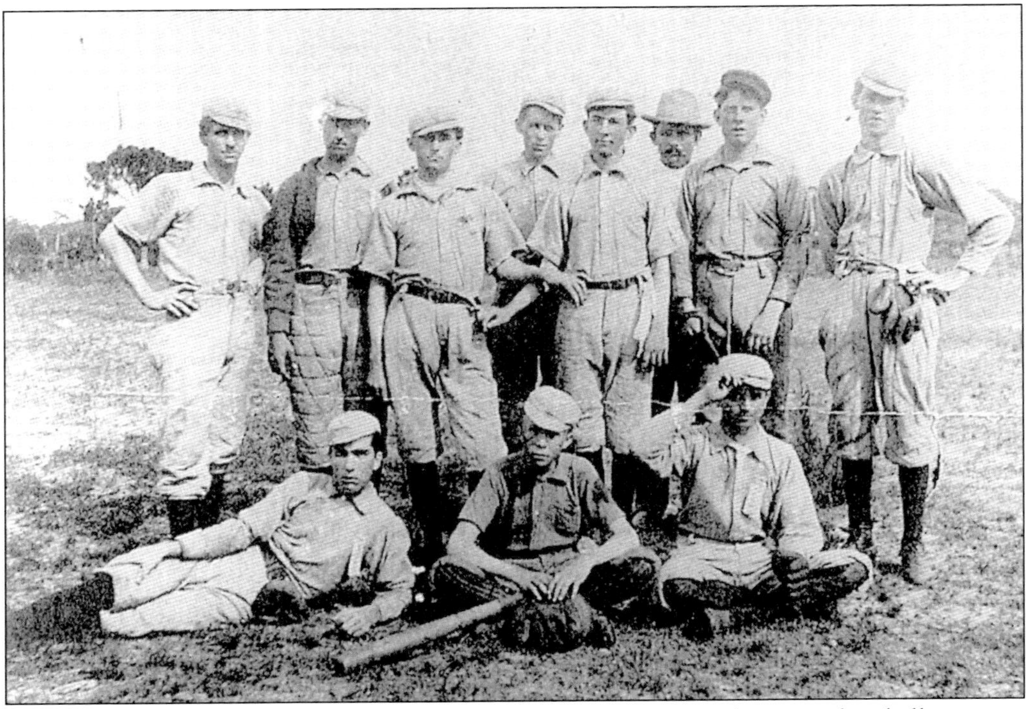

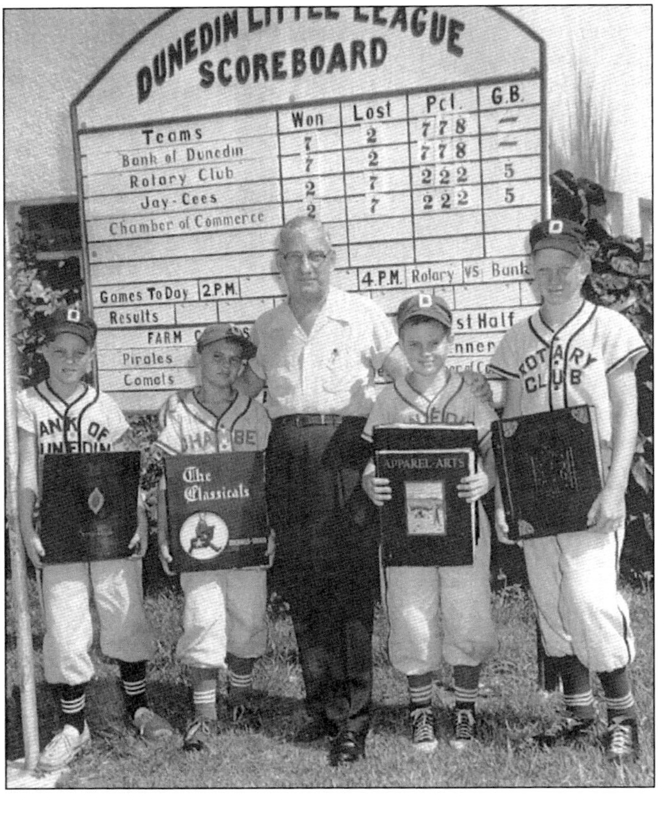

A Clearwater baseball team posed for this photograph about 1914. Notice the "PC," representing Pinellas County, on some of the players' shirts. Pinellas County had just formally separated from Hillsborough County in 1912. (Courtesy of Pinellas County Historical Museum.)

Edward H. Eckert (center) is flanked by Little Leaguers from teams sponsored by the Bank of Dunedin, the chamber of commerce, the jaycees, and the rotary club. Little League baseball was started in Dunedin in 1954 by the Dunedin Jaycees. The four teams formed by the above organizations played their games at Fisher Field. A second league, called the American League, was formed in 1960 and played at Grant Field. (Courtesy of Dunedin Historical Museum.)

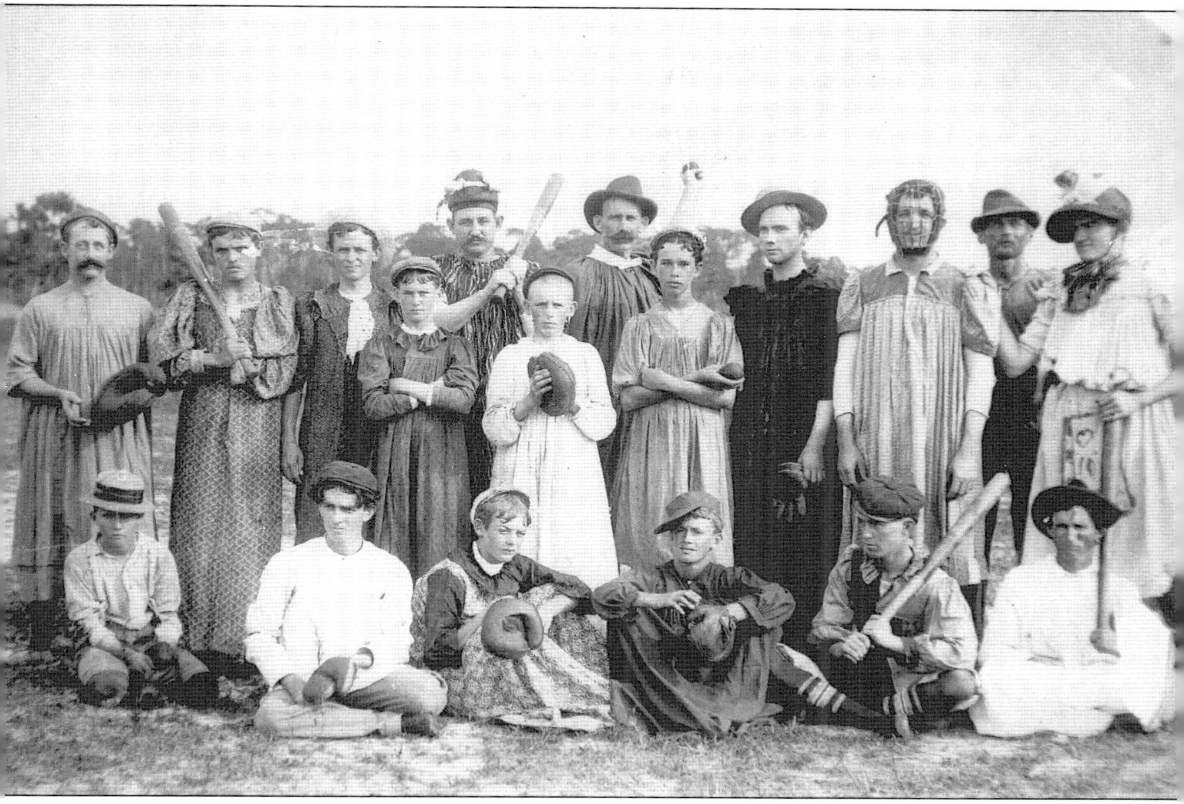

Members of a Clearwater baseball team enjoy a day of ball games while wearing women's clothing to amuse the crowd of spectators, *c.* 1895. This was not an unusual practice by local teams, as other teams would perform similar stunts to attract crowds to the games. (Courtesy of Pinellas County Historical Museum.)

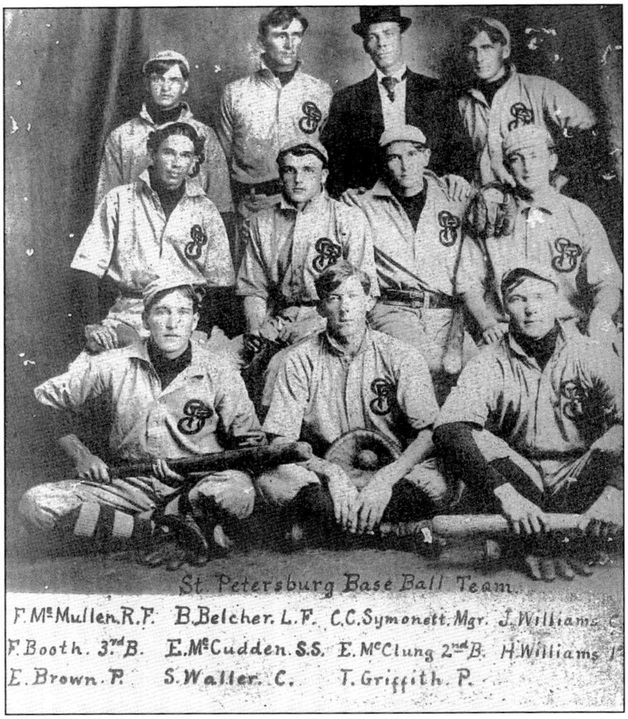

An early 1900s view of a St. Petersburg team shows them wearing the logo "SP" on their shirt pockets. If one were to take notice of the names under the photo, one would see that many pioneering families in Pinellas County had young boys who were interested in the game of baseball. (Courtesy of Pinellas County Historical Museum.)

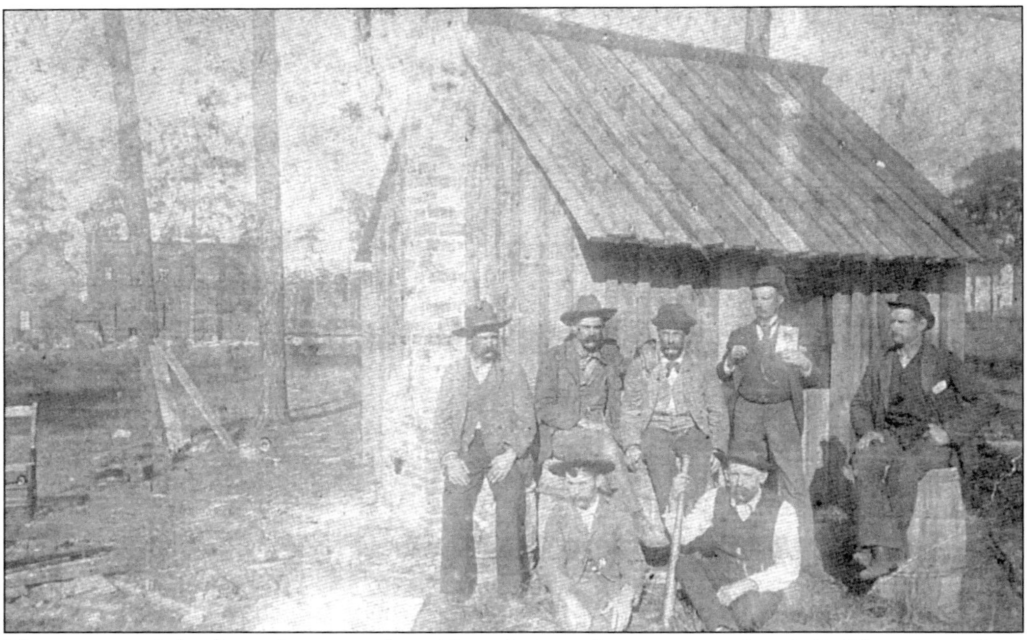

This is one of the first photos to show Dunedin's early interest in baseball. The photo from the early 1880s shows seven team members posing after a game of "townball." Captain Fred Emerson (top row, second from right) displays the scorecard. Home plate is to the left of the group, and team members on the bottom row hold the bat. (Courtesy of Dunedin Historical Museum.)

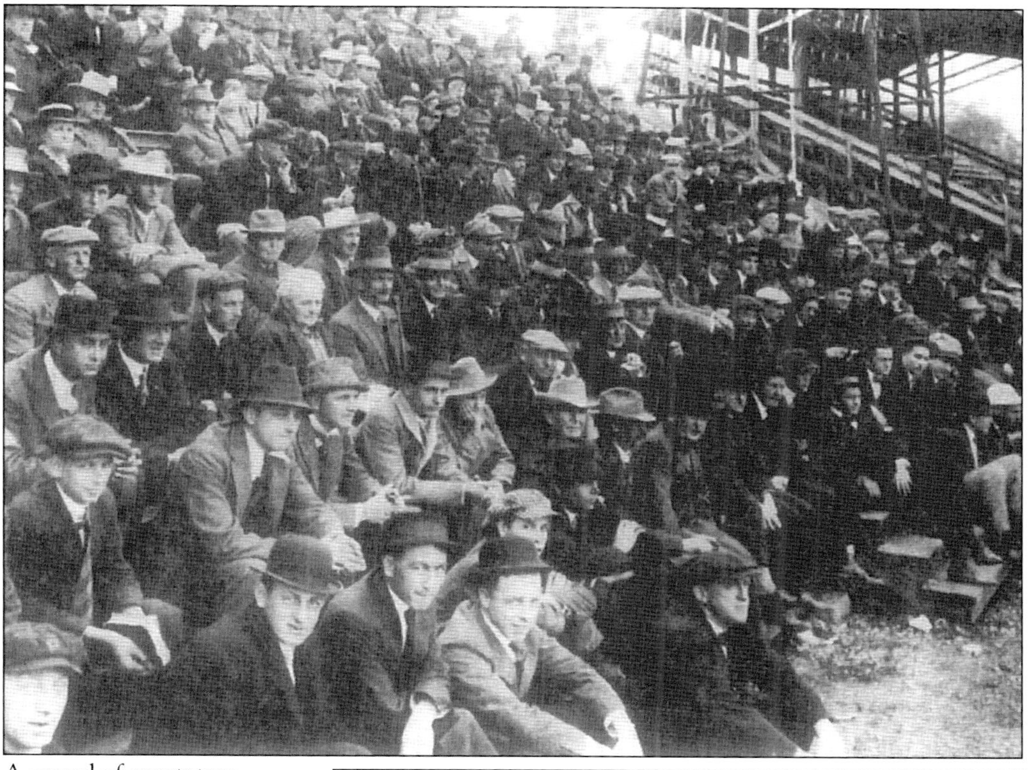

A crowd of spectators watches a game between the Philadelphia Phillies and the St. Louis Browns in St. Petersburg, c. 1915. (Courtesy of Pinellas County Historical Museum.)

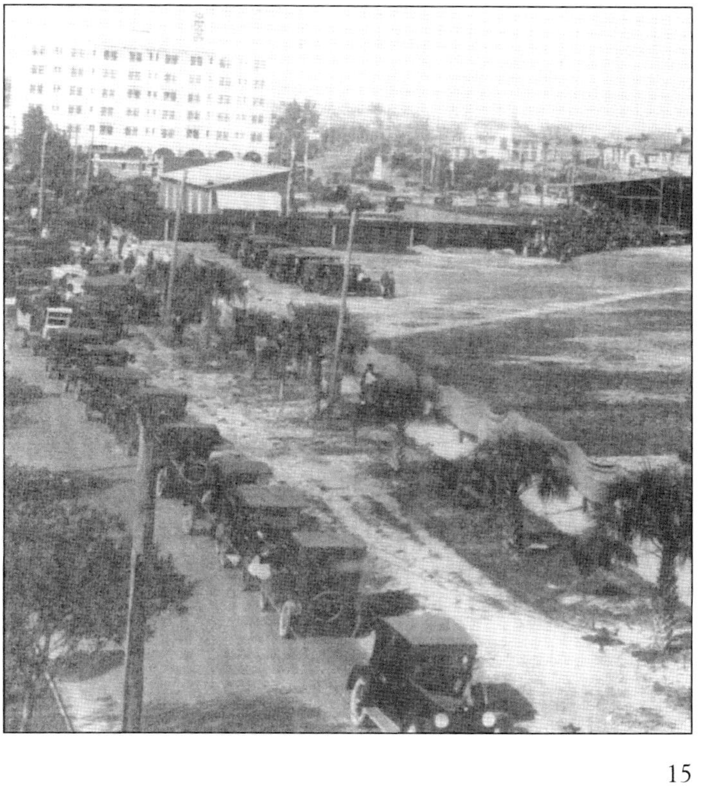

Waterfront Field in St. Petersburg was used by the Boston Braves during the 1920s. (Courtesy of Pinellas County Historical Museum.)

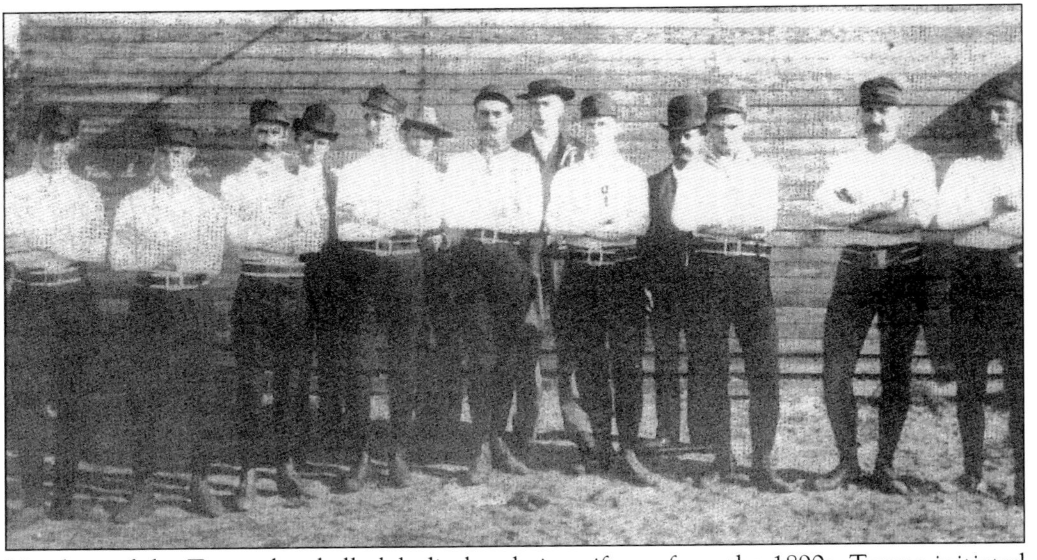

Members of the Tampa baseball club display their uniforms from the 1890s. Tampa initiated baseball clubs starting in the early 1880s, and many young boys from prominent Tampa families participated in the game. In this photo, Samuel Lowry is fourth from the left. (Courtesy of Special Collections, University of South Florida.)

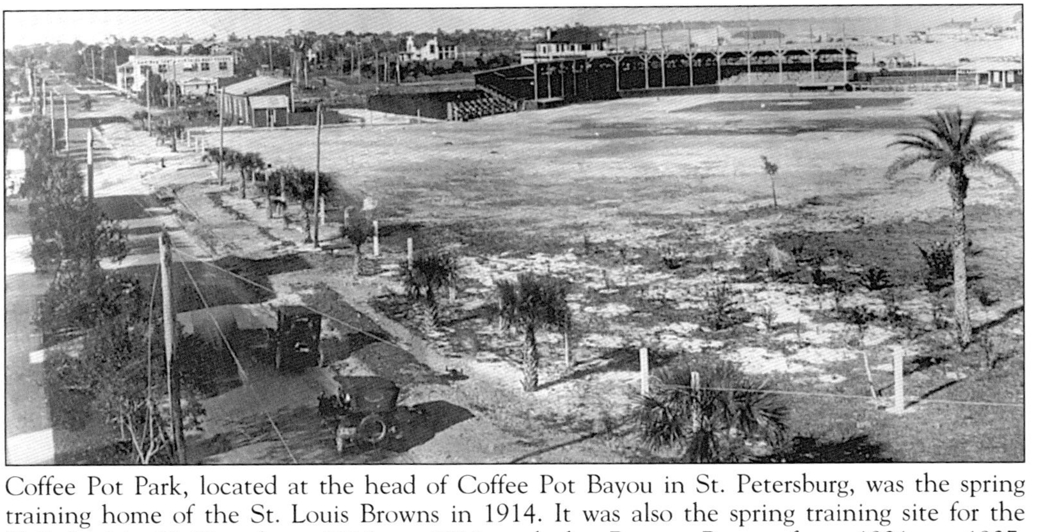

Coffee Pot Park, located at the head of Coffee Pot Bayou in St. Petersburg, was the spring training home of the St. Louis Browns in 1914. It was also the spring training site for the Philadelphia Phillies from 1915 to 1918 and the Boston Braves from 1921 to 1937. The scoreboard measured only 3 feet high and was located on the old plank fence in the outfield. This photo dates to *c.* 1918. (Courtesy of Pinellas County Historical Museum.)

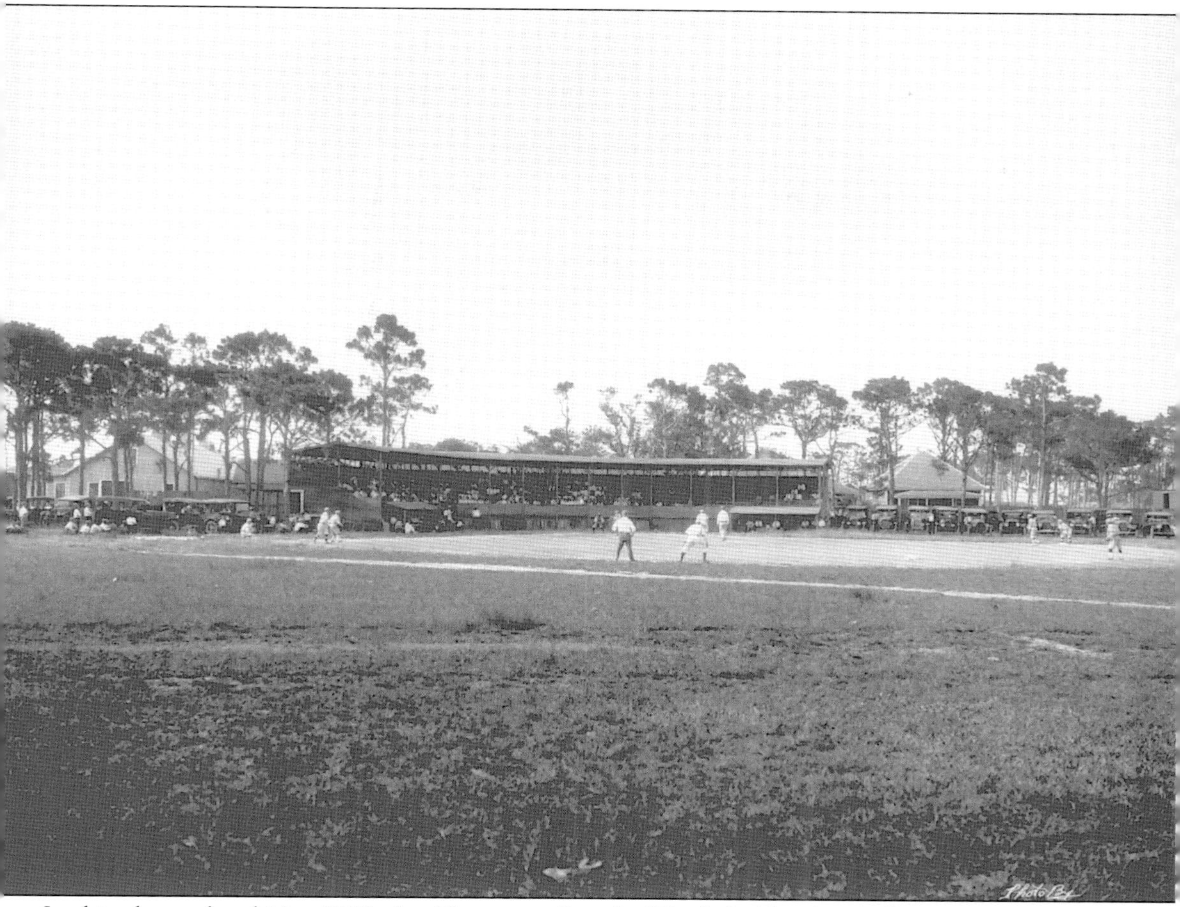

In this photo, dated May 1922, the Clearwater Board of Trade holds a baseball demonstration to help promote baseball in Clearwater. In 1924, a relocated Florida State franchise team called the Daytona Beach Islanders became the Clearwater Pelicans. (Courtesy of Tampa-Hillsborough County Public Library System.)

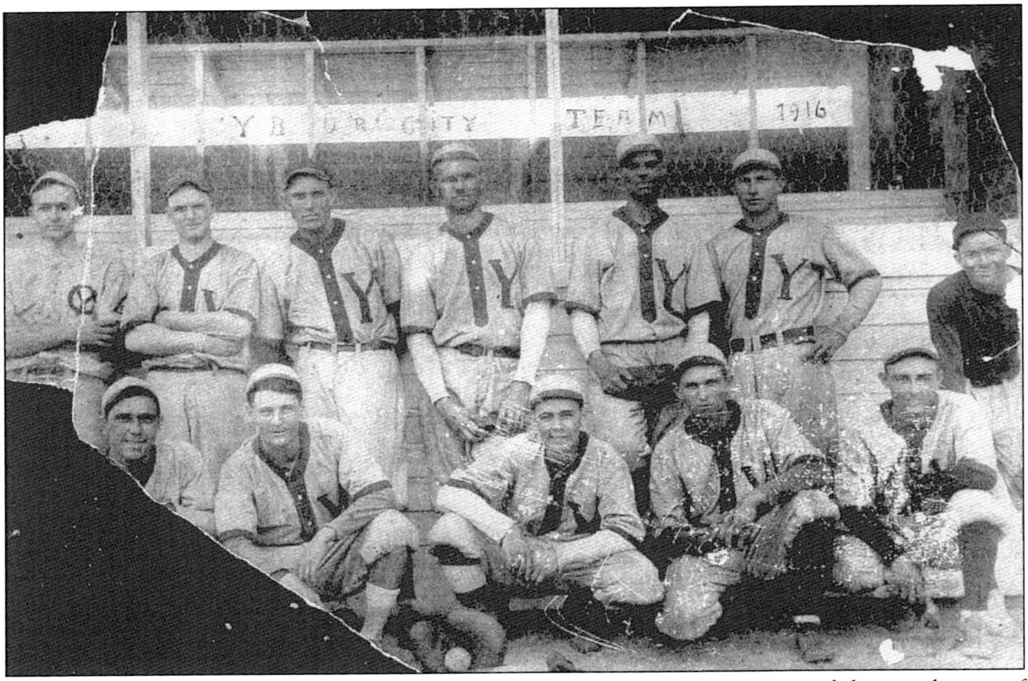

This is a rare 1916 photo of one of the earliest teams in Ybor City. Many of the employees of the cigar factories (the majority of whom were of Cuban, Spanish, and Italian heritage) would participate on company teams. Notice that the emblem on most of the shirts was a large "Y," but one team member in the top row on the far right has a "Y" within a circle on his shirt pocket. (Courtesy of Andrew Espolita.)

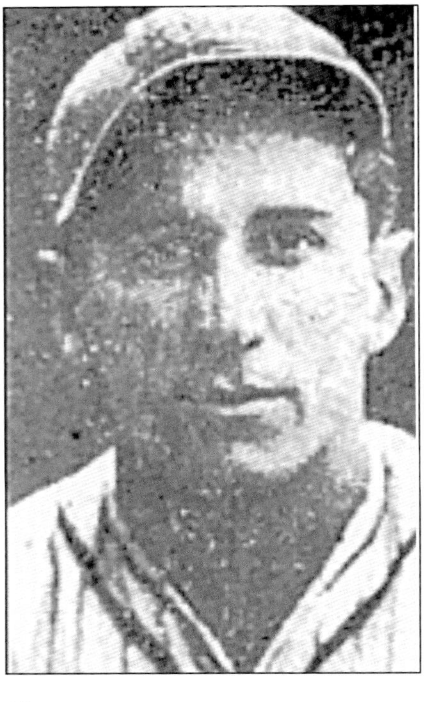

Alfonso Raymond Lopez (a.k.a. Al Lopez) was a product of Ybor City's sandlot baseball teams. Born on August 20, 1908, Al was the first Tampanian and Florida native to make the major leagues. He was elected to the Baseball Hall of Fame in 1977. This image of Al Lopez was taken in 1930. (Courtesy of *La Gaceta*.)

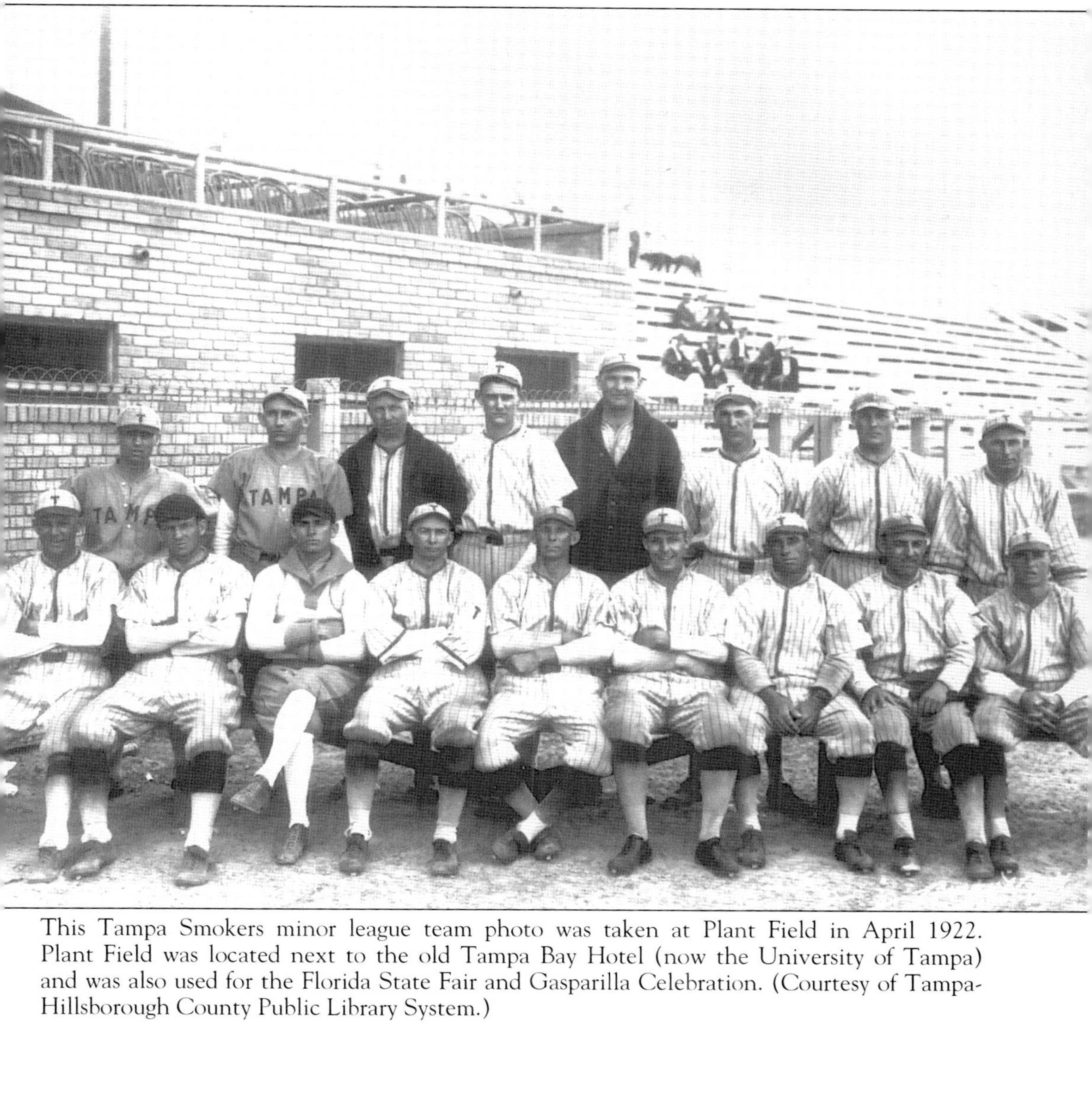

This Tampa Smokers minor league team photo was taken at Plant Field in April 1922. Plant Field was located next to the old Tampa Bay Hotel (now the University of Tampa) and was also used for the Florida State Fair and Gasparilla Celebration. (Courtesy of Tampa-Hillsborough County Public Library System.)

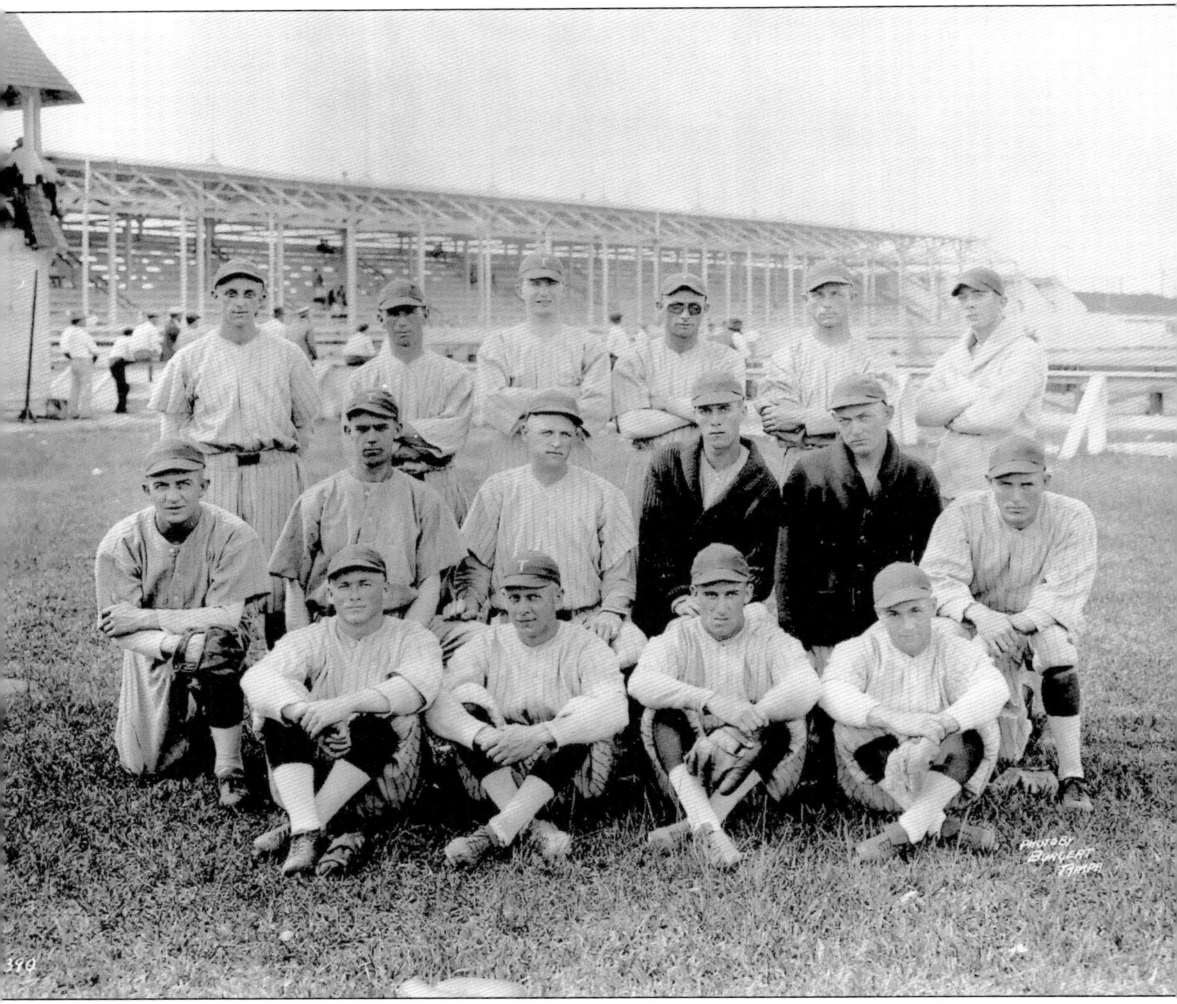

The Tampa Smokers used Plant Field for their home team games. Notice the color variation of uniforms and hats from their 1922 photograph. The section of uncovered stands in the far distance to the right was the "colored" section and was reserved for African-American spectators during the days of Jim Crow in the South. (Courtesy of Tampa-Hillsborough County Public Library System.)

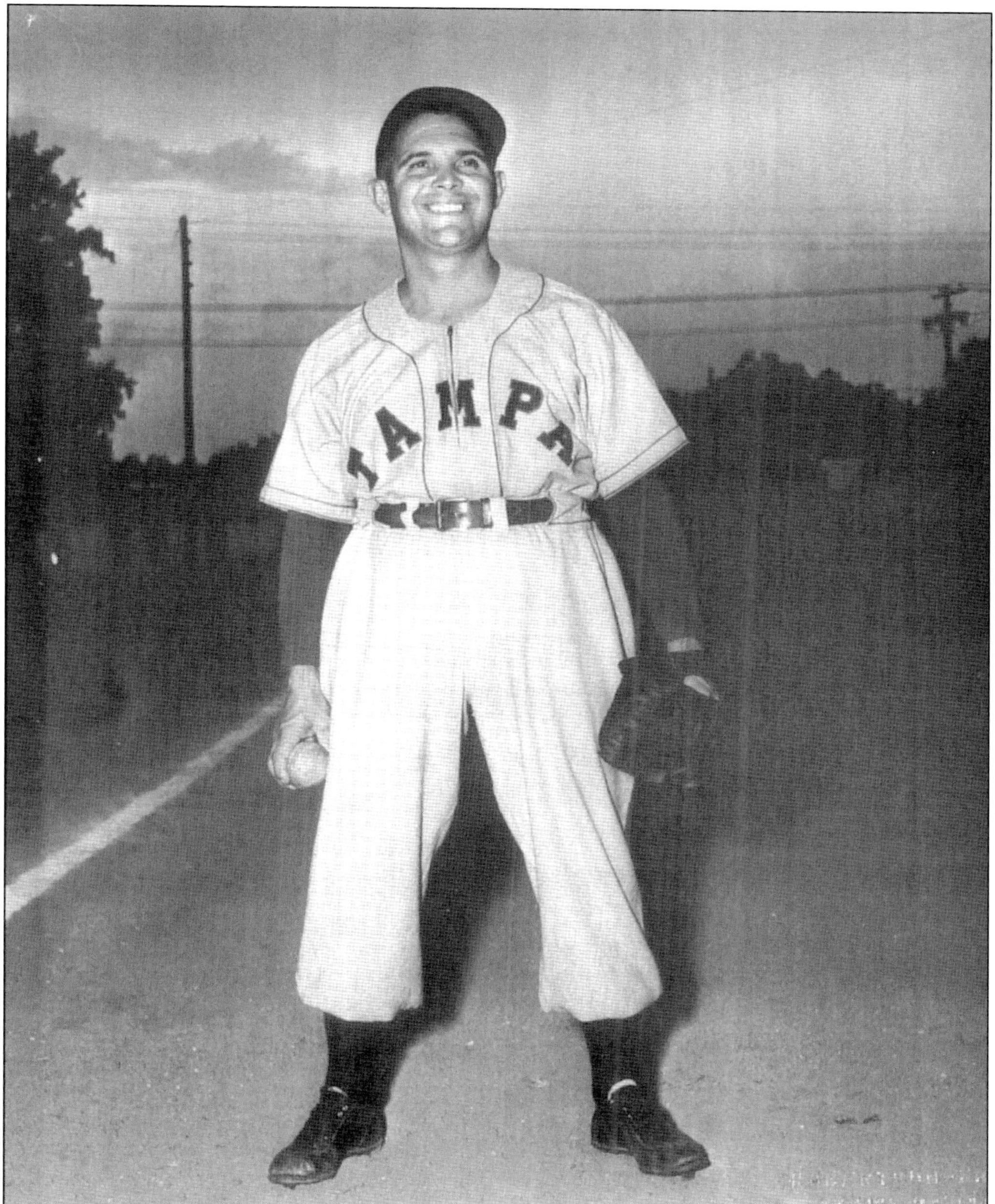

Andrew Espolita was a former member of the Tampa Smokers. He played with stars such as Al Lopez and taught players such as Tony La Russa the techniques and rules of the game. In the 1920s and 1930s, Andrew was also a member of the Pan-American ball team that traveled to Central and South America for many competitive games. He is considered by many to be one of the pioneers of baseball in Tampa Bay. (Courtesy of Andrew Espolita.)

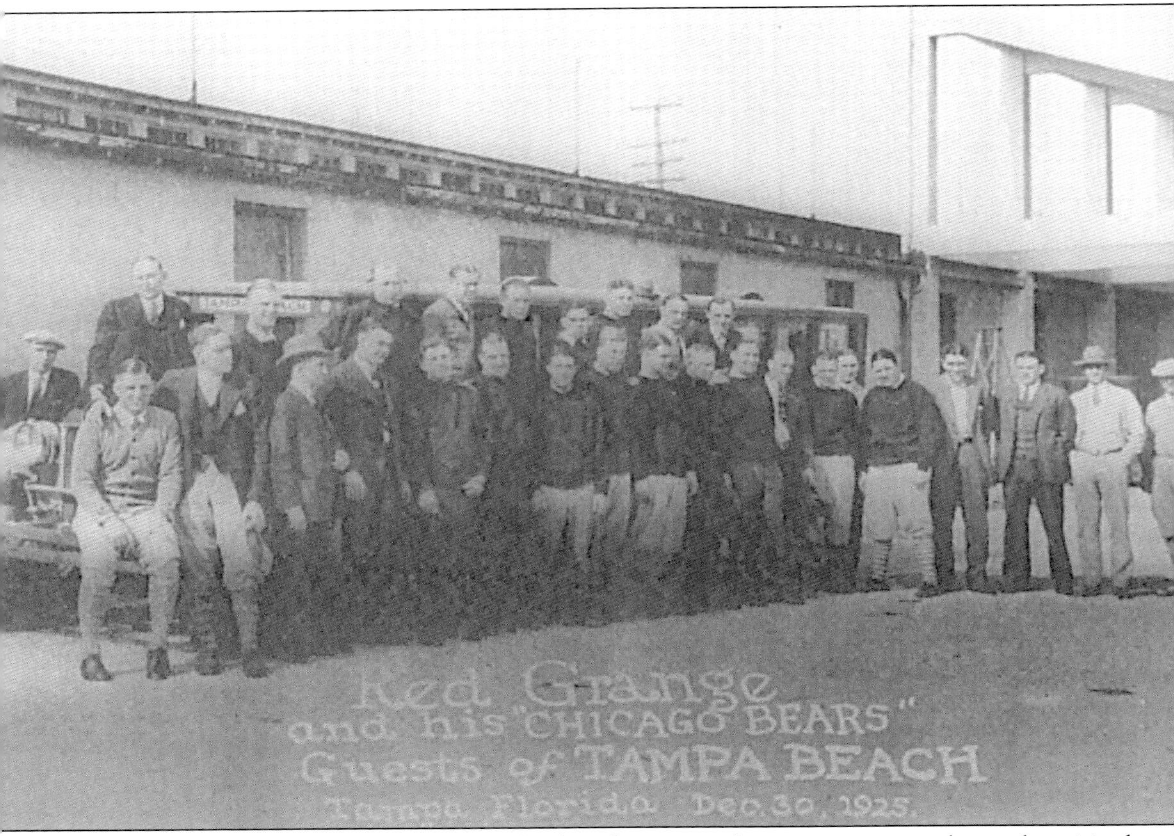

Though baseball is the topic of this book, other teams from various sports have also visited Tampa Bay. Most notably, Red Grange and his Chicago Bears football team visited Tampa as guests of Tampa Beach. The team members are photographed on the grounds of Plant Field on December 30, 1925. (Courtesy of Tampa-Hillsborough County Public Library System.)

Two

Youth Baseball and Little League

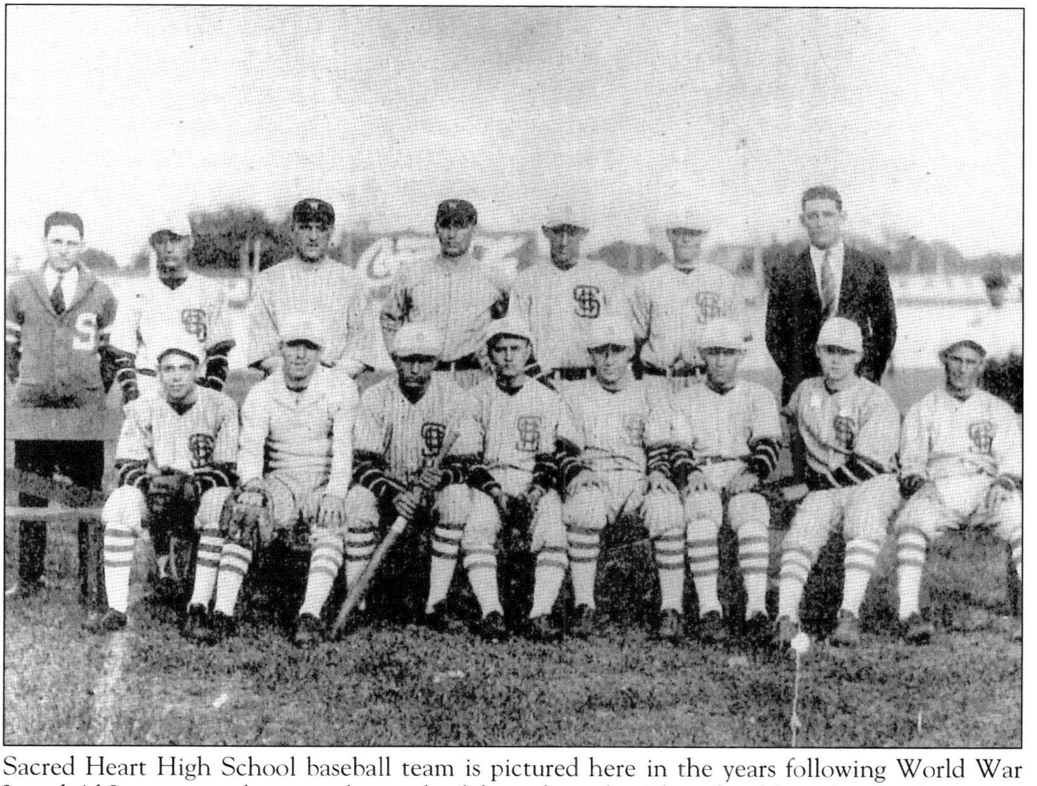

Sacred Heart High School baseball team is pictured here in the years following World War I, and Al Lopez is in the second row, third from the right. The school later became known as Jesuit High School. (Courtesy of Special Collections, University of South Florida.)

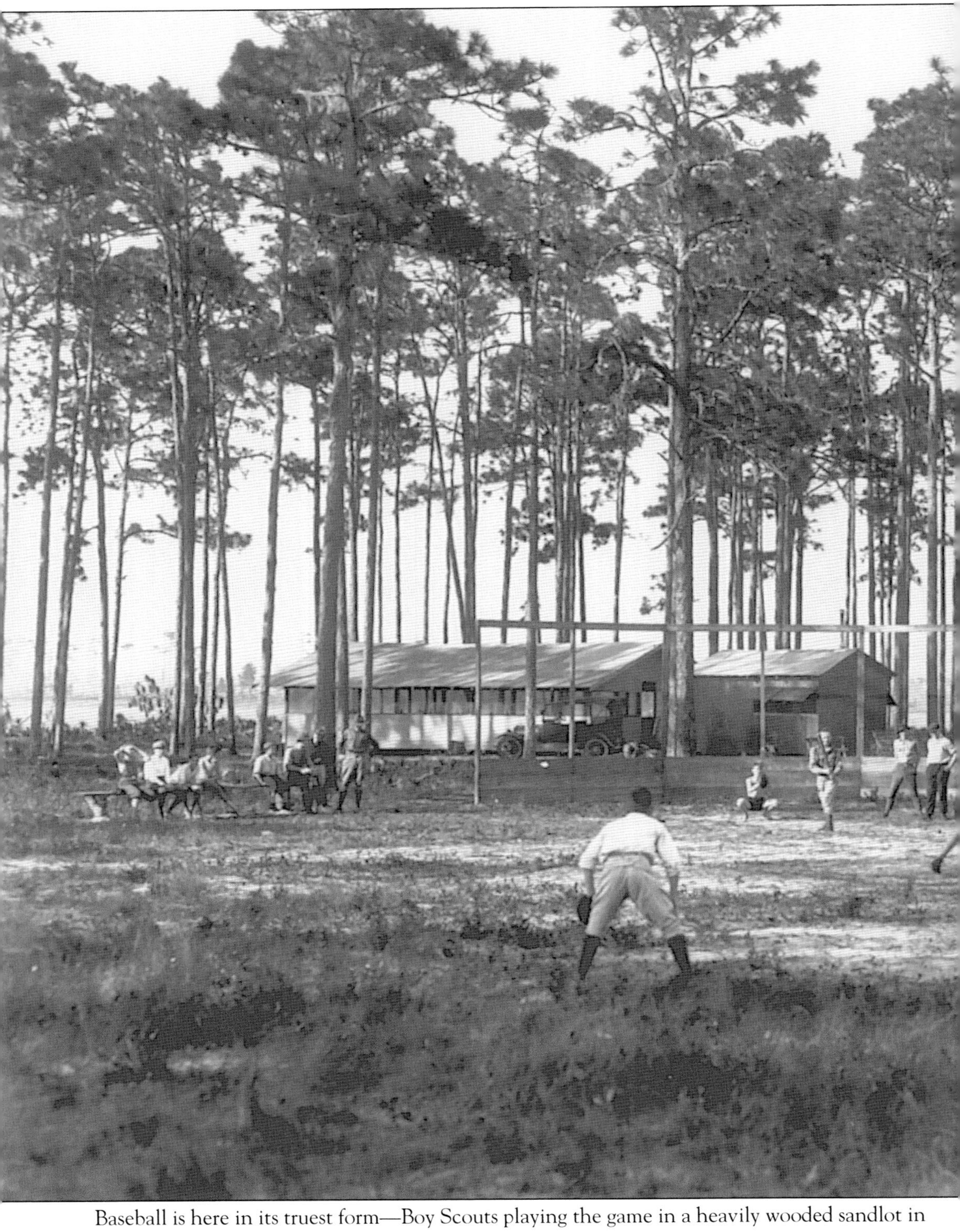

Baseball is here in its truest form—Boy Scouts playing the game in a heavily wooded sandlot in

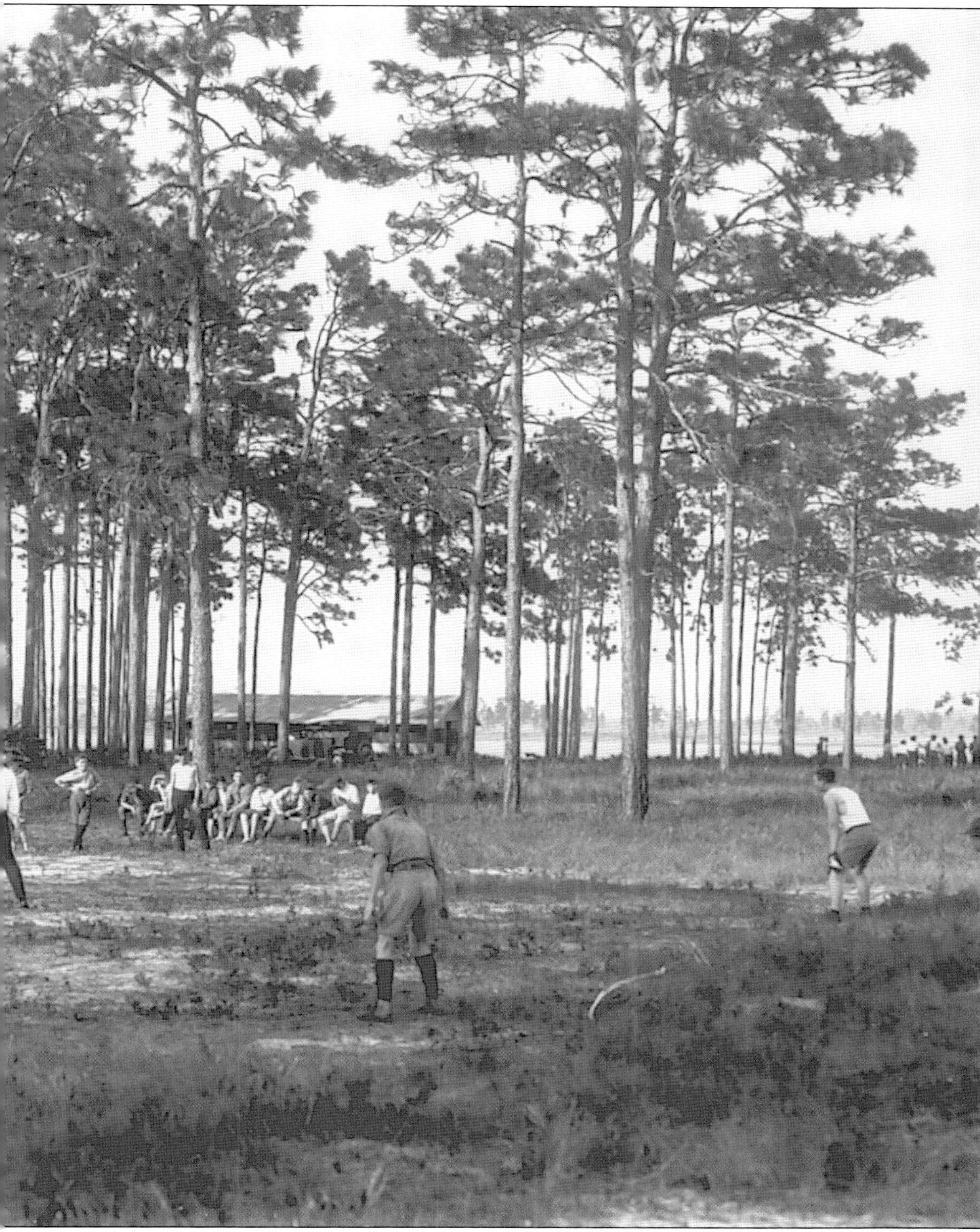

1921. (Courtesy of Tampa-Hillsborough County Public Library System.)

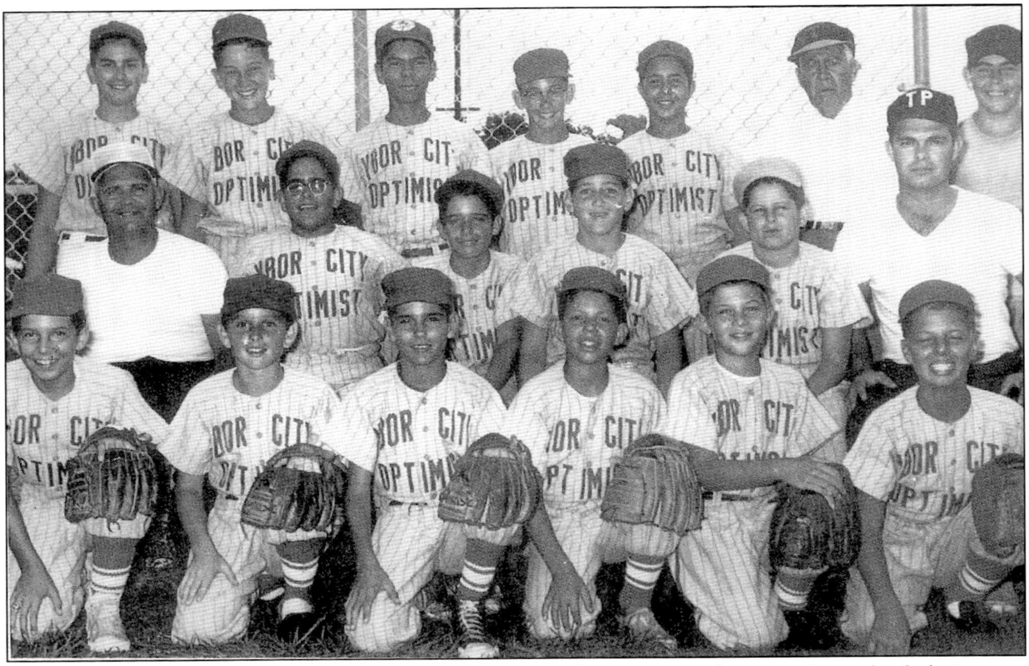

Since the founding of Little League in 1939, many future major leaguers have had their start on local Little League teams. Seen here are members of the Ybor City Optimist Club All-Stars, who traveled to Miami for a three-game series in 1959. The team's manager, Andrew Espolita, is on the far left of the middle row. (Courtesy of *La Gaceta*.)

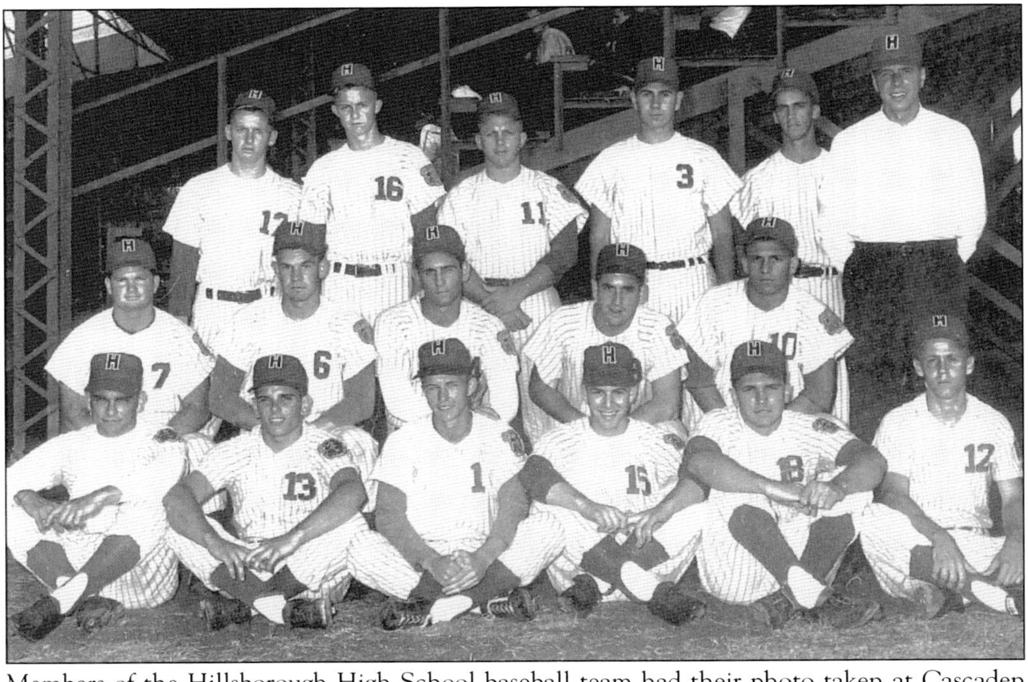

Members of the Hillsborough High School baseball team had their photo taken at Cascaden Park in Ybor City in March 1961. (Courtesy of *La Gaceta*.)

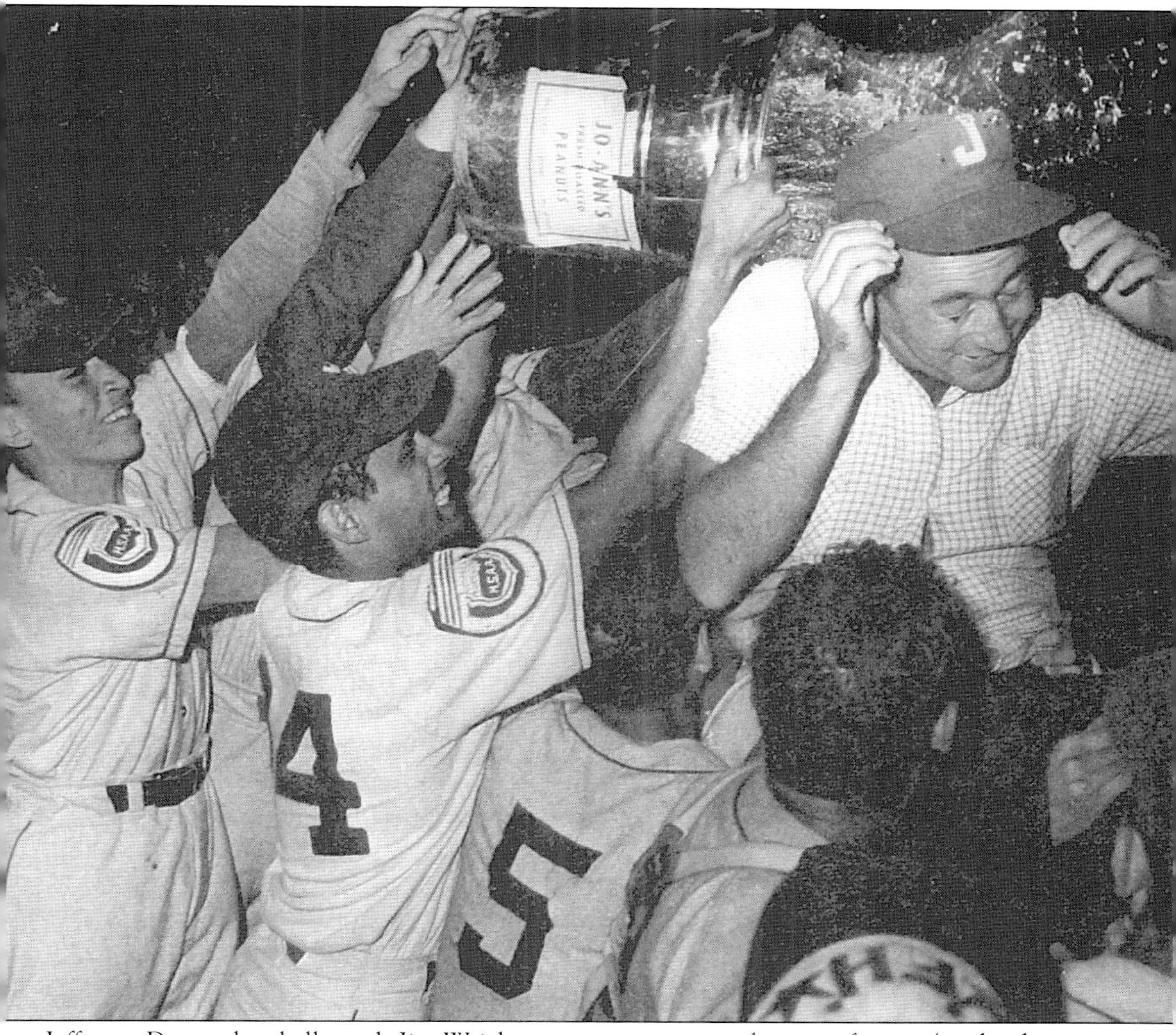

Jefferson Dragon baseball coach Jim Wright gets an appropriate dousing of water (in the days before the dousing of the winning coach with Gatorade) by his players after the Dragons won the right to play in the state baseball tournament by defeating Chamberlain High School. The photo was taken *c.* April 25, 1962. Tony La Russa, former Tampanian and Oakland baseball manager, now the manager of the St. Louis Cardinals, played on this Jefferson High School team. (Courtesy of *La Gaceta.*)

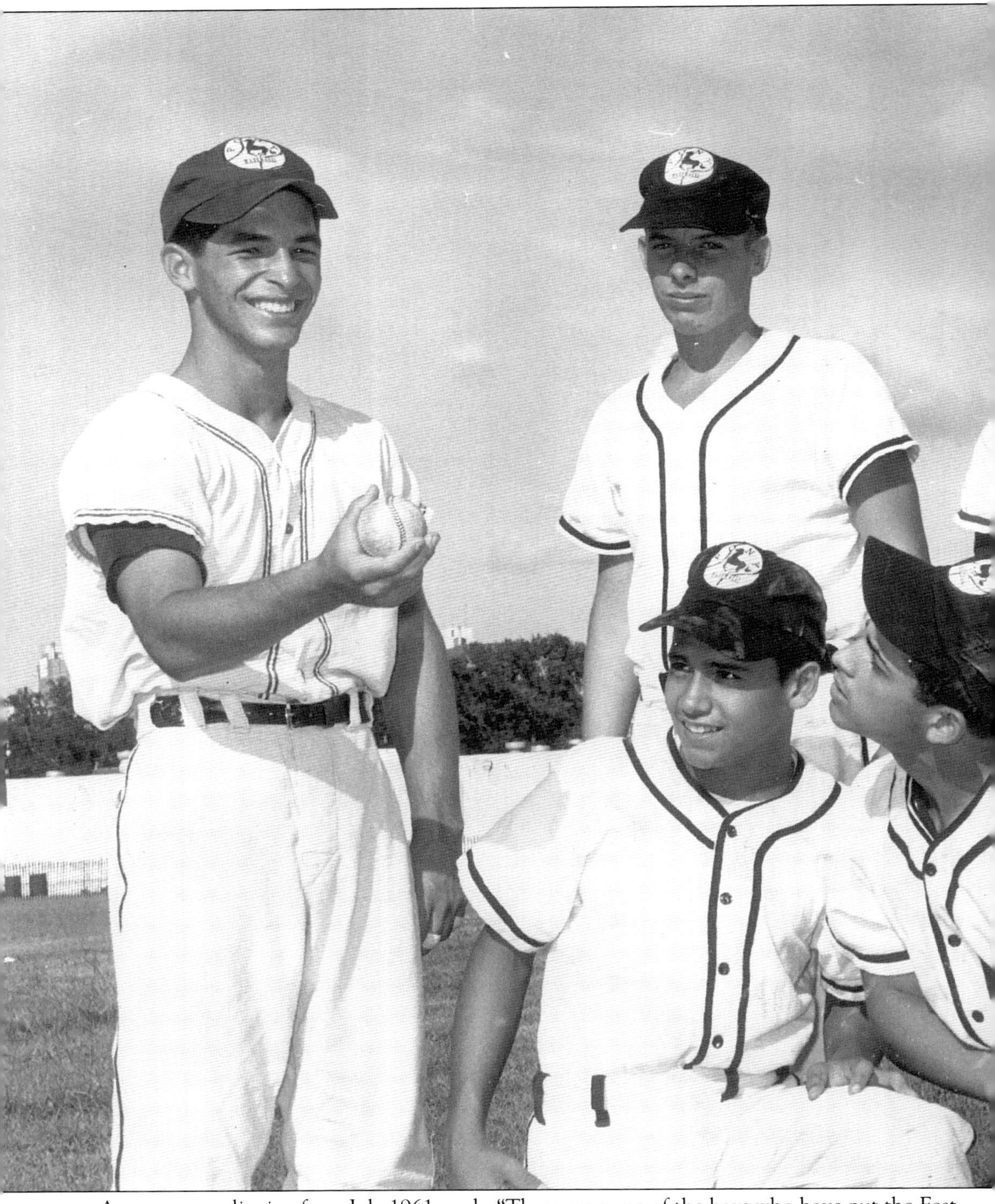

A newspaper clipping from July 1961 reads, "These are some of the boys who have put the East Shetland Pony League All-Stars into tonight's final of the District C tournament at Clearwater. Standing at left is Oscar Gonzalez, who was the winning hurler last night. Kneeling, from left to

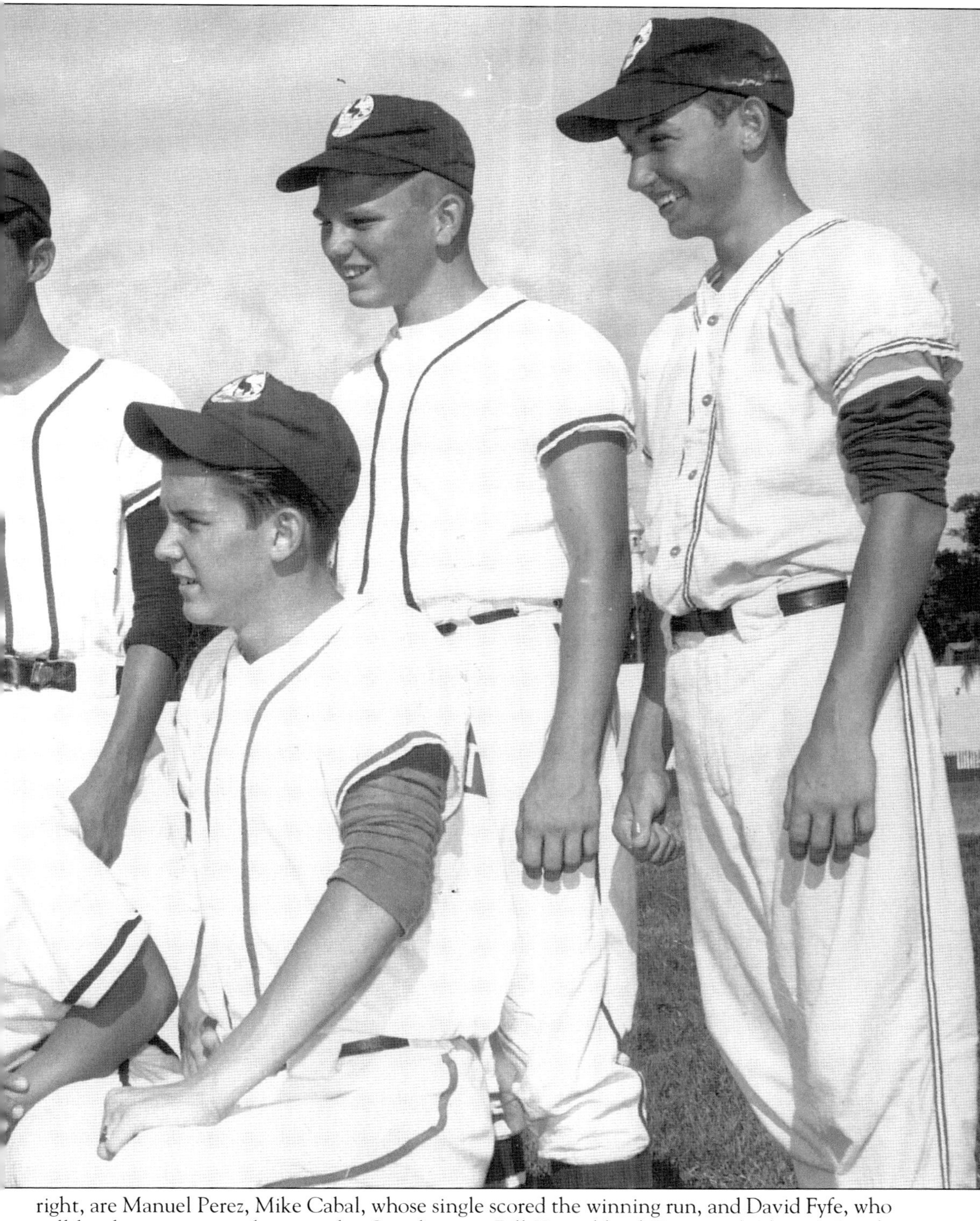

right, are Manuel Perez, Mike Cabal, whose single scored the winning run, and David Fyfe, who will be the starting pitcher tonight. Standing are Bill Youngblood, Raymond Alvarez, Randy Canal and Terry Jarvis." (Courtesy of *La Gaceta*.)

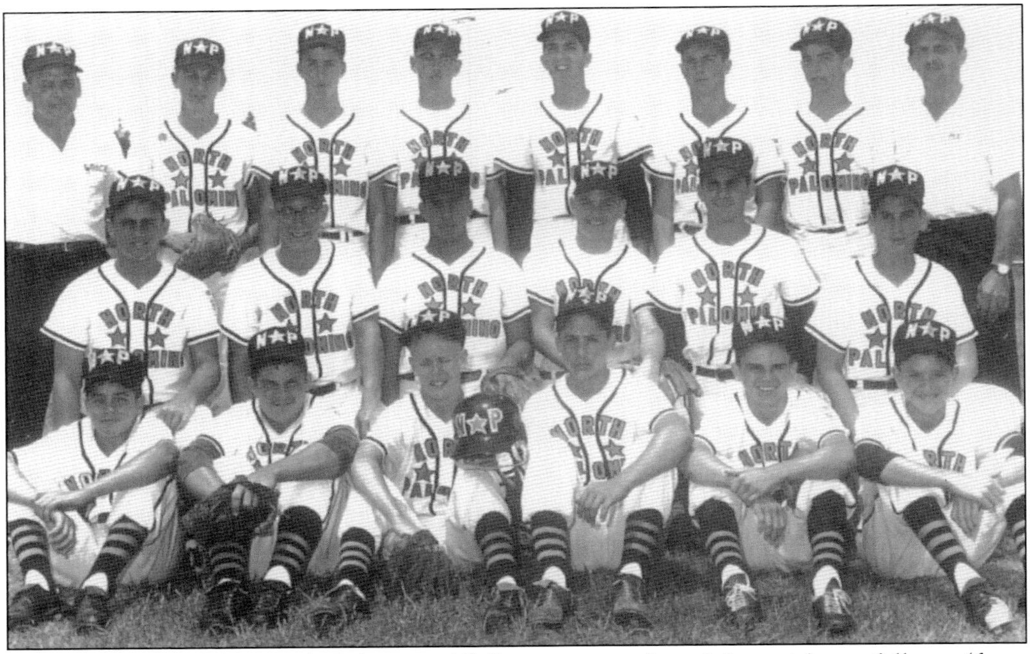

These members of the North Palomino All-Star nine are, from left to right, as follows: (front row) Ed Morassi, Dick Cigarran, Bill Graham, Tony Leto, Ralph Bosek, and Chick Nunez; (middle row) Ed Ellis, Ricky Catlett, Ray Morejon, Chris Corral, Tony DiGiovanni, and Glen Permuy; (back row) coach Manuel Corral, Curt Suchan, Paul Hopper, James Fender, Tom Cavalieri, Bob Thornley, Ronnie Bidwell, and manager Don Suchan. The photo dates to *c.* July 21, 1964. (Courtesy of *La Gaceta*.)

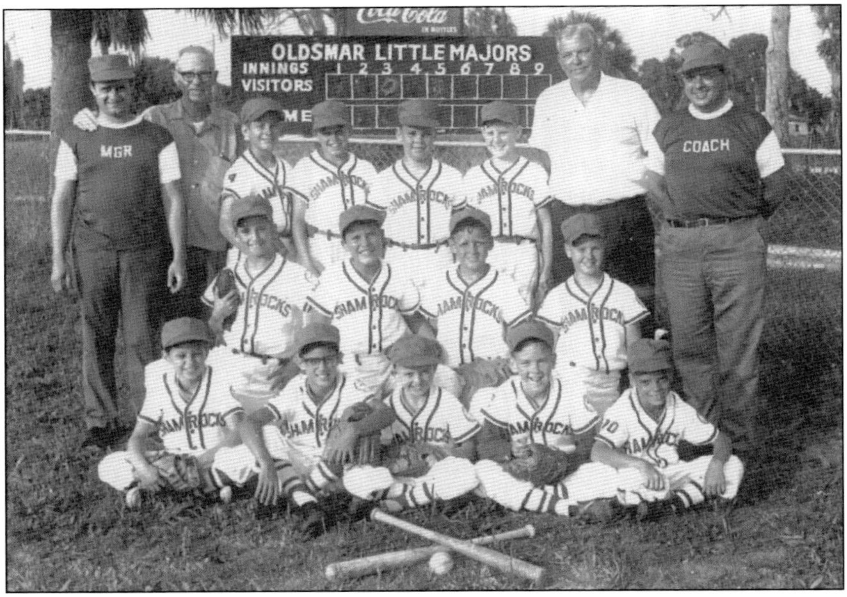

R.E. Olds Park has a picnic area, a fishing pier, a nature walk, and a baseball field for Little League teams like the Shamrocks, a local Oldsmar team of the 1960s. (Courtesy of Oldsmar Cultural Affairs Department and Oldsmar Public Library.)

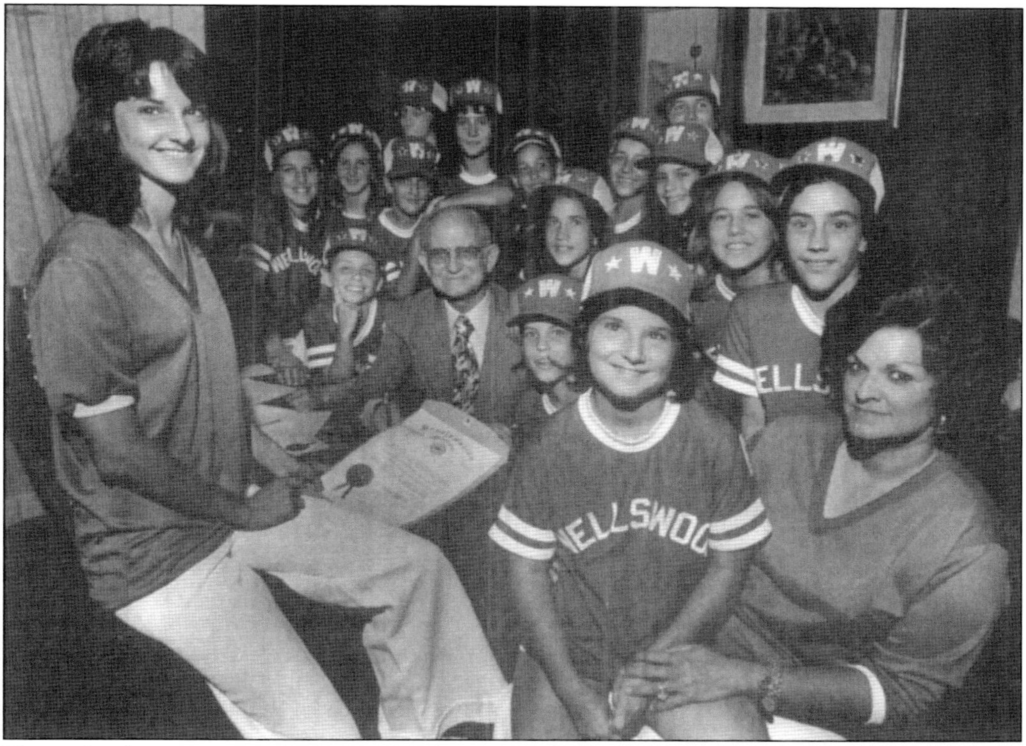

The girls take over! Acting Mayor Lloyd Copeland is upstaged and overrun in his City Hall office by members of the 1974 World Champion Wellswood Little League girls' team as he makes public the proclamation declaring it their week in Tampa. In the foreground, from left to right, are coach Yoli Espino, pitcher Sandra Espino, and their mother-manager, Sylvia Espino. (Courtesy of *La Gaceta*.)

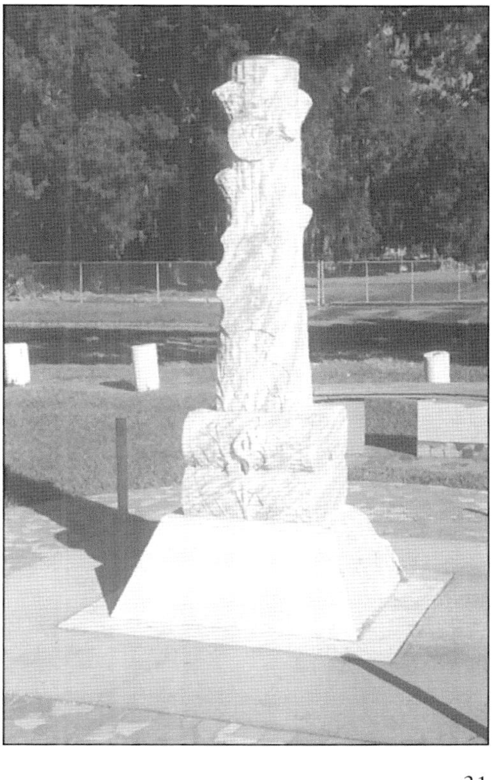

It is rare to find baseball monuments in the Tampa Bay area, especially those dedicated to Little League. Seen here is the 1967 West Tampa All-Star Team Memorial upon which are listed the names of the team members and the team's accomplishments, including their ranking as fifth in the 1967 World Series. It is interesting to note that the memorial was made from a stock tombstone usually reserved for Woodsmen of the World, a fraternal order. The memorial can be found on the baseball grounds near MacFarlane Park, off MacDill Avenue. (Photo by the author.)

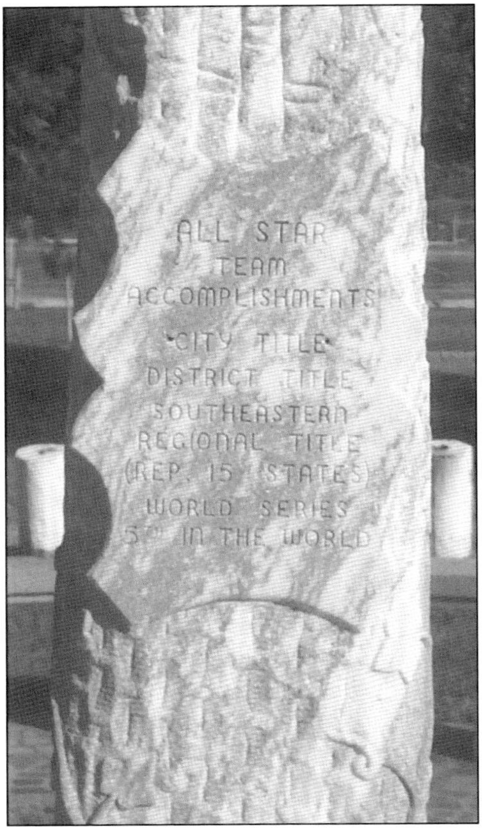

This is a close-up of the 1967 West Tampa All-Star Team Memorial, showing the team's accomplishments. (Photo by the author.)

This is another close-up showing the names of the team members. (Photo by the author.)

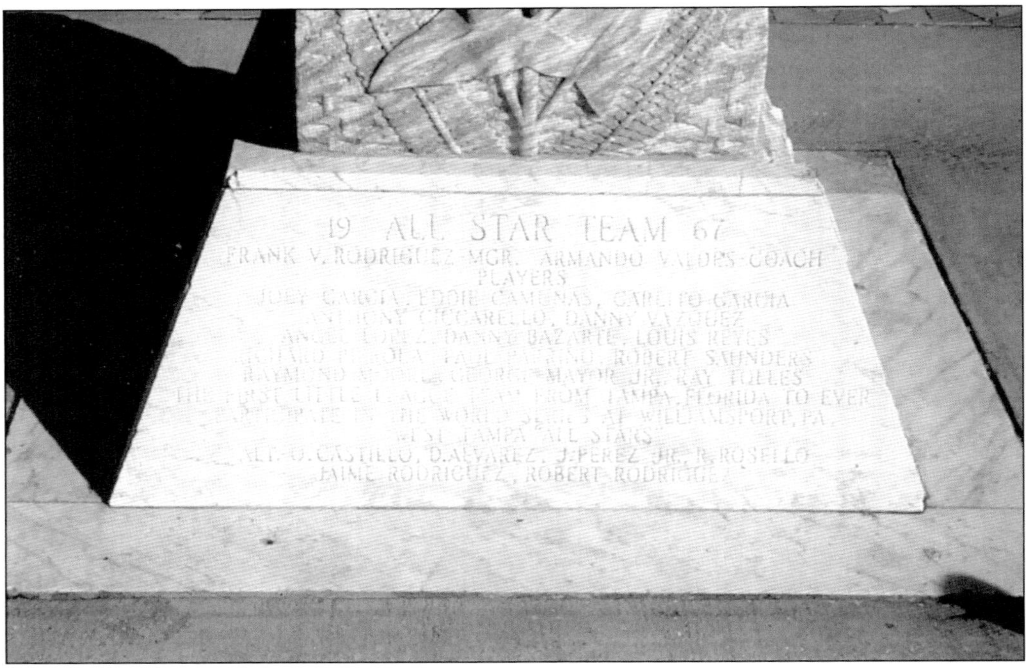

Located nearby the 1967 memorial is another memorial built in the following year and dedicated to "The First Senior Little League Team from the Tampa Bay Area to ever participate in World Series Play at Gary Ind. finishing Second in the World." (Photo by the author.)

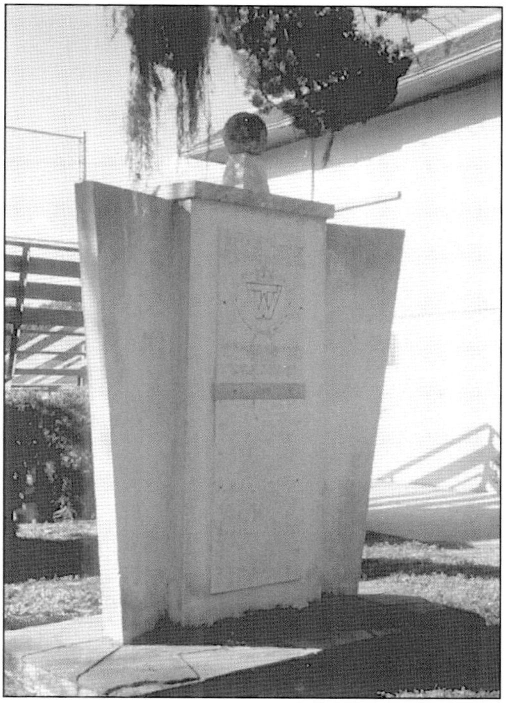

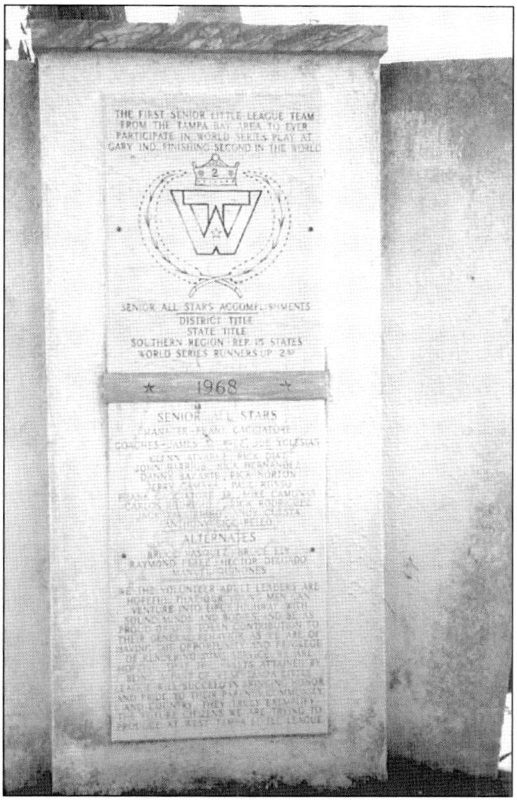

This is the 1968 memorial, which lists the names of the coaches and team members. (Photo by the author.)

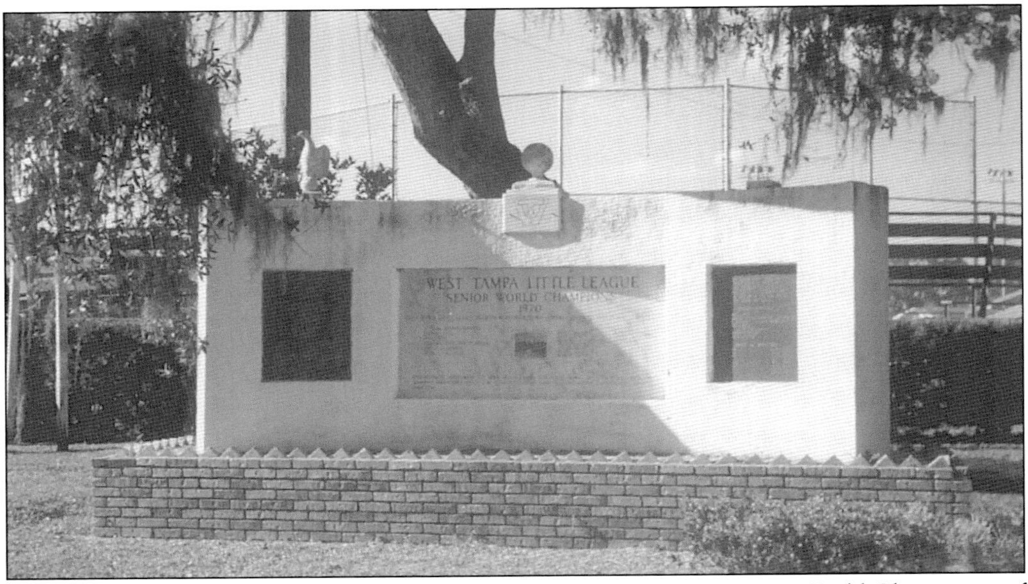

The most extravagant memorial is the one dedicated to the 1970 Senior World Champions of the West Tampa Little League. (Photo by the author.)

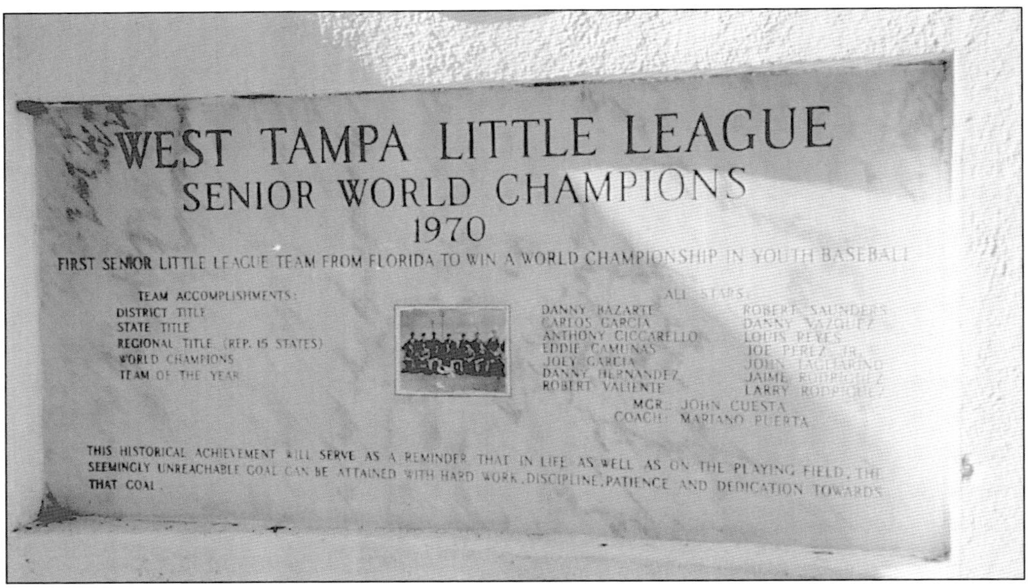

The 1970 memorial lists the team's accomplishments, the team members' names, and even includes a team photo. (Photo by the author.)

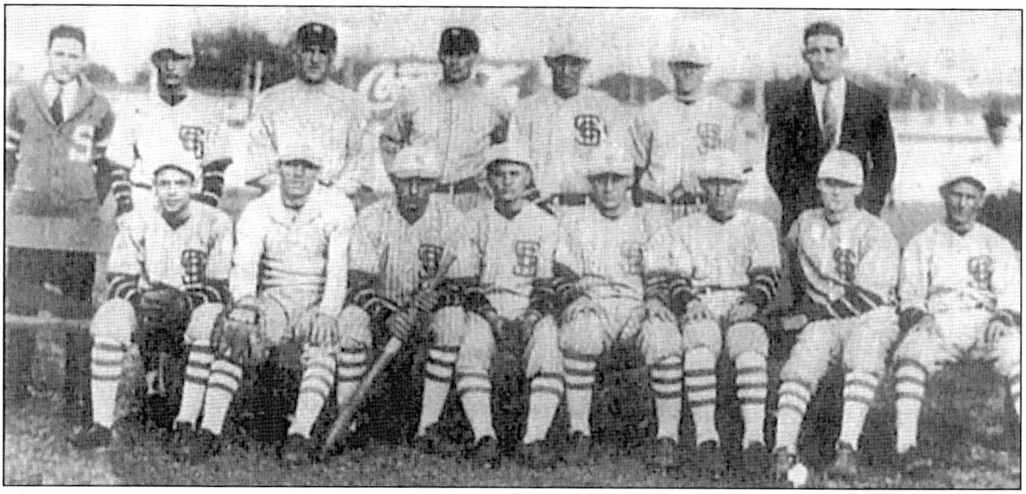

The Sacred Heart High School team appears here in 1924. Al Lopez is identified as the third from the right, in the back row. (Courtesy of Special Collections, University of South Florida.)

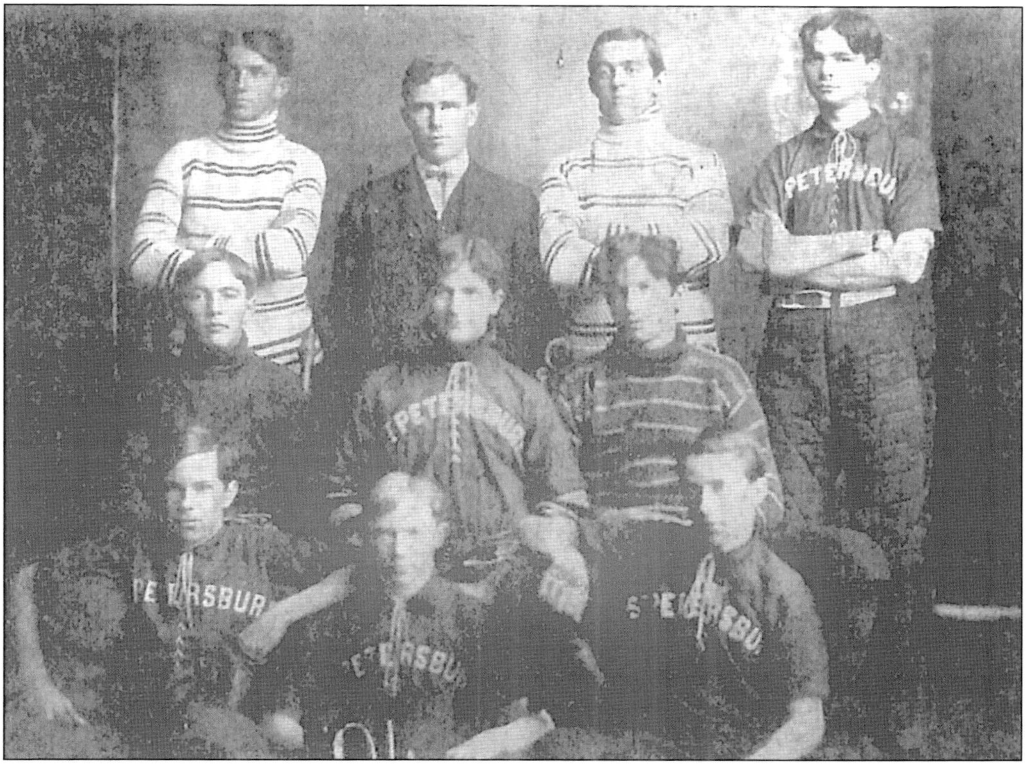

This 1904 baseball team was from St. Petersburg High School. (Courtesy of Pinellas County Historical Museum.)

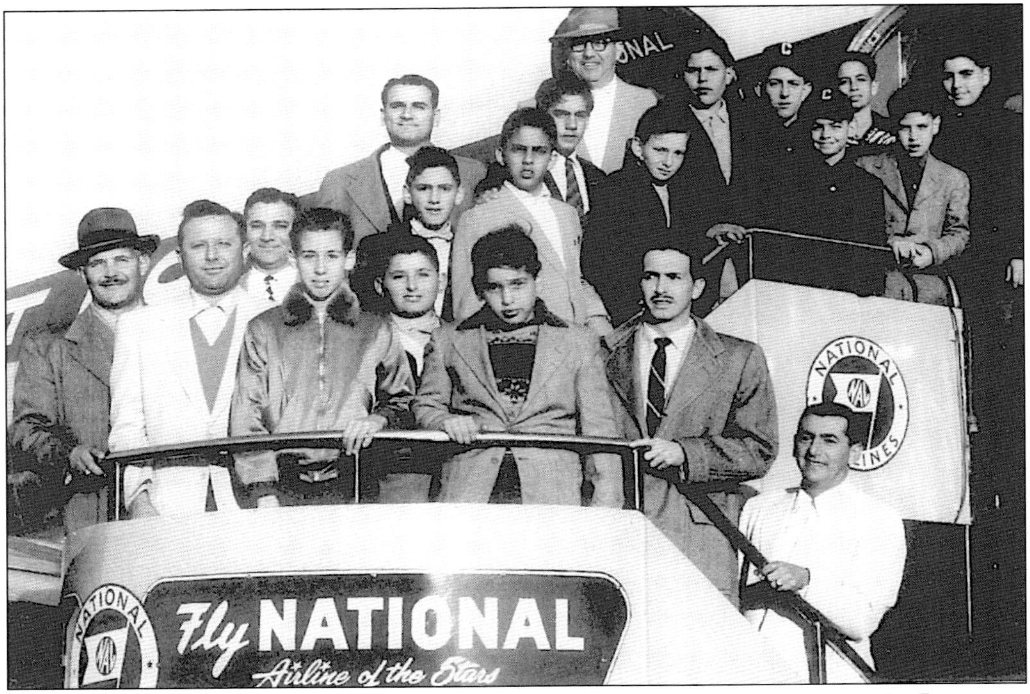

Andrew Espolita (at far left, in fedora) and a group of children, including Tony La Russa, are seen boarding a plane for a Little League game in the 1950s. Espolita served as a coach for La Russa's team from Tampa. (Courtesy of Andrew Espolita.)

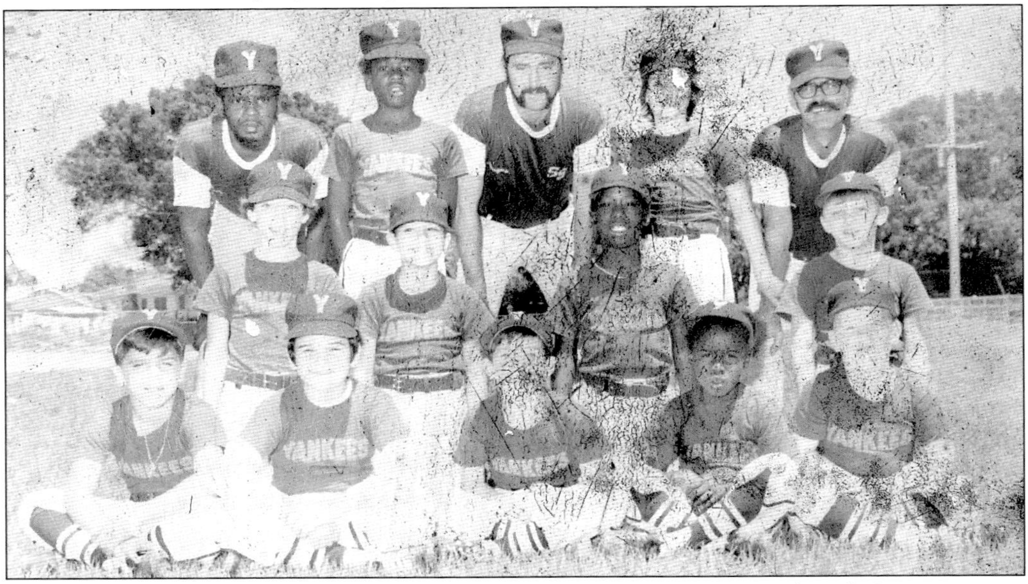
In the 1960s and 1970s, many of the ethnic clubs in Ybor City sponsored Little League teams, such as the Circulo Cubano Yankees of 1974. Many children of immigrants were becoming more "Americanized" with each passing generation, and today many Tampaños who are third or fourth generation do not know the language of their immigrant forebears. (Courtesy of El Museo del Circulo Cubano.)

Three

LEAGUES OF THEIR OWN:

MINORITIES IN BASEBALL

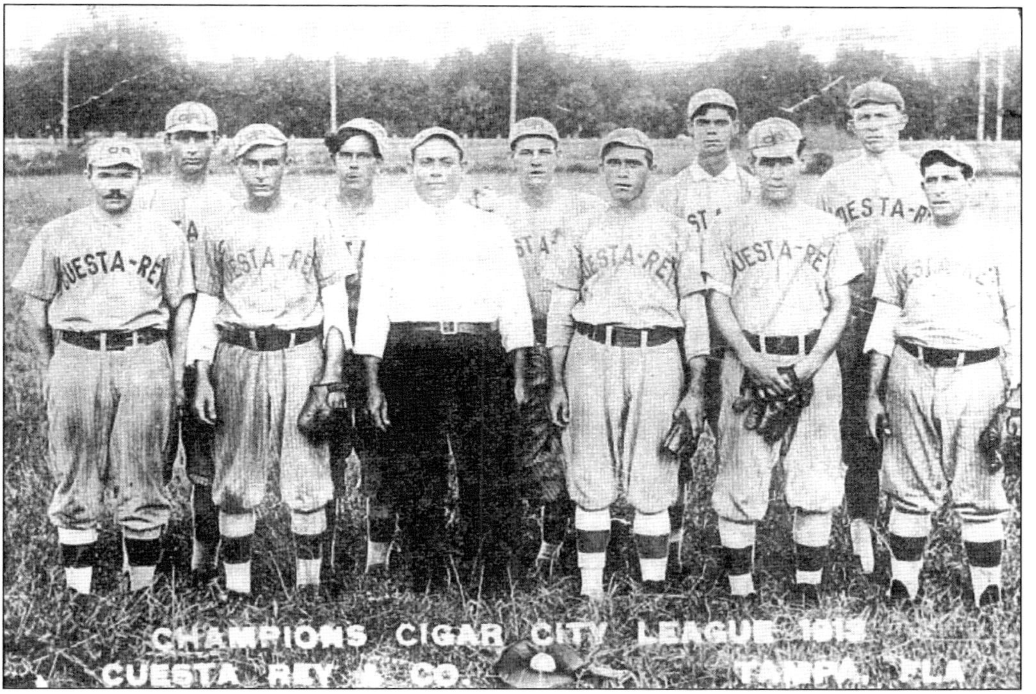

In a segregated South, as well as in the North, many African Americans, Hispanics, and other ethnic minorities were not allowed to participate in the game with their white counterparts. In Ybor City, some of these minorities formed their own teams and leagues in order to play against each other. Seen here are Cuban, Italian, and Spanish ballplayers for the Cuesta Rey Cigar Company. This team was the 1913 champion of the Cigar City League. (Courtesy of Andrew Espolita.)

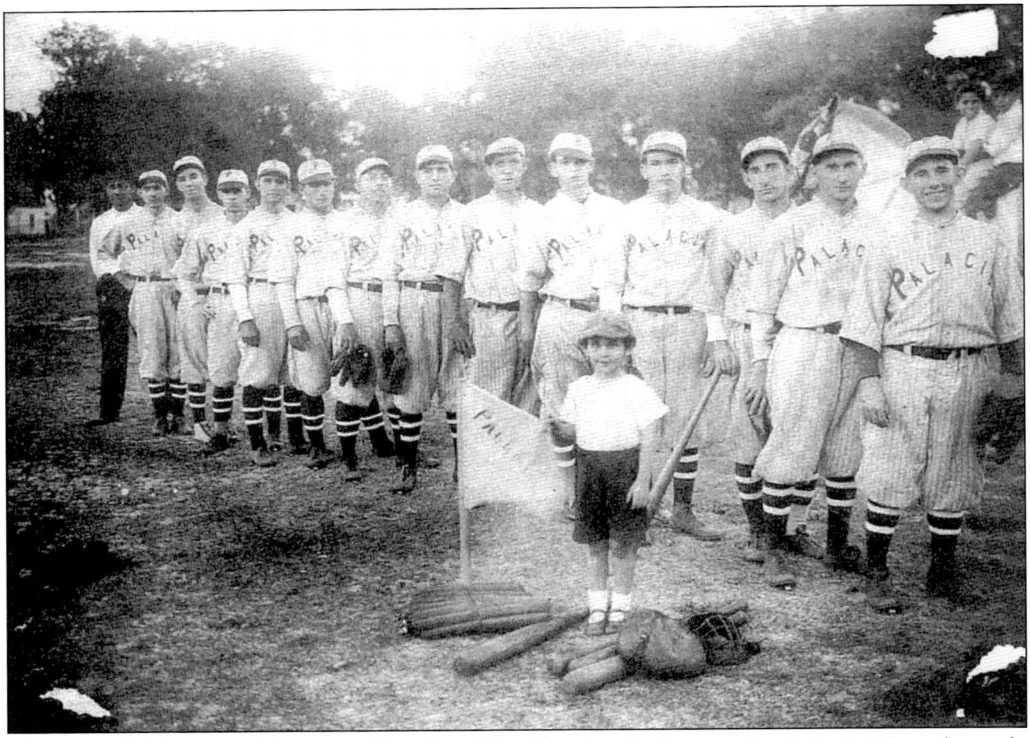

This is a World War I–era scene of another Ybor City baseball team, the Palacio. Note the early baseball equipment in the foreground. (Courtesy of Andrew Espolita.)

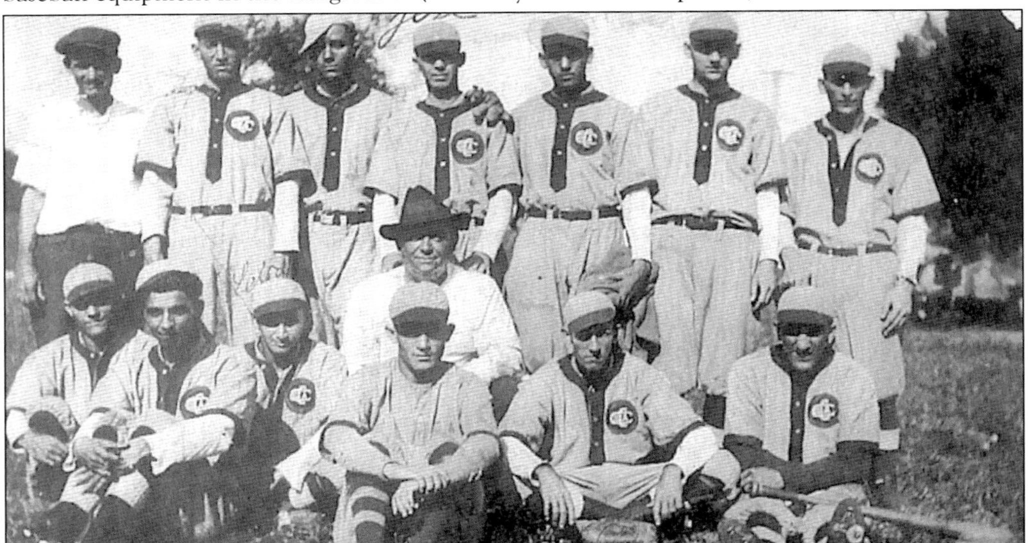

Many of the ethnic clubs banded together and formed the Intersocial League in which they could compete against each other. Seen here are members of the Circulo Cubano (Cuban Club) during the years of the First World War (1914–1919). Note their distinctive team patch with "CCA," which stands for Circulo Cubano Atletica. (Courtesy of Paul Dosal.)

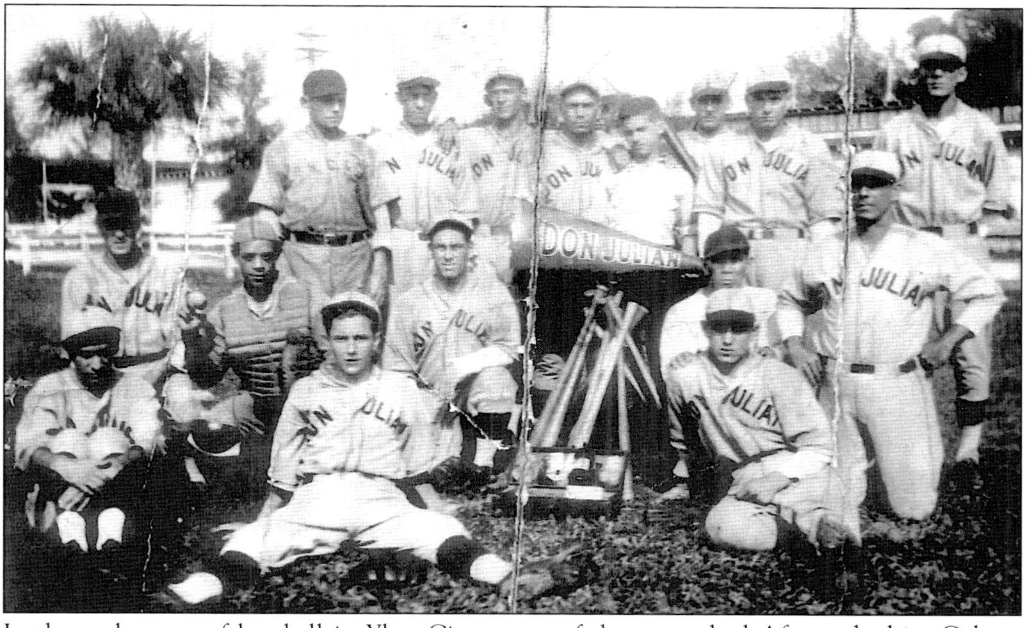

In the early years of baseball in Ybor City, many of the teams had Afro and white Cubans playing together, as can be seen by the catcher in the far left and his teammates in this *c.* 1918 image. Many Afro Cubans and African Americans were forced to play only in the Negro Leagues due to Jim Crow laws and racism in the South and the rest of the country. Players like Juanelo Mirabel of Tampa and Jimmy Hill of Plant City played on area teams like the St. Petersburg Stars and the Lakeland Tigers. Eventually, a few moved on to the major league from Negro League teams, when baseball was desegregated in 1946 by the signing of Jackie Robinson by the Dodgers. (Courtesy of Andrew Espolita.)

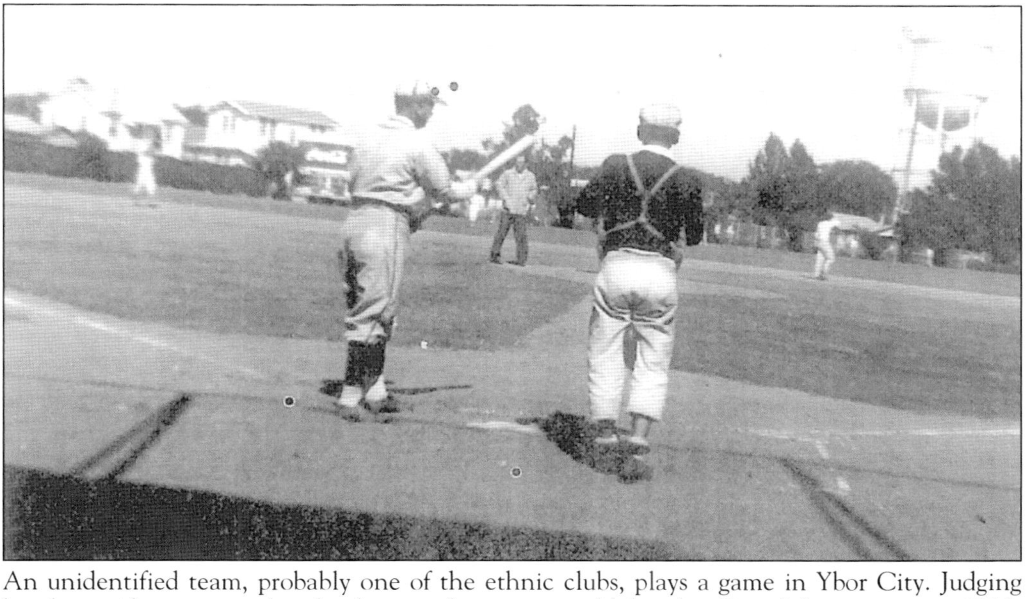

An unidentified team, probably one of the ethnic clubs, plays a game in Ybor City. Judging by the uniforms worn by the batter, the team could be the Don Julian team, *c.* 1918. (Courtesy of *La Gaceta*.)

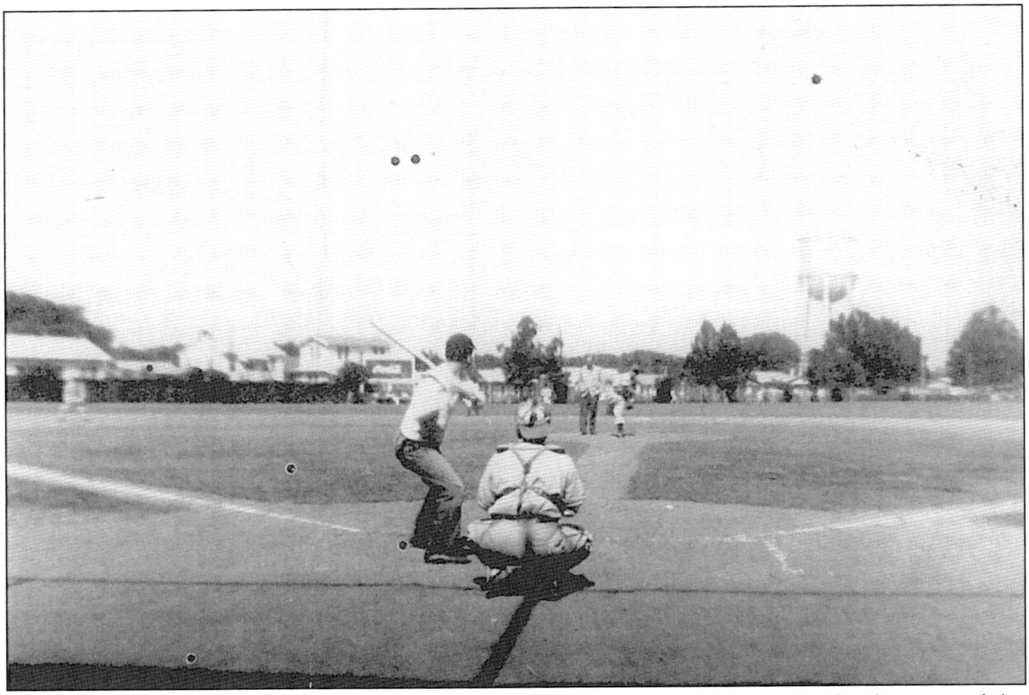

In this view of the same game, an the early Coca Cola sign is visible in the far distance of the field. (Courtesy of *La Gaceta*.)

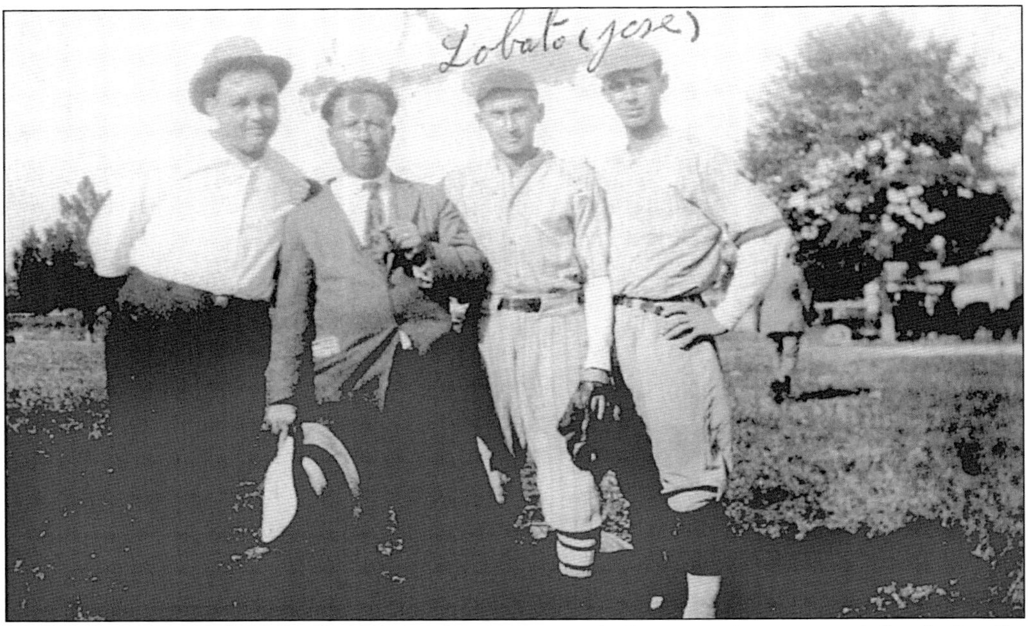

Andrew Espolita and José Lobato, in uniform, pose with their team's sponsor while playing for one of the local business leagues in the late 1920s. (Courtesy of Andrew Espolita.)

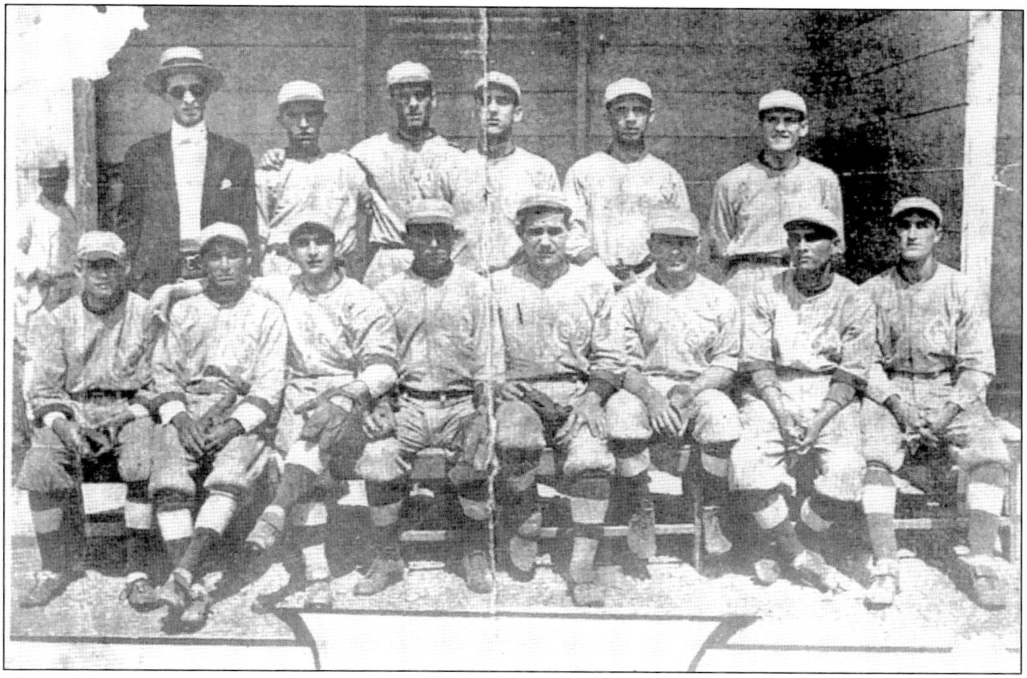

The Circulo Cubano team of Ybor City is pictured here during World War I. Note the mirrored and connected letter "C" as the team logo on their jerseys. (Courtesy of Andrew Espolita.)

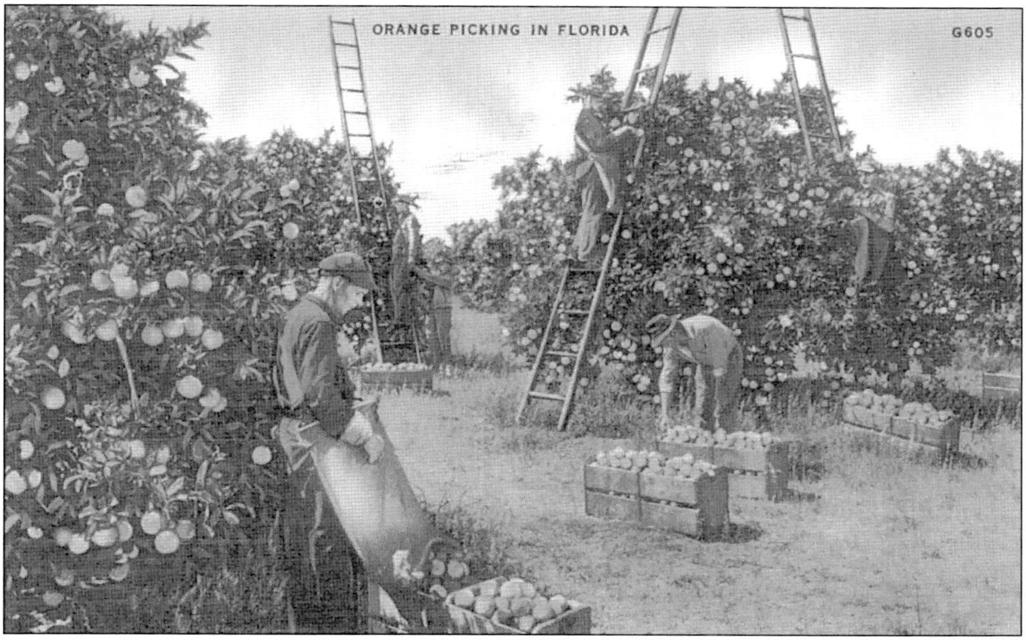

The Centro Asturiano, another ethnic club from Ybor City, was mainly reserved for Asturians from Spain. This photo was probably taken at Cascaden Park in the 1930s. (Courtesy of *La Gaceta*.)

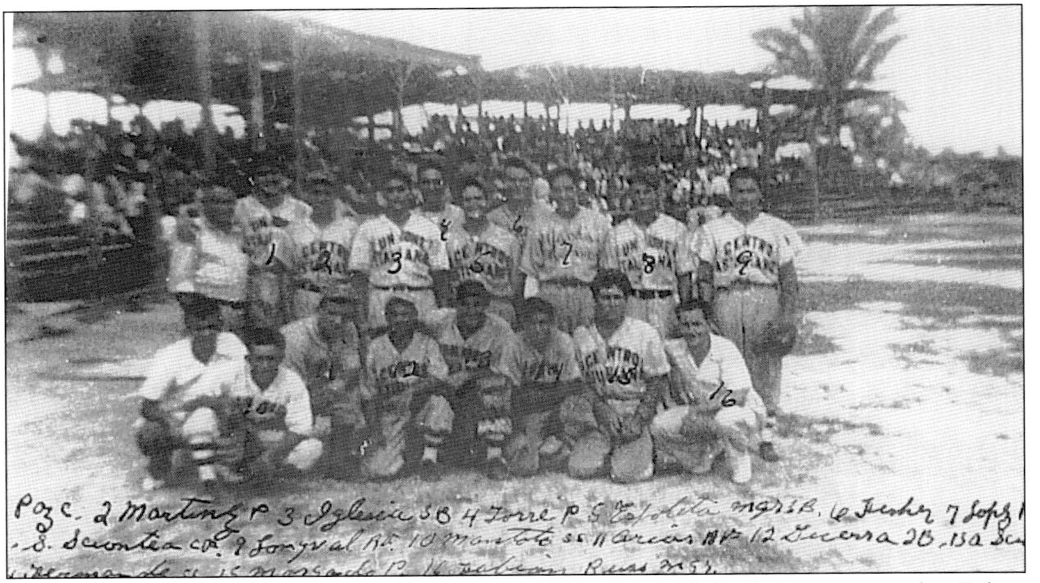

Team members from the Centro Asturiano pose for a photo while playing against the Cuban national team in Key West on July 4, 1939. Andrew Espolita played third base and was a manager for the team. (Courtesy of Andrew Espolita.)

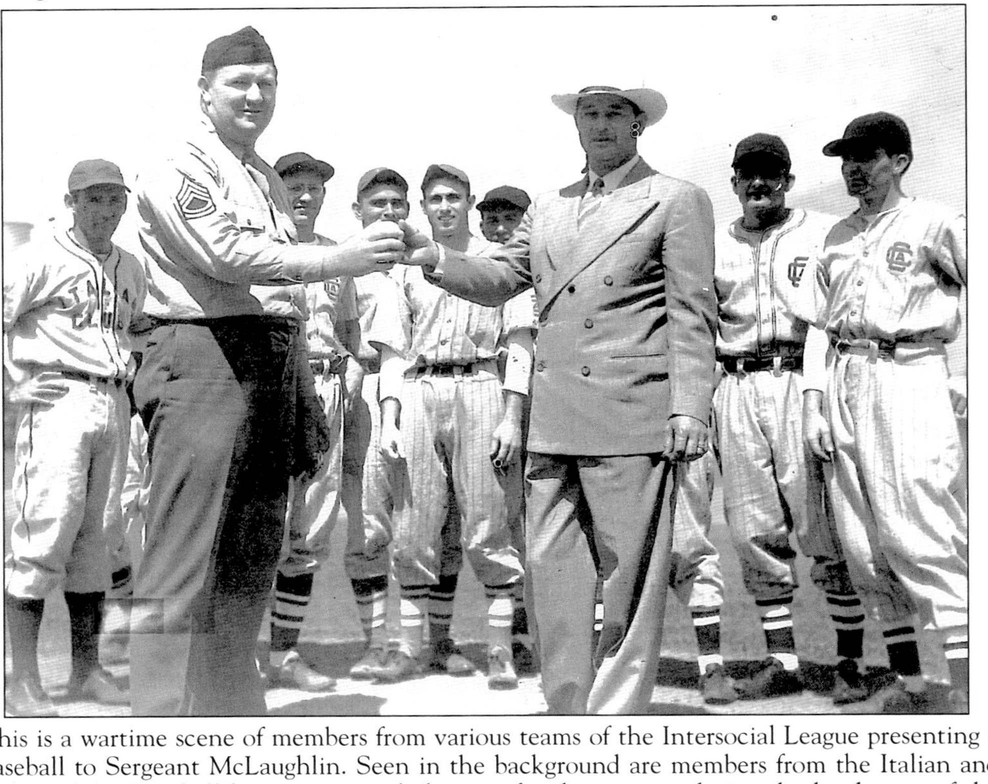

This is a wartime scene of members from various teams of the Intersocial League presenting a baseball to Sergeant McLaughlin. Seen in the background are members from the Italian and Cuban clubs. Baseball became a morale booster for the country during the hard years of the Second World War (1941–1945). (Courtesy of *La Gaceta*.)

Twin sisters Mary and Myra Crisman were very involved in athletic activities in Dunedin. Here, the pair is dressed in their softball uniforms for the Clearwater team, Peggy's Girls. This team would participate in the Women's Softball Championship in Chicago in the late 1930s. When the men went off to fight in World War II, many women entered baseball when the All-American Girls Professional Baseball League was formed. The women kept baseball alive at a time when public interest would have waned because of the war. Eventually, training camps for the league were established in Havana, Cuba, and in Fort Lauderdale, Florida. The league ceased to exist after 1954, but there was an increase in the public's awareness of women's role in baseball because of the 1992 film *A League of Their Own*. A permanent exhibit highlighting the role of women in baseball now stands in the Baseball Hall of Fame. (Courtesy of Dunedin Historical Museum.)

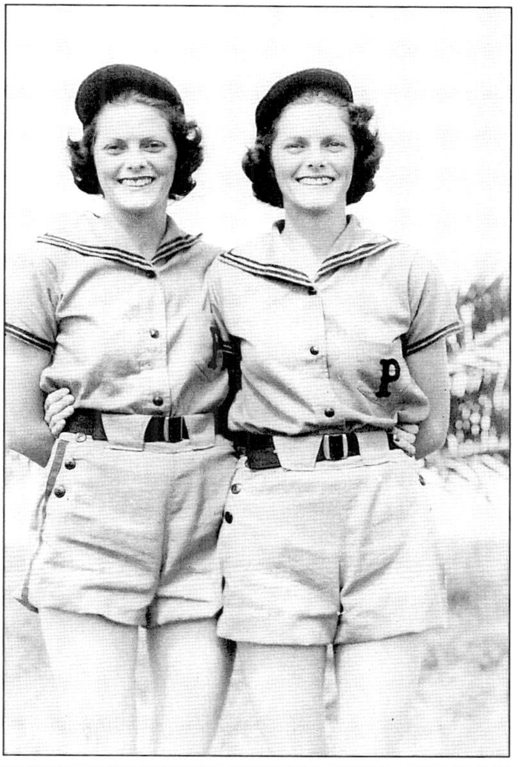

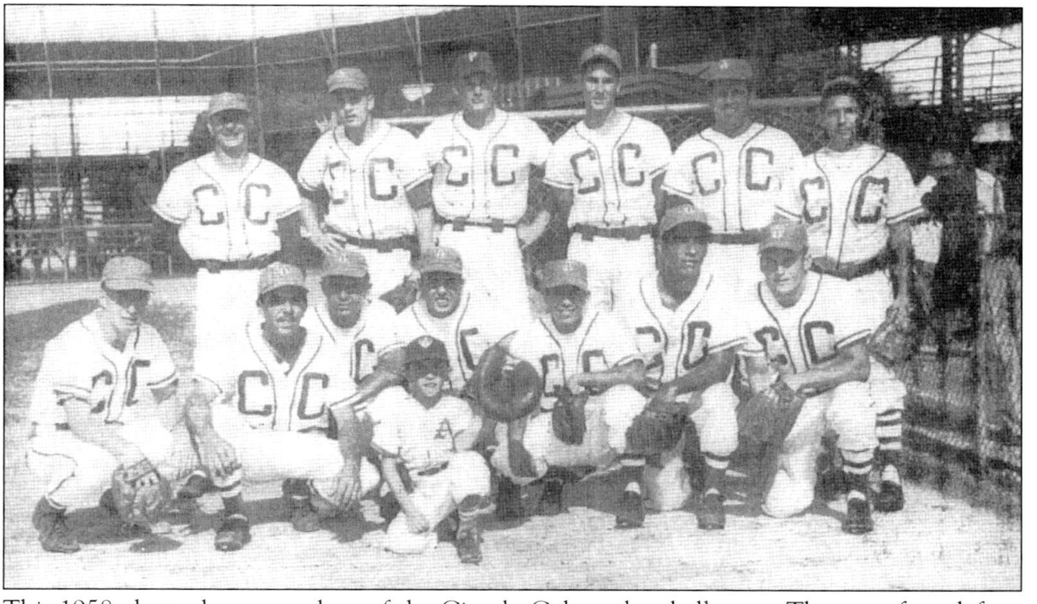

This 1958 photo shows members of the Circulo Cubano baseball team. They are, from left to right, as follows: (kneeling) Tommy Burkhan, Frank Lanza, Richard Grant, Billy River, Luis Digedierrt, Richard Bravo, Tomy King, and Frank Lanza Jr.; (standing) Camilo Bello, Edward Kansriddle, Ronald Dinner, Howard Prescott, Luis Vigil, and Isidoro Lanza. (Courtesy of El Museo del Circulo Cubano.)

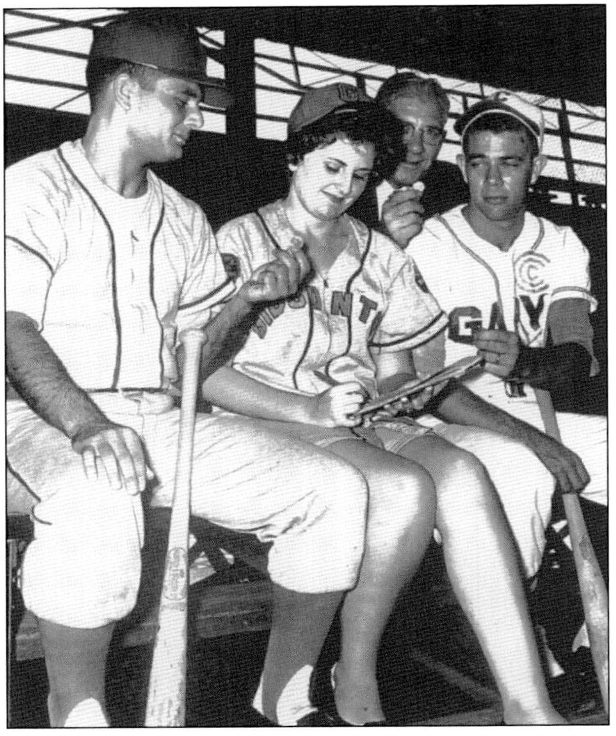

The Intersocial League is chipping into the "good luck" telegram being prepared by Tampa fans for the Tampa-trained Cincinnati Reds, who were nearing the National League pennant in 1961. Tampans contributed quarters toward a telegram to be sent to the Reds. The money was raised to help youth baseball in the Tampa area. The drive was held during games of the Intersocial League at Cuscaden Park. Players Pete Busciglio (left) of Brandon and Nolan Tillman (right) of Gary and Intersocial president Pete Leto give their quarters to Miss Nellie Mae Leto. (Courtesy of *La Gaceta*.)

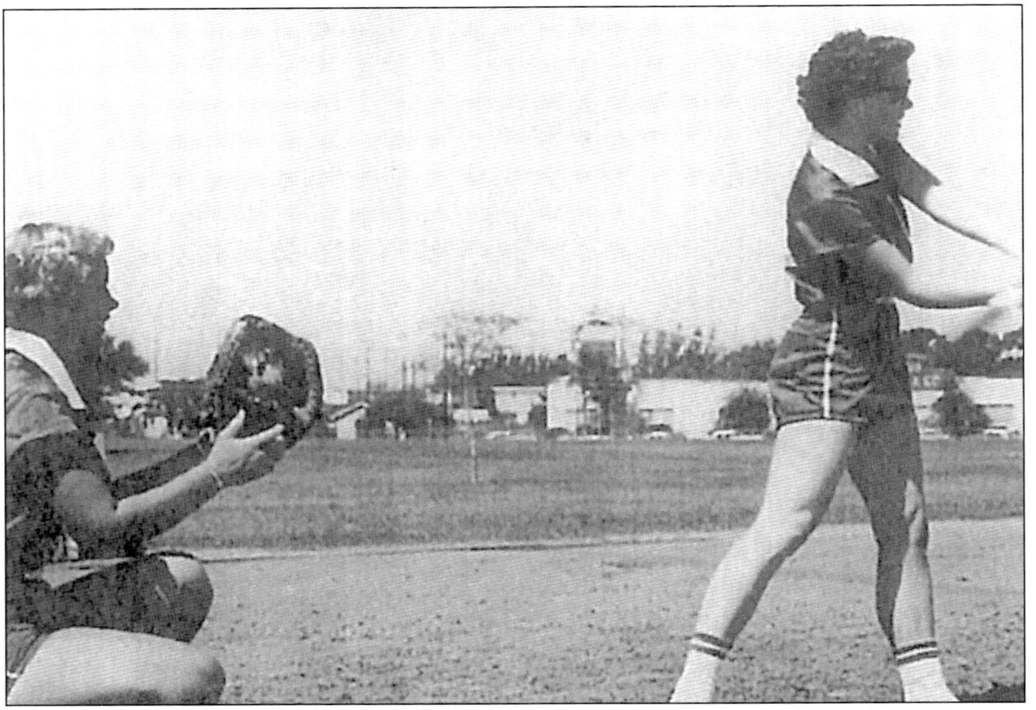

A girls' baseball team practices somewhere in St. Petersburg in the late 1950s to the early 1960s. (Courtesy of Pinellas County Historical Museum.)

Four

The Minor Leagues

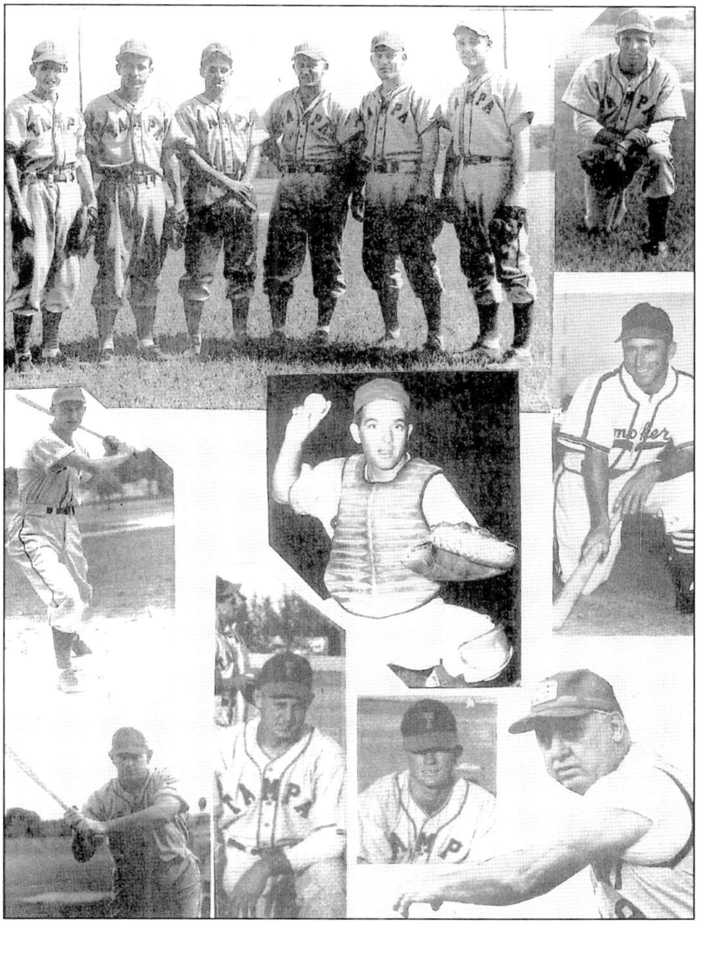

The Tampa Smokers was one of Tampa's earliest teams. This collage of images spans the glory years of the team from the 1930s to the late 1940s. Local natives such as Al Lopez and Andrew Espolita were members of this famous baseball team. (Courtesy of *La Gaceta*.)

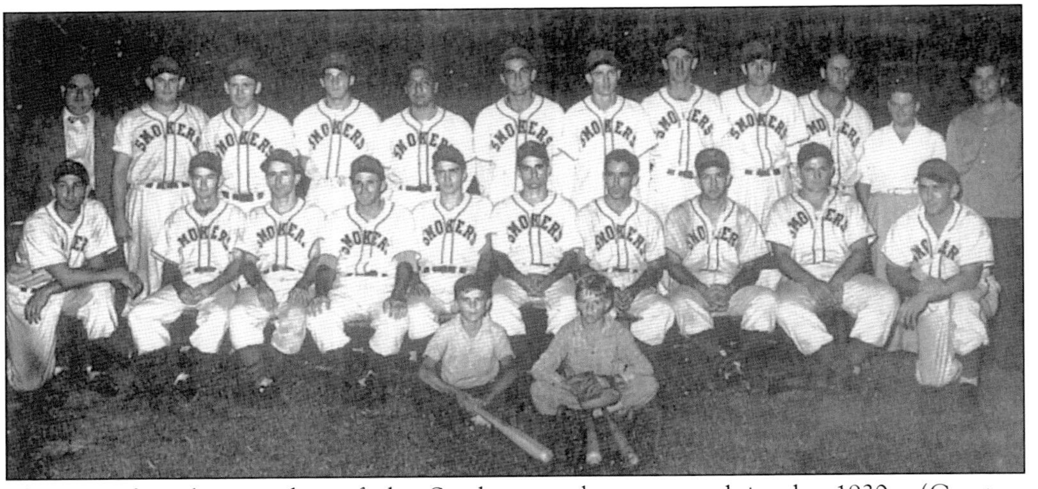

This is a formal team shot of the Smokers as they appeared in the 1930s. (Courtesy of *La Gaceta*.)

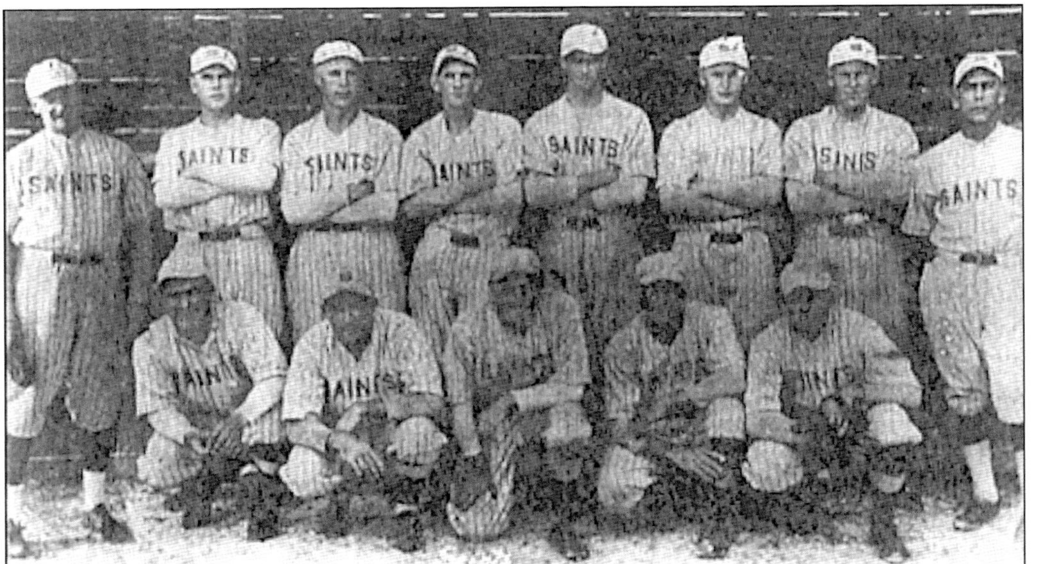

Across the bay, the 1922 St. Petersburg Saints were champions of the Florida State League. (Courtesy of Pinellas County Historical Museum.)

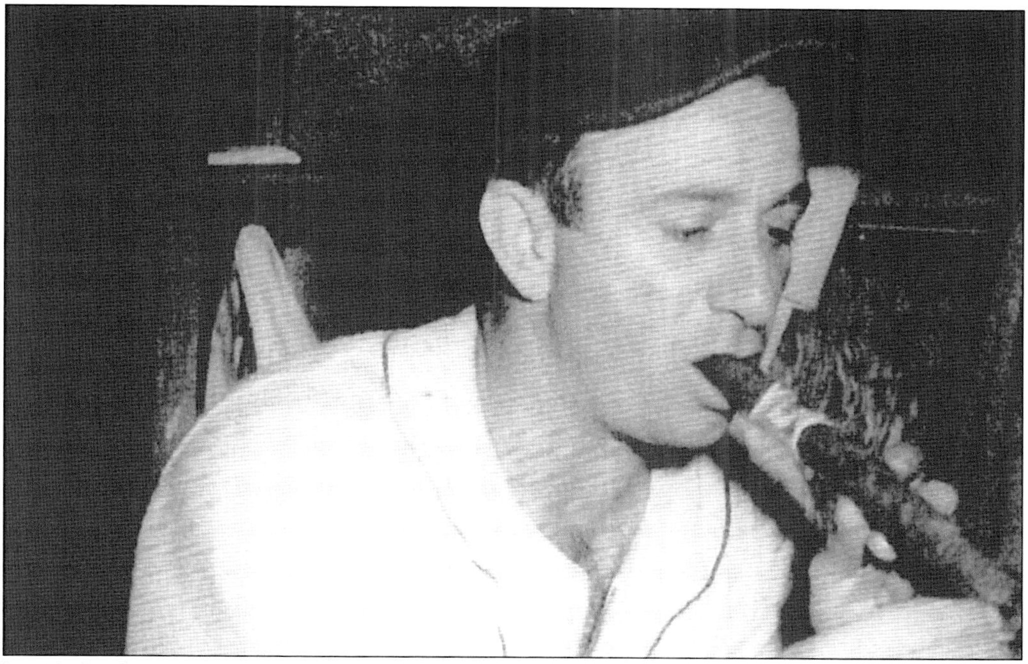

In 1947, the manager for the Tampa Smokers was Tony Cucinello. (Courtesy of Florida State Archives.)

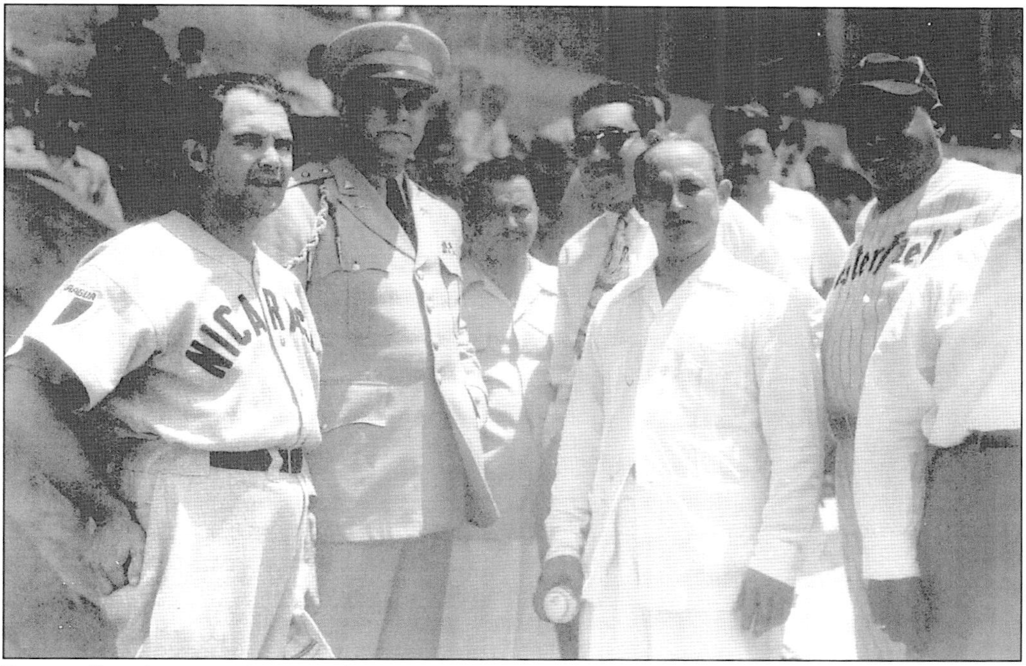

Eventually, players with years of experience can coach or manage a team of their own. Andrew Espolita, who began playing baseball as a young child in Ybor City in 1913, coached the Nicaraguan baseball team in the 1930s. Espolita (left) is pictured in Managua with the son (second from left) of dictator General Somoza. (Courtesy of Andrew Espolita.)

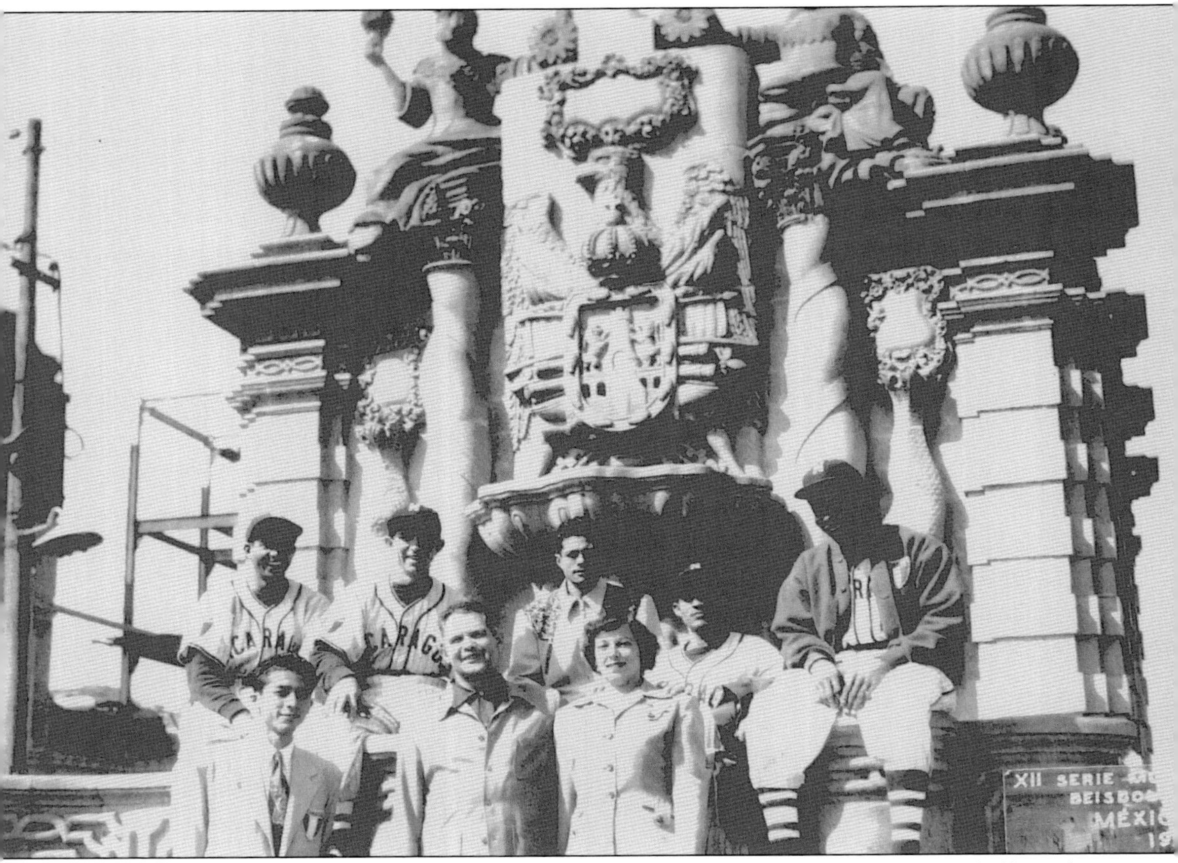

In the 1920s and 1930s, many Hispanics and African Americans who played baseball sought out professional foreign teams willing to accept them. This was due to rampant racism in American teams of all professional leagues. Andrew Espolita and his fellow players from Ybor City went to Nicaragua and played for that country's team. Espolita (second from left, back row) is pictured with other teammates from the national Nicaraguan baseball team during a series in Mexico City, 1931. (Courtesy of Andrew Espolita.)

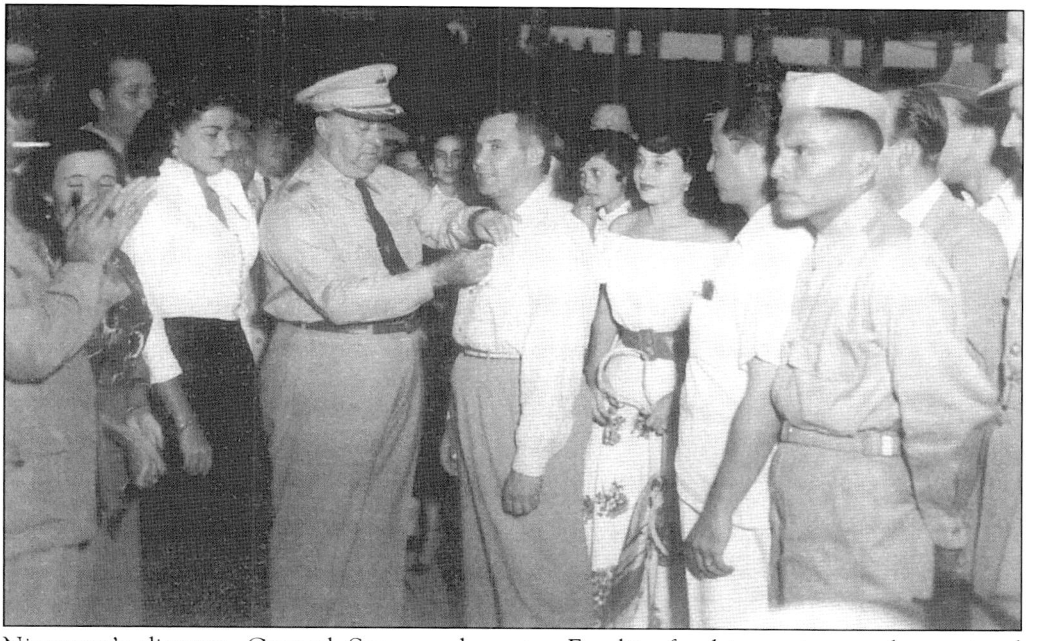

Nicaragua's dictator, General Somoza, decorates Espolita for his service to the national Nicaraguan baseball team, *c.* 1940s. (Courtesy of Andrew Espolita.)

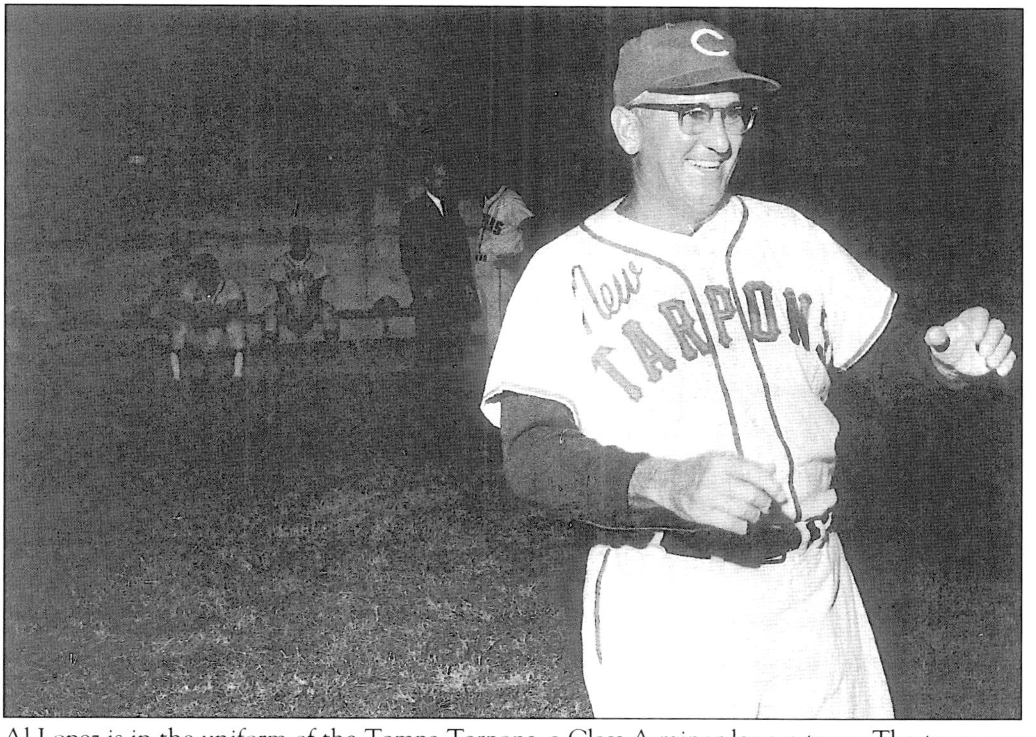

Al Lopez is in the uniform of the Tampa Tarpons, a Class A minor league team. The team was affiliated with the Cincinnati Reds and was based out of Al Lopez Field. The team ceased to exist after the Reds' 1987 move to Plant City from Tampa. (Courtesy of *La Gaceta*.)

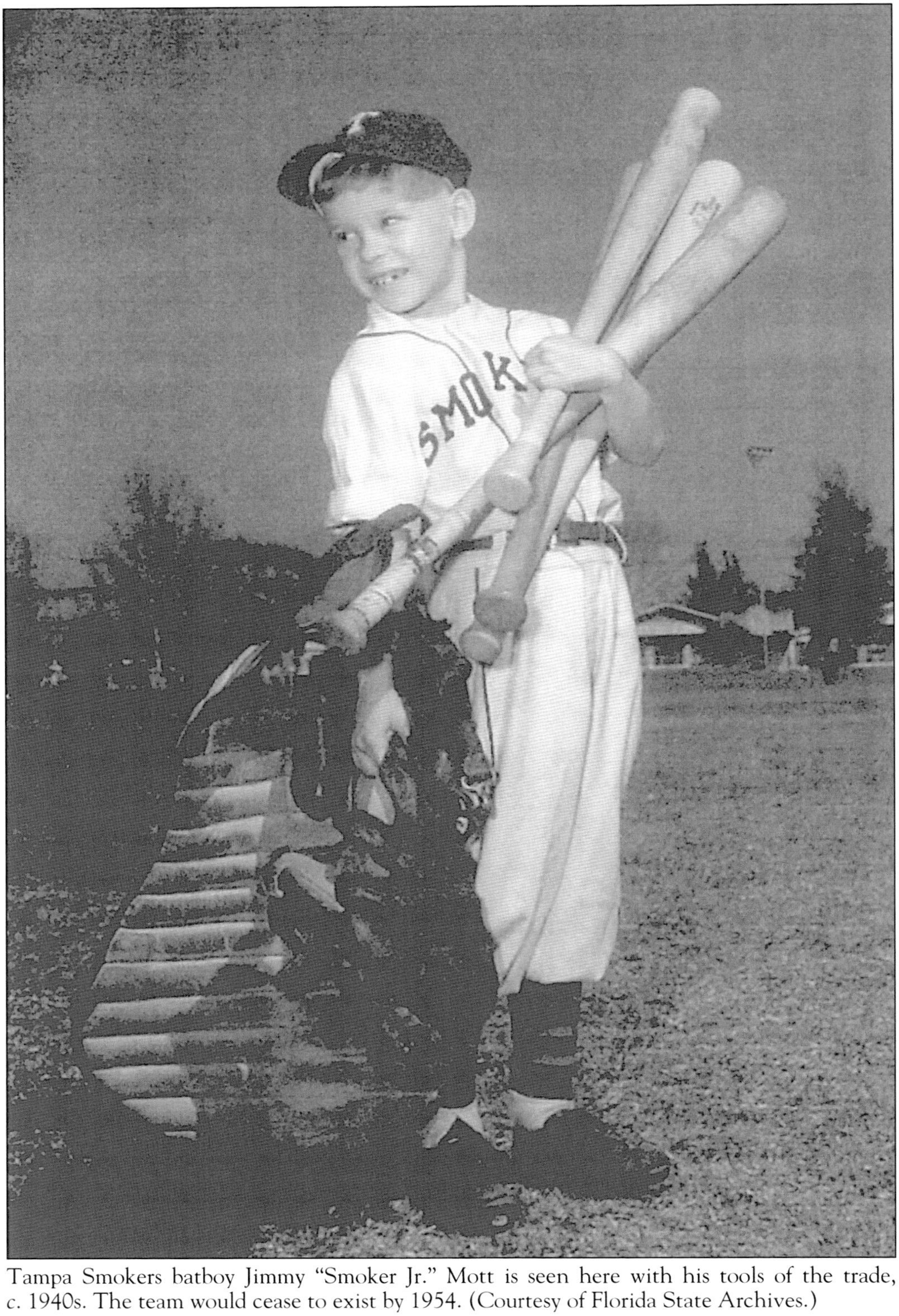

Tampa Smokers batboy Jimmy "Smoker Jr." Mott is seen here with his tools of the trade, c. 1940s. The team would cease to exist by 1954. (Courtesy of Florida State Archives.)

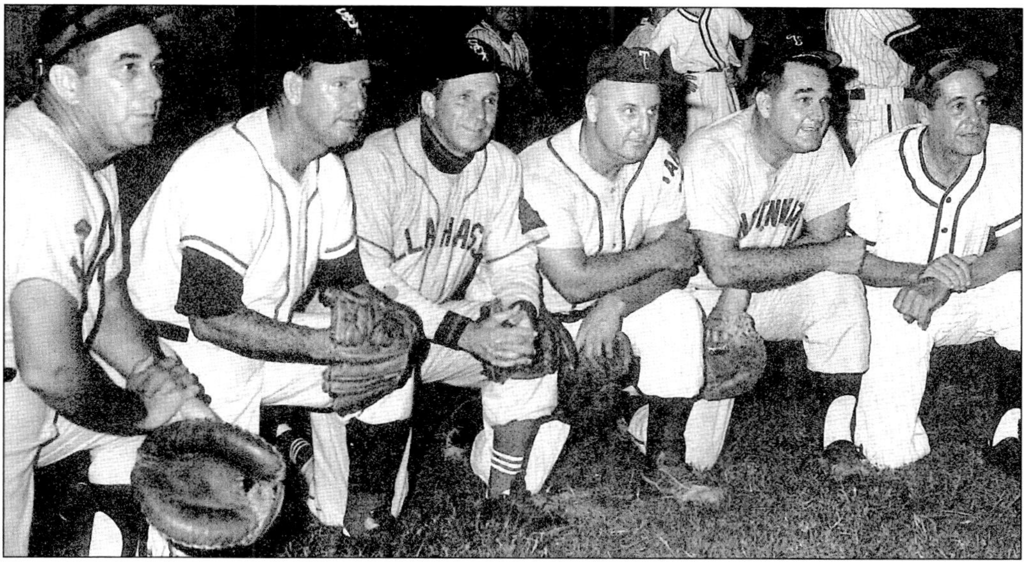

Back in uniform again—these former Smokers were on hand to see action in a game against the Tampa Tarpons, who won 2-0, at Al Lopez Field on August 22, 1964. They are, from left to right, Manny Fernandez, Marcela Maseda, Charlie Cuellar, Chet Covington, Benny Fernandez and Manuel Lopez. (Courtesy of *La Gaceta*.)

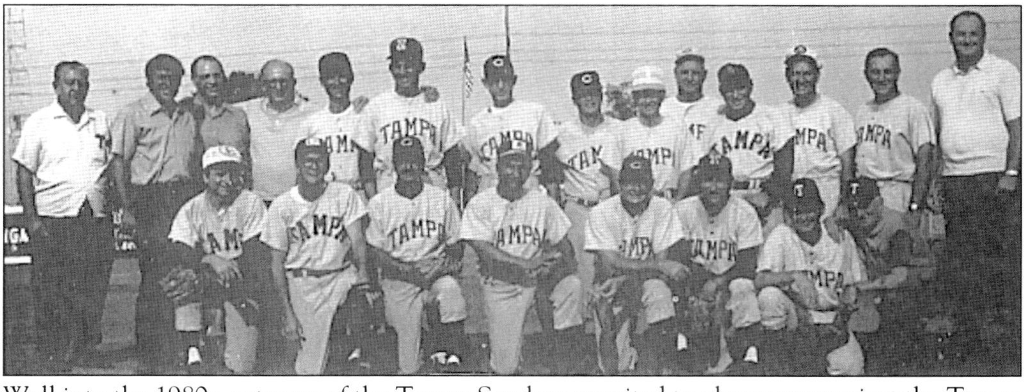

Well into the 1980s, veterans of the Tampa Smokers reunited to play games against the Tampa Tarpons. This photograph dates to the early 1970s. (Courtesy of *La Gaceta*.)

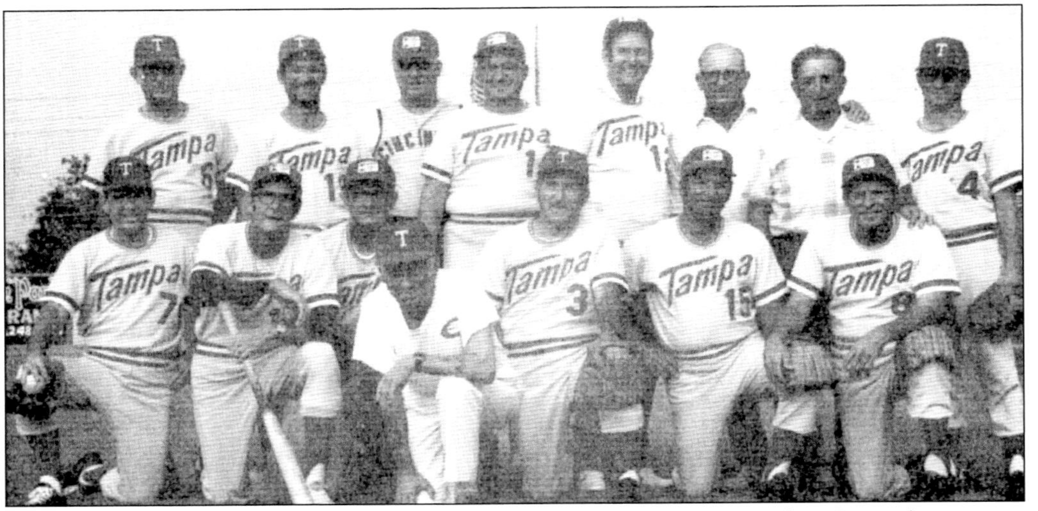

Here is another reunion of Tampa Smokers players, c. 1974. (Courtesy *of La Gaceta.*)

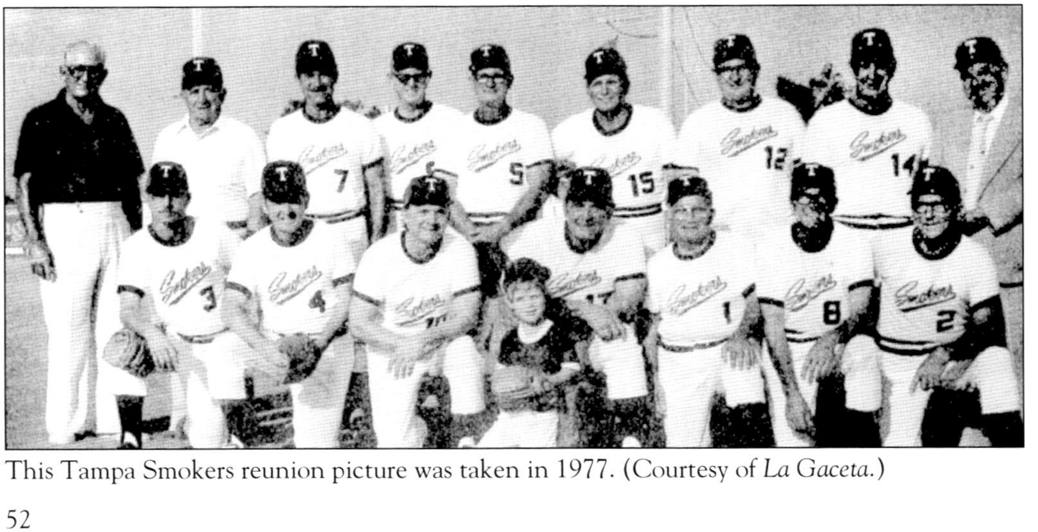
This Tampa Smokers reunion picture was taken in 1977. (Courtesy of *La Gaceta.*)

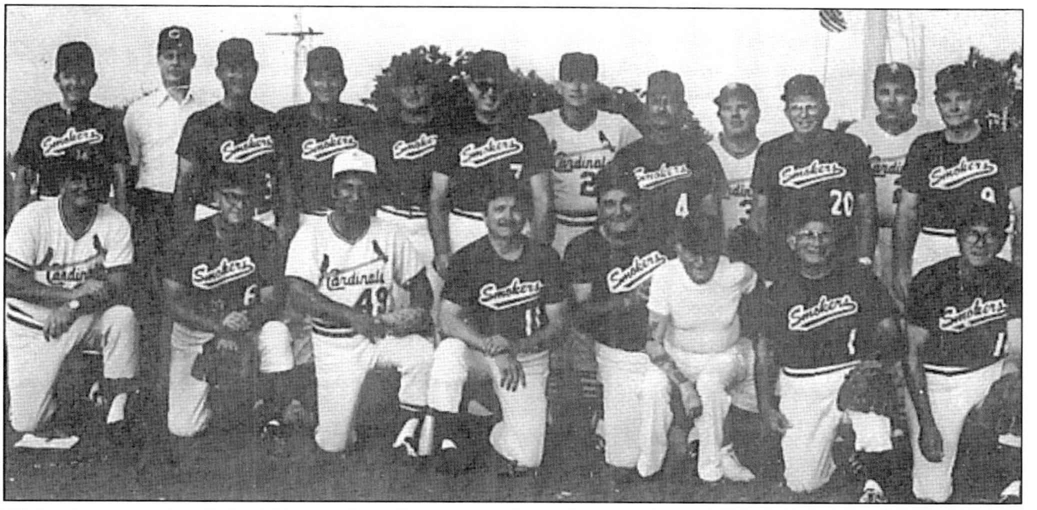

This photograph of the Tampa Smokers was taken during their 1978 "Oldtimers" game at Al Lopez Field. (Courtesy of *La Gaceta*.)

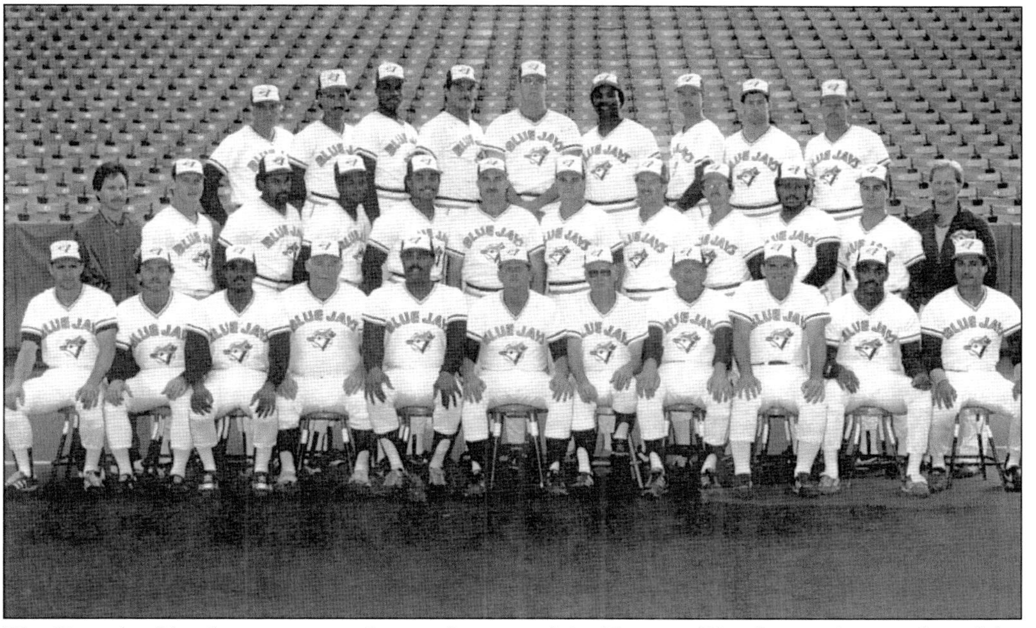

The Dunedin Blue Jays is a minor league division of the Toronto Blue Jays and a member of the Florida State League since 1987. The Dunedin Blue Jays play their home games at Grant Field in Dunedin, located on Douglas Avenue, which is also the spring training site of the Toronto Blue Jays. (Courtesy of Dunedin Historical Museum.)

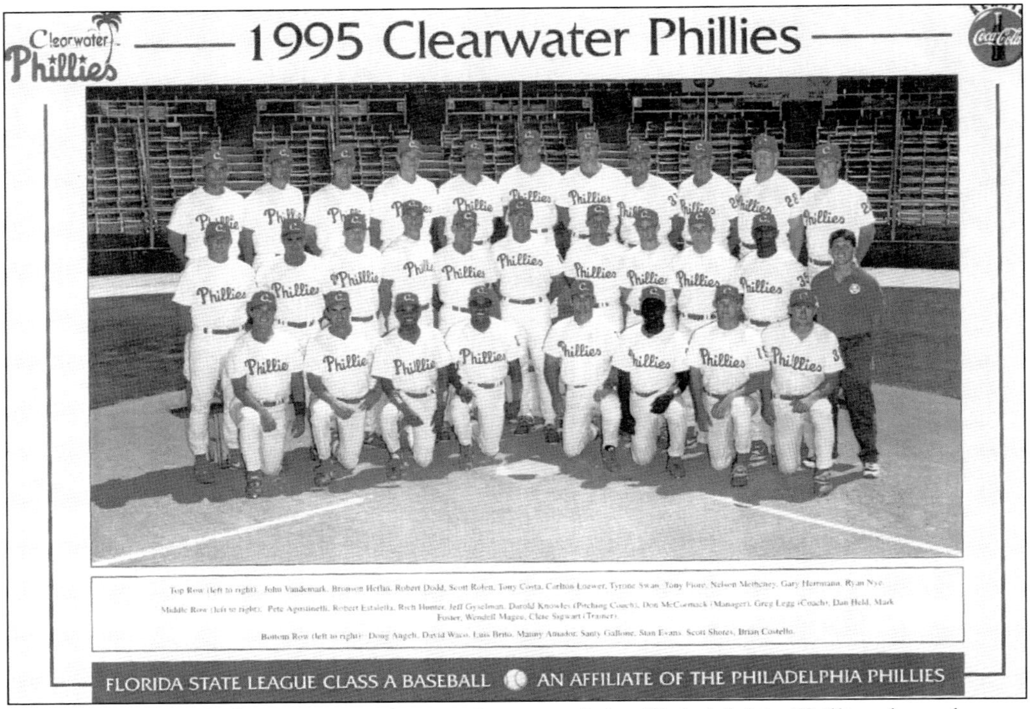

The Clearwater Phillies, a minor league division of the Philadelphia Phillies, have been a member of the Florida State League since 1985. Their home games are played at the Jack Russell Field, located in Clearwater, on Phillies Drive. (Courtesy of Clearwater Phillies.)

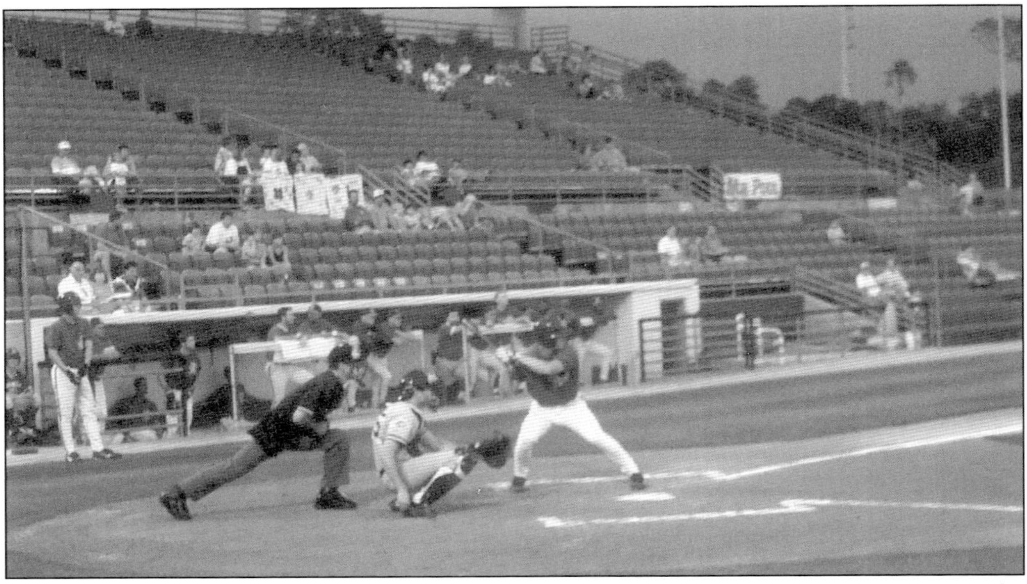

A batter from the Dunedin Blue Jays is about to take a swing in a game against the St. Petersburg Devil Rays at Al Lang Field in June 1998. (Photo by the author.)

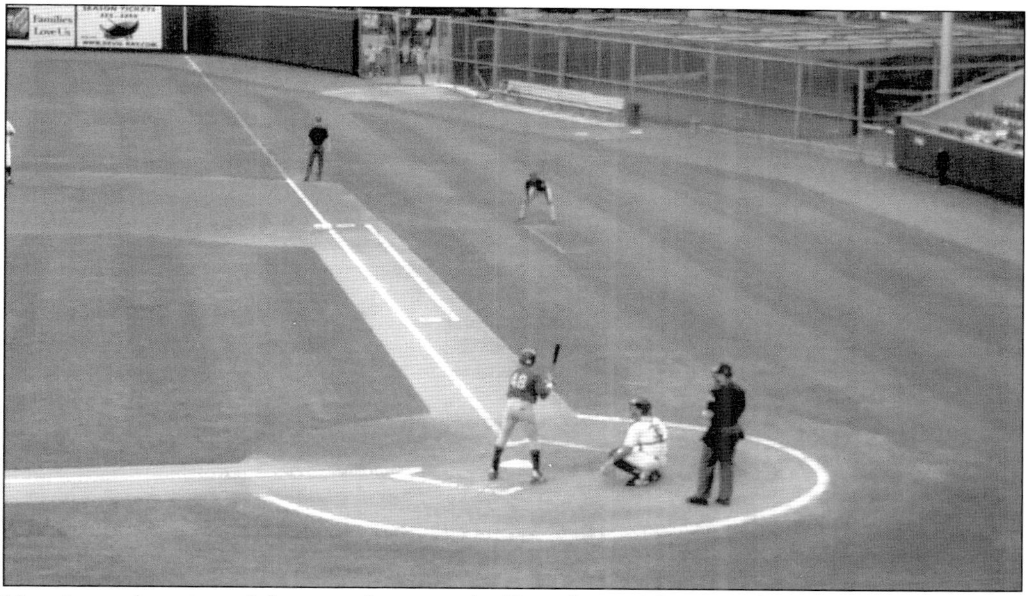

Here is another view of the game between the Dunedin and St. Petersburg teams in June 1998. (Photo by the author.)

Al Lang stadium served as a winter home for the Cardinals and the Mets until the Tampa Bay Devils Rays was created. The facility serves both the Tampa Bay Devil Rays and the St. Petersburg Devil Rays. (Photo by the author.)

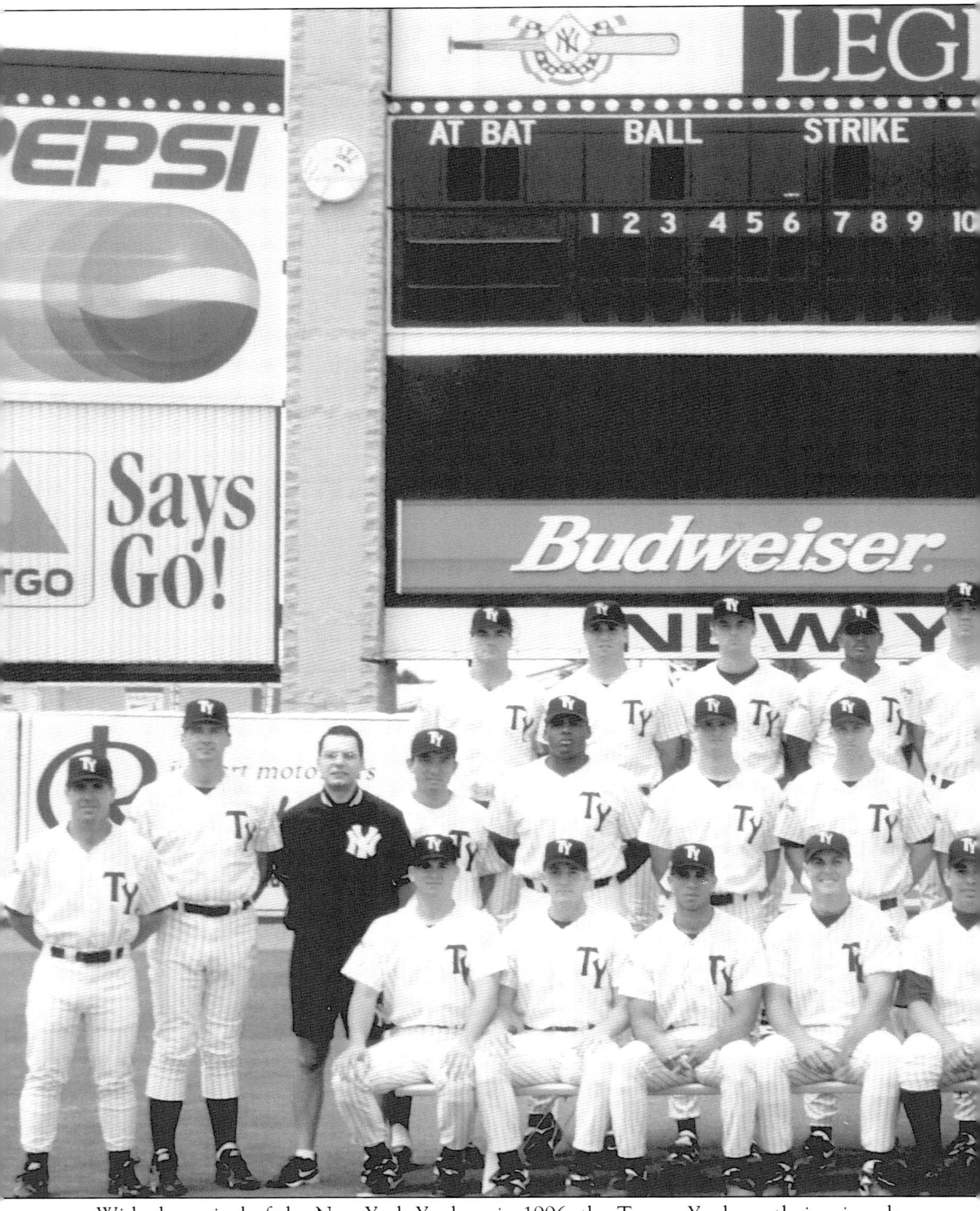

With the arrival of the New York Yankees in 1996, the Tampa Yankees, their minor league team, filled in the gap left by the Tampa Tarpons when they were disbanded in 1987. Seen

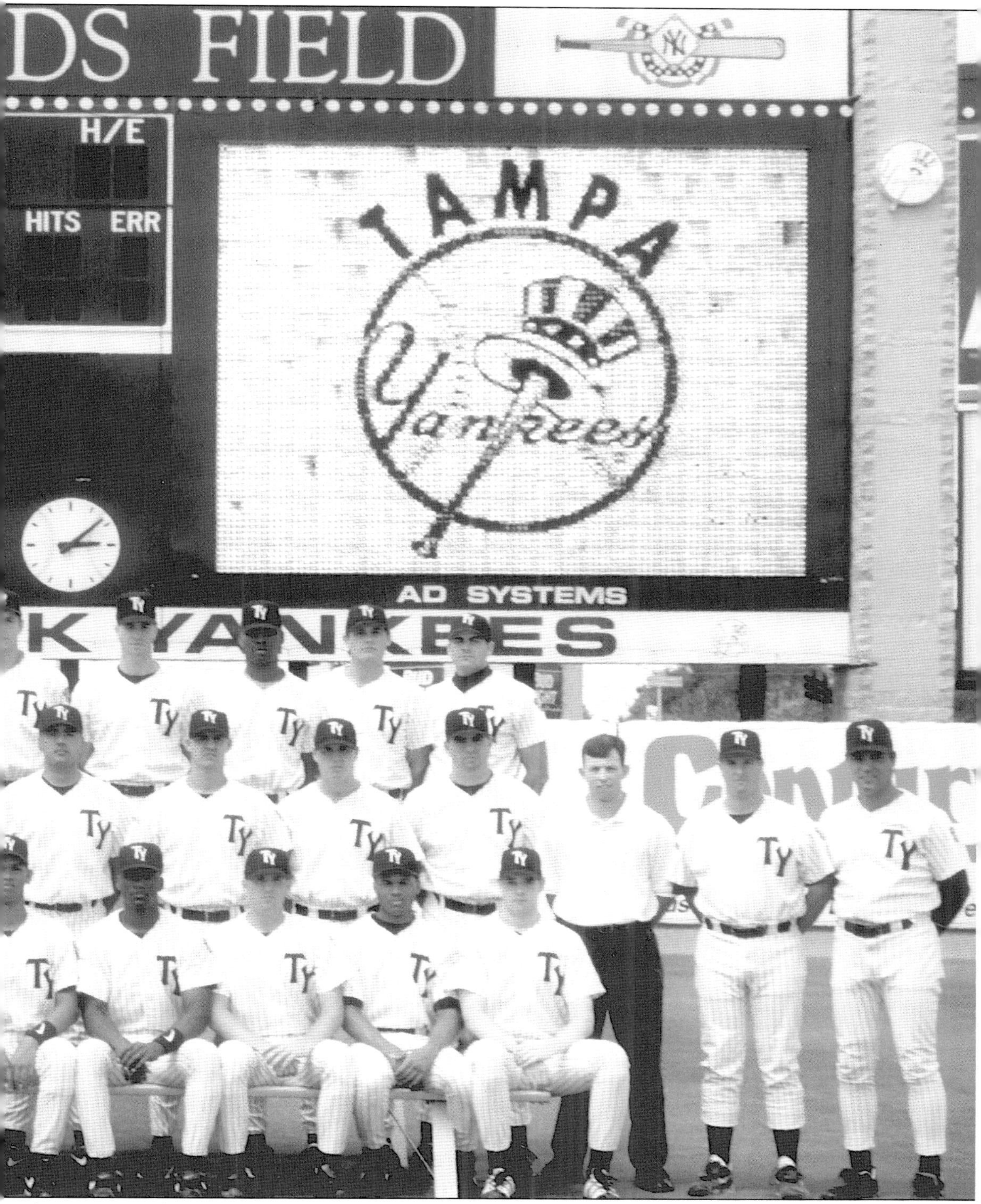

here are members of the 1997 Tampa Yankees team at Legends Field, Tampa. (Courtesy of Tampa Yankees.)

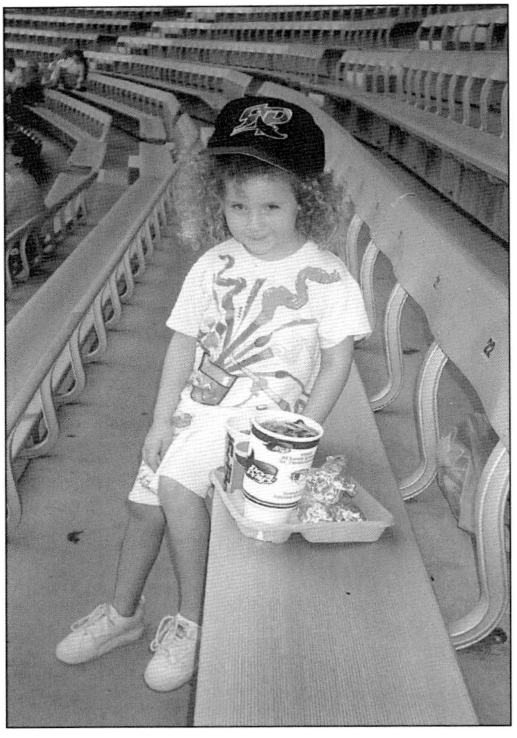

Though there are fewer spectators at most minor league games than at major league games, some diehards go to see the game itself, in its truest form, being played by players without multi-million dollar contracts. This is the case with 6-year-old Caroline (the author's daughter) sporting her St. Petersburg Devil Rays Hat and souvenir cup at a game in Al Lang Field, 1999. (Photo by the author.)

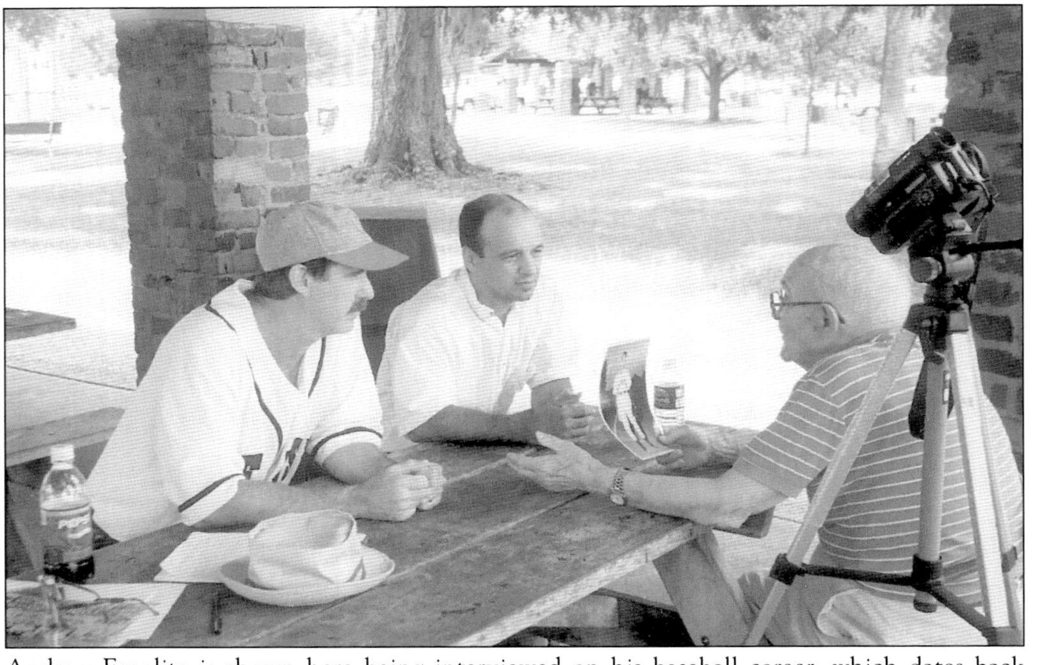

Andrew Espolita is shown here being interviewed on his baseball career, which dates back to 1913. From playing with various teams in Ybor City to becoming a member of the Tampa Smokers and the Nicaraguan national baseball team, Espolita is considered by many to be an early baseball pioneer in Tampa Bay. (Photo by the author.)

Five

The Major Leagues and Spring Training

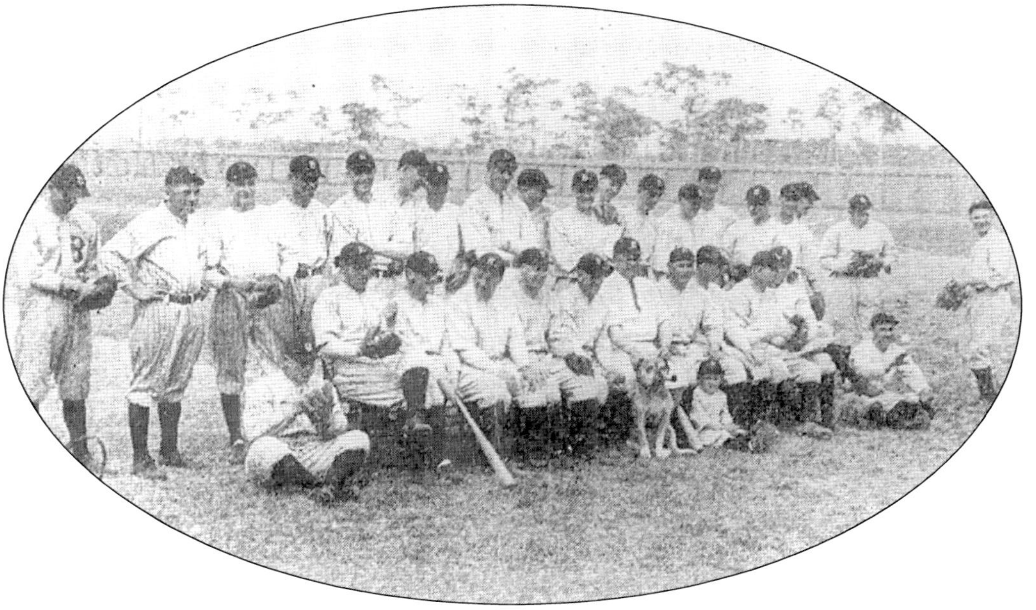

Between 1923 and 1932 (and again between 1936 and 1940), the Brooklyn Dodgers used Clearwater as a base for their spring training. Seen here is a 1926 image of the team while in Clearwater. (Courtesy of Pinellas County Historical Museum.)

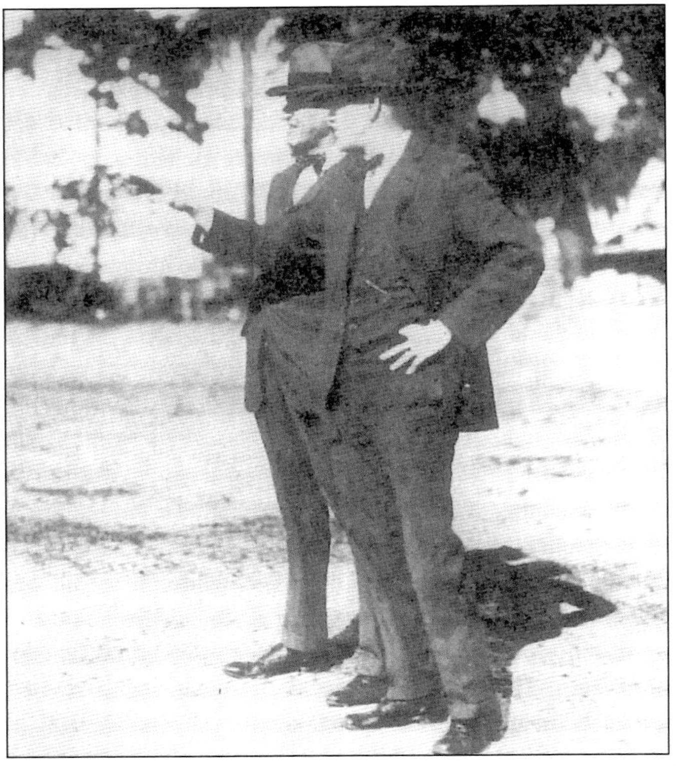

Miller Huggins (foreground) initially tried to bring the St. Louis Cardinals to St. Petersburg in 1912. When the Cardinals backed out of the deal, Tampa succeeded in bringing in another team to the bay area the following year. On February 26, 1913, the Chicago Cubs held Tampa Bay's first spring training game against the Cuban Athletics at Plant Field; the score was 4-2. (Courtesy of Pinellas County Historical Museum.)

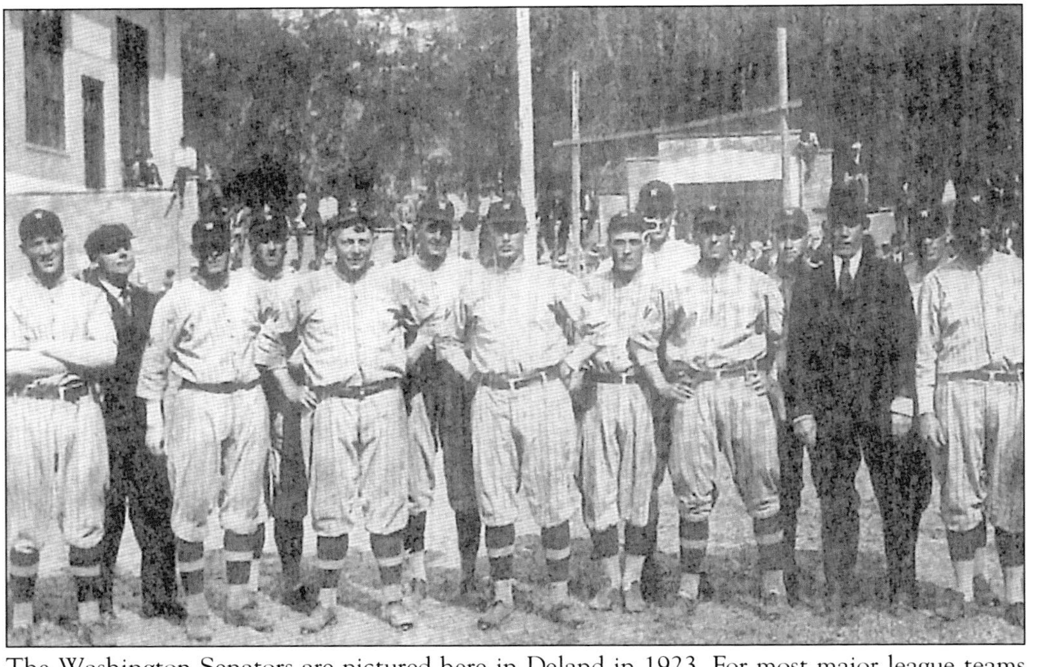

The Washington Senators are pictured here in Deland in 1923. For most major league teams wintering in Florida, training consisted of traveling to other Florida towns to play against other major league or local semi-professional teams. (Courtesy of Florida State Archives.)

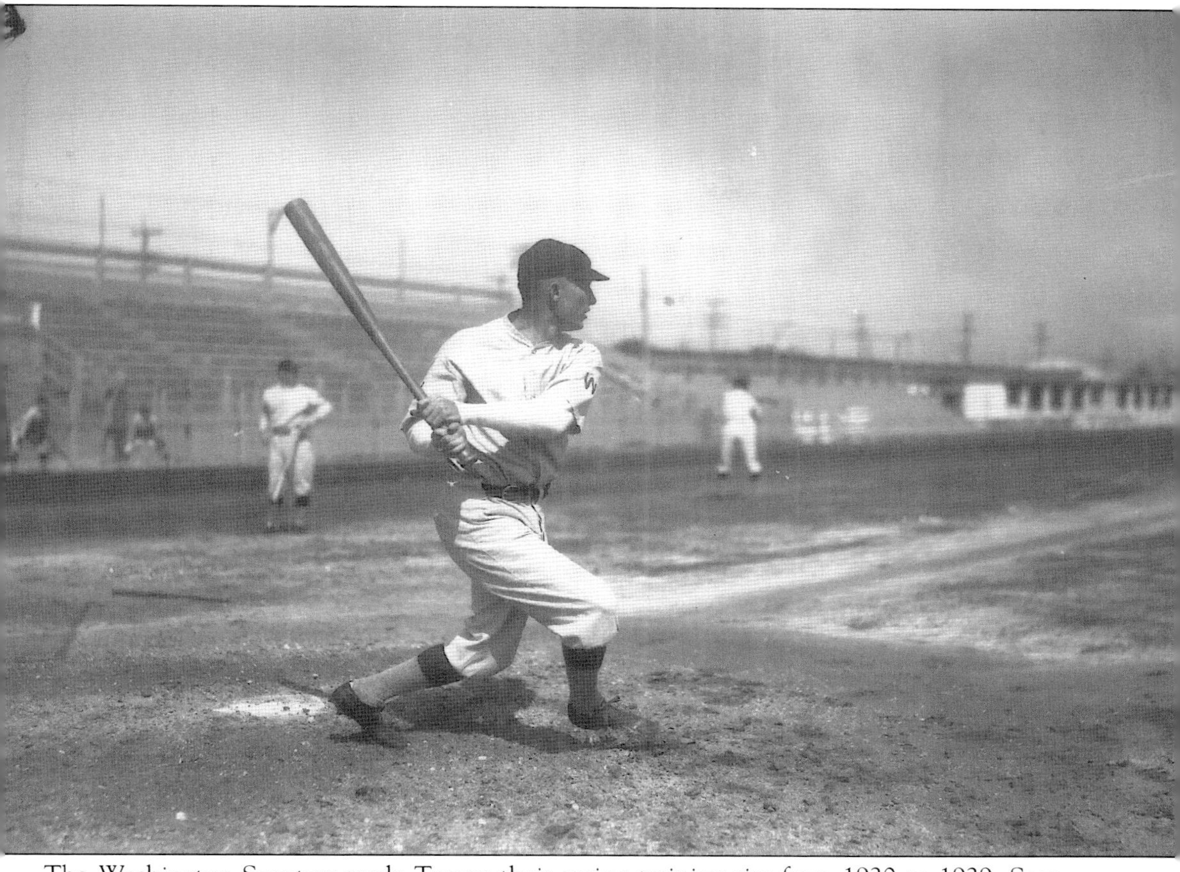

The Washington Senators made Tampa their spring training site from 1920 to 1929. Seen here is Sam Rice taking a swing at a pitch on the diamond at Plant Field (site of the University of Tampa). The photograph is dated March 1925. (Courtesy of Tampa-Hillsborough County Public Library System.)

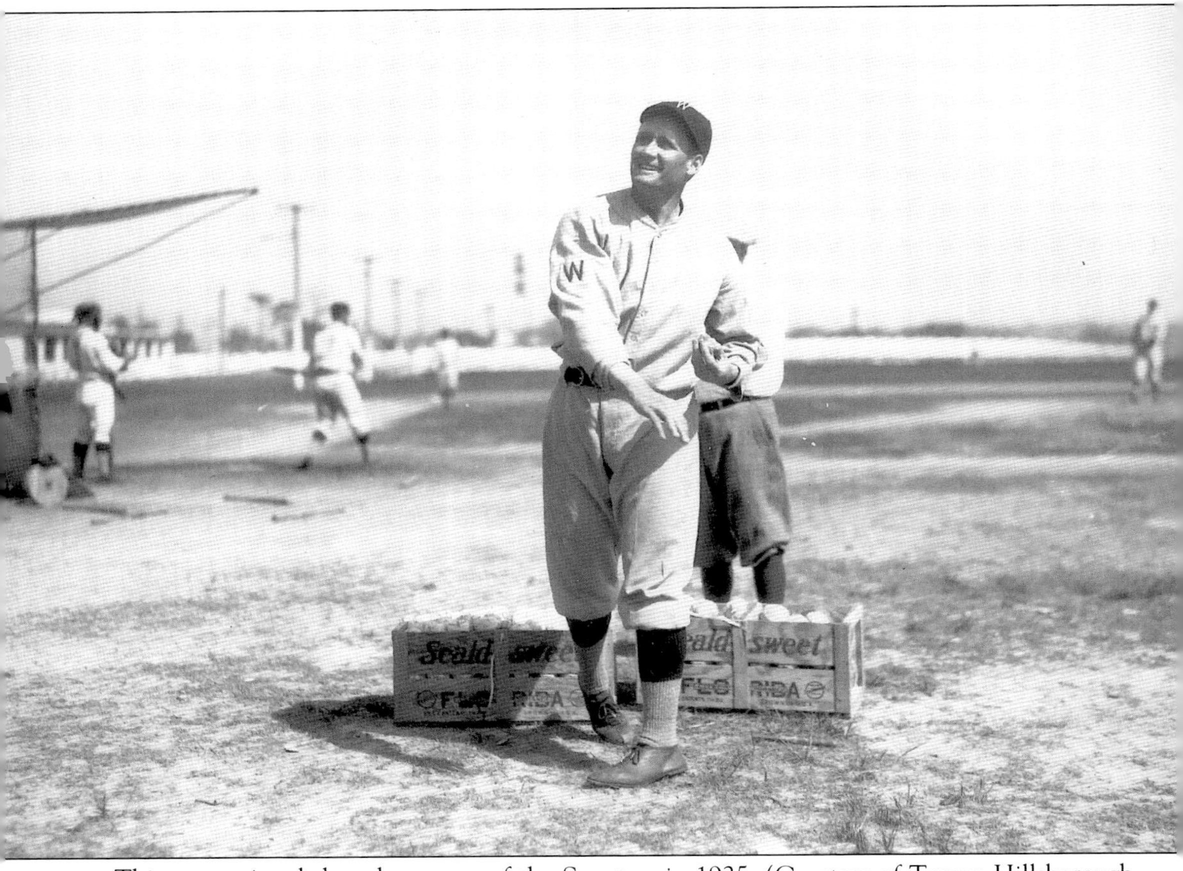

This promotional shot shows one of the Senators in 1925. (Courtesy of Tampa-Hillsborough County Public Library System.)

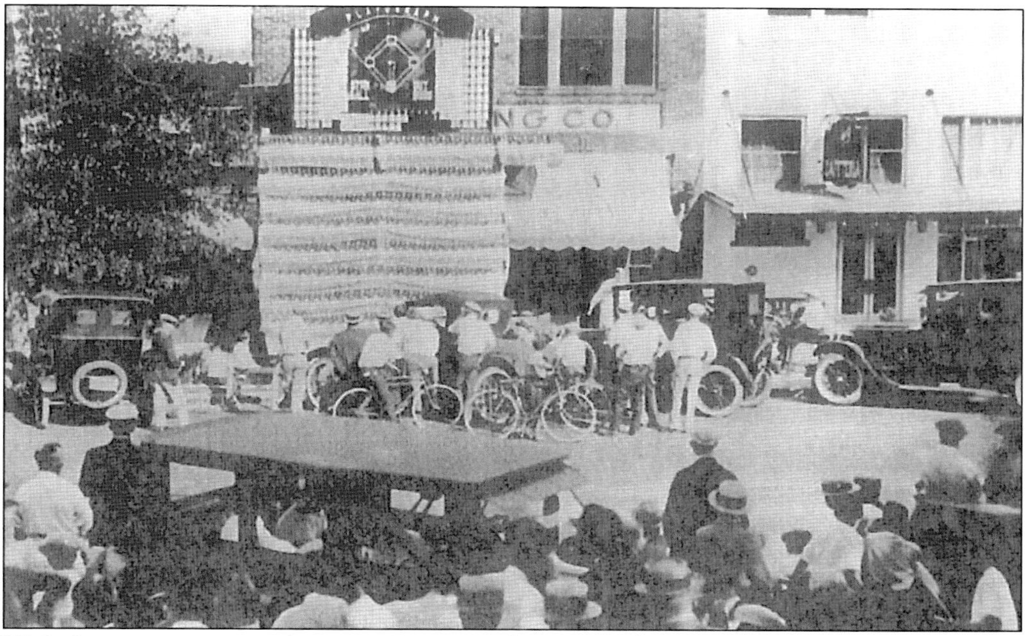

With fierce competition between Tampa and St. Petersburg to bring professional baseball to the area, ploys were used to create interest in the game, such as this baseball scoreboard located in front of the offices of the *St. Petersburg Times* in 1924. (Courtesy of Pinellas County Historical Museum.)

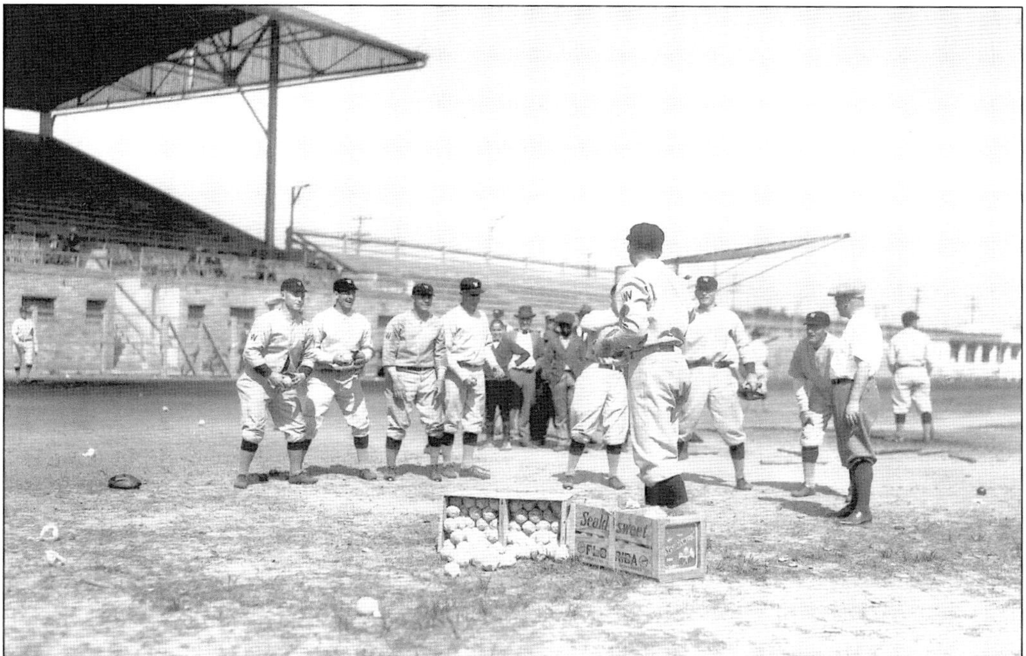

Clowning around for the camera, these baseball players have substituted oranges for their baseballs! (Courtesy of Tampa-Hillsborough County Public Library System.)

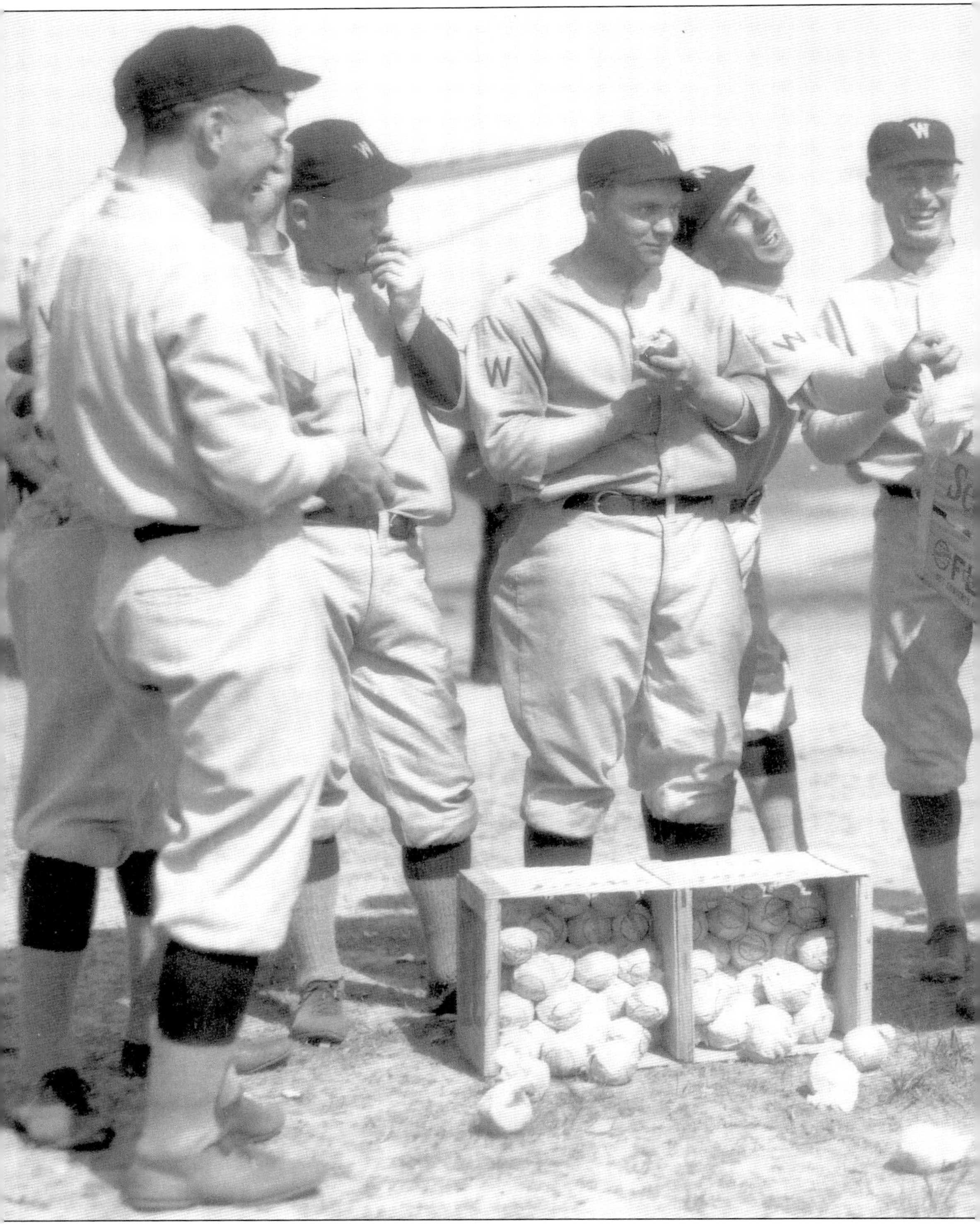

This image is simply titled "View of Washington Senators sampling some oranges, 9 March

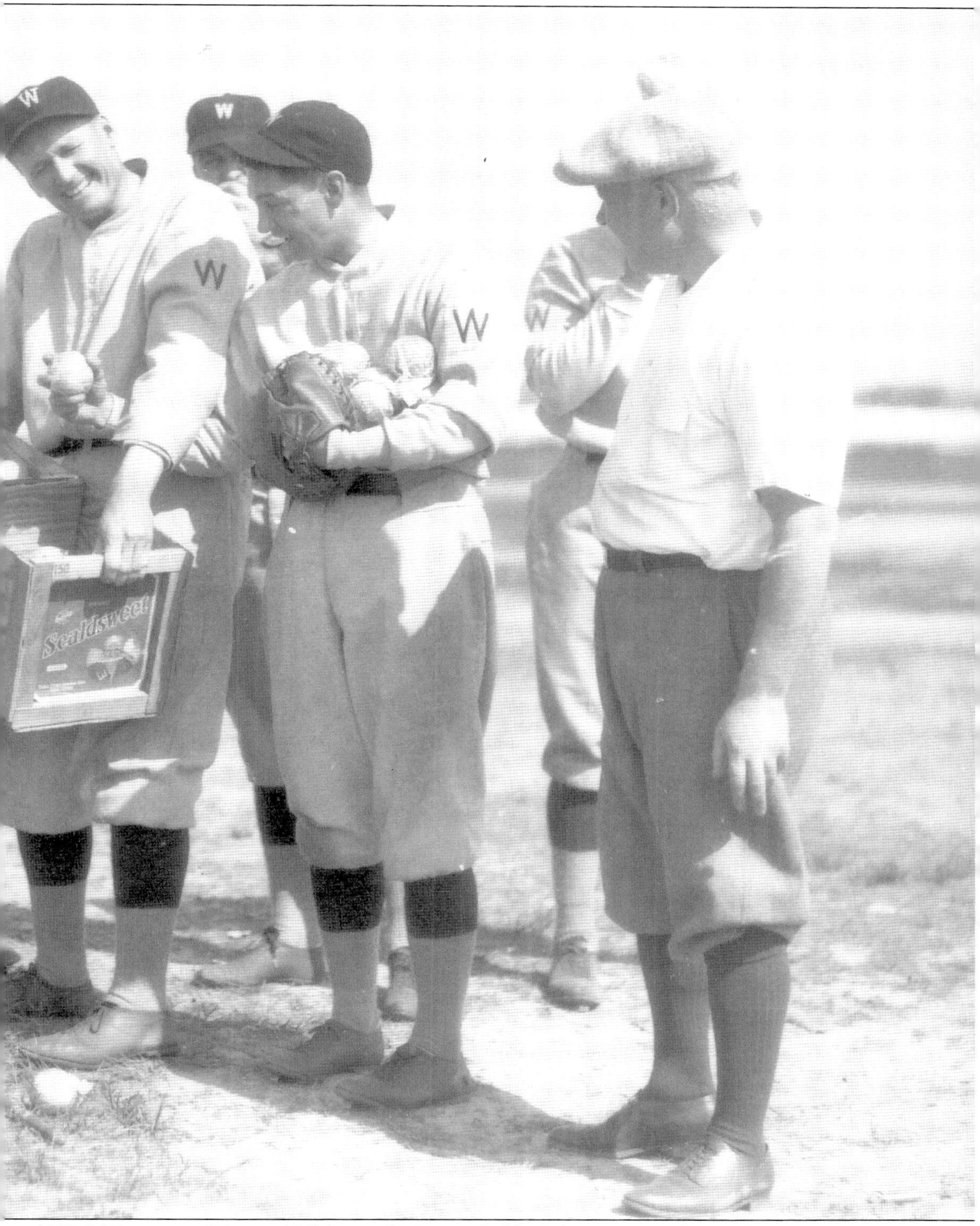

1925." (Courtesy of Tampa-Hillsborough County Public Library System.)

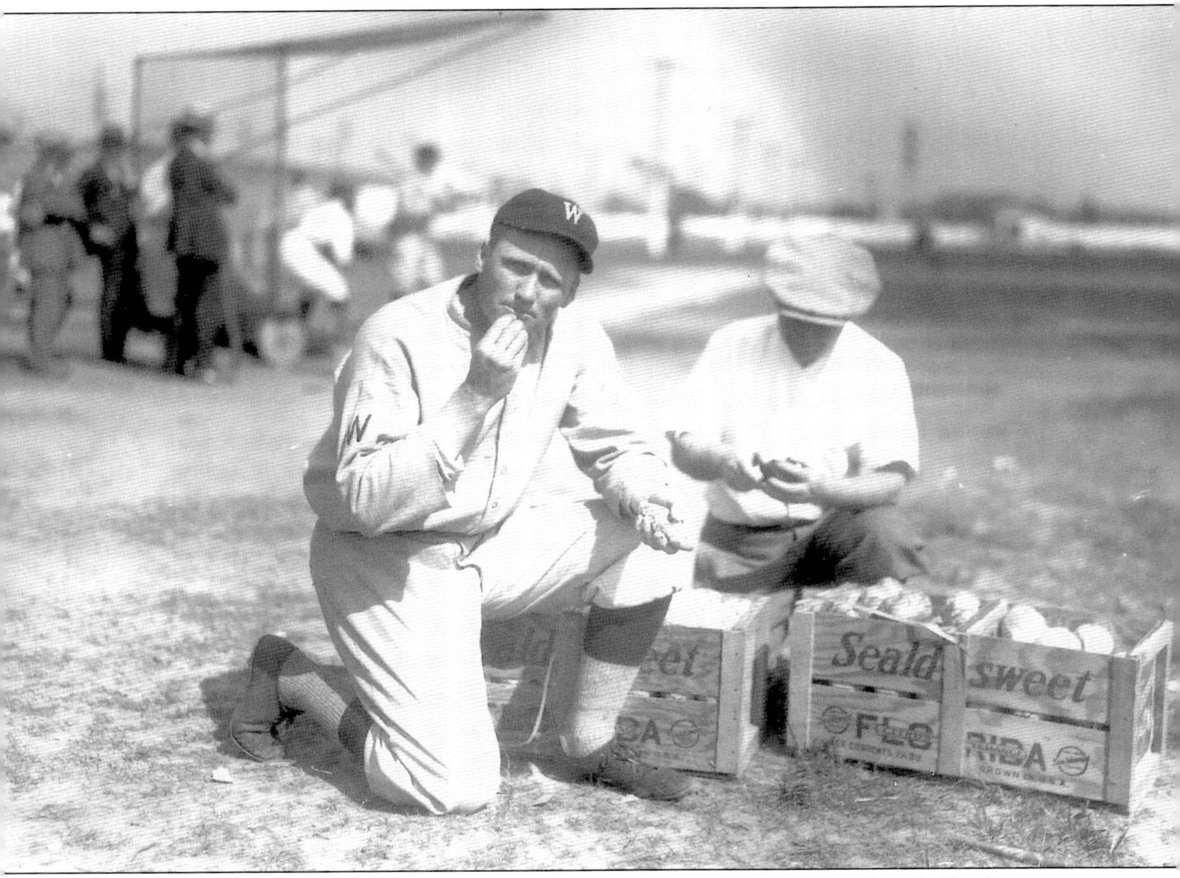

The promotional line for this image was "Washington Senators baseball players get an energy boost with oranges, 9 March 1925." (Courtesy of Tampa-Hillsborough County Public Library System.)

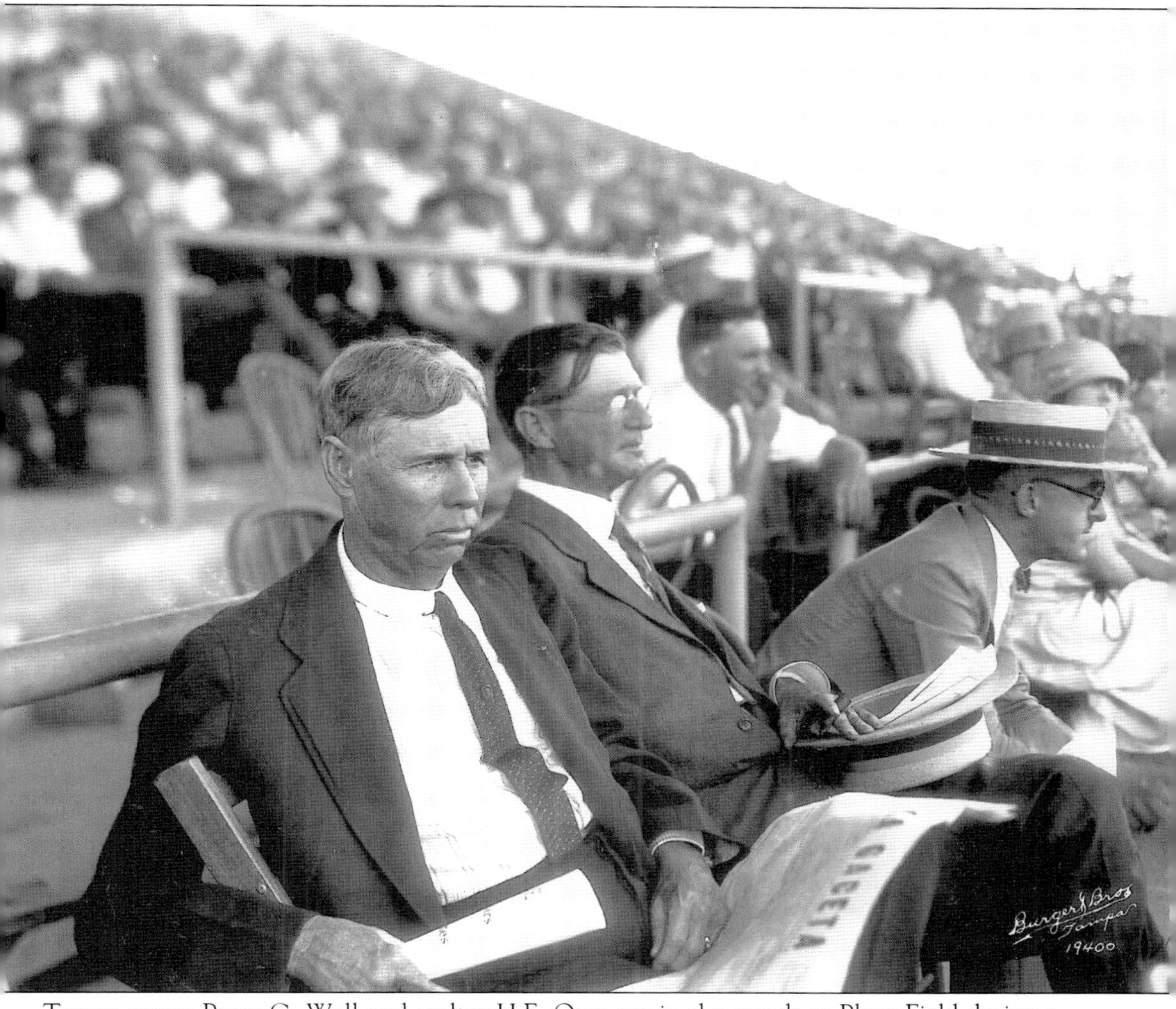

Tampa mayor Percy G. Wall and realtor H.E. Opre are in the stands at Plant Field during a Washington Senators baseball game, May 14, 1926. Note an early edition of *La Gaceta* on the mayor's lap. The paper was a tri-lingual (Spanish, Italian, and English) publication that catered to the Cuban and Italian immigrant communities in Ybor City and West Tampa. (Courtesy of Tampa-Hillsborough County Public Library System.)

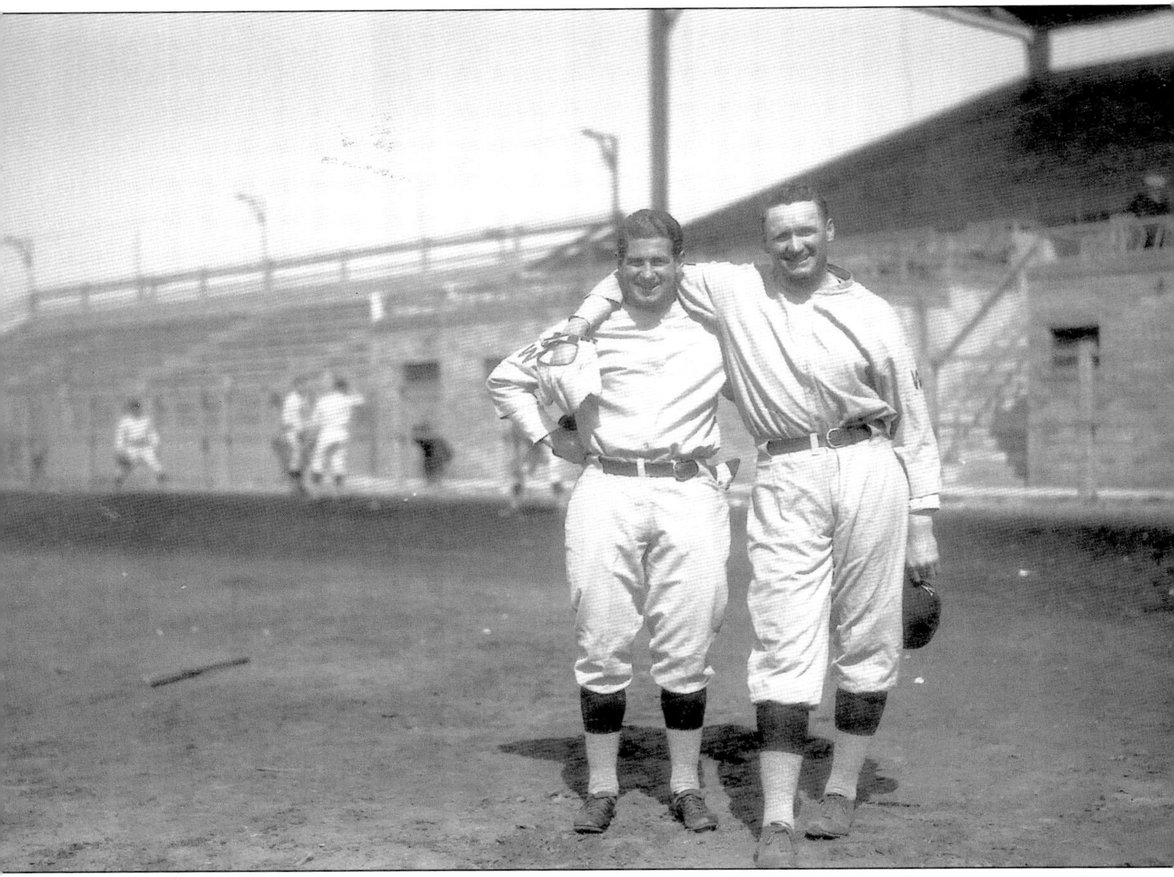

Washington Senators teammates Walter Johnson and Bucky Harris pause for a moment to have their picture taken during spring training at Plant Field, March 9, 1925. (Courtesy of Tampa-Hillsborough County Public Library System.)

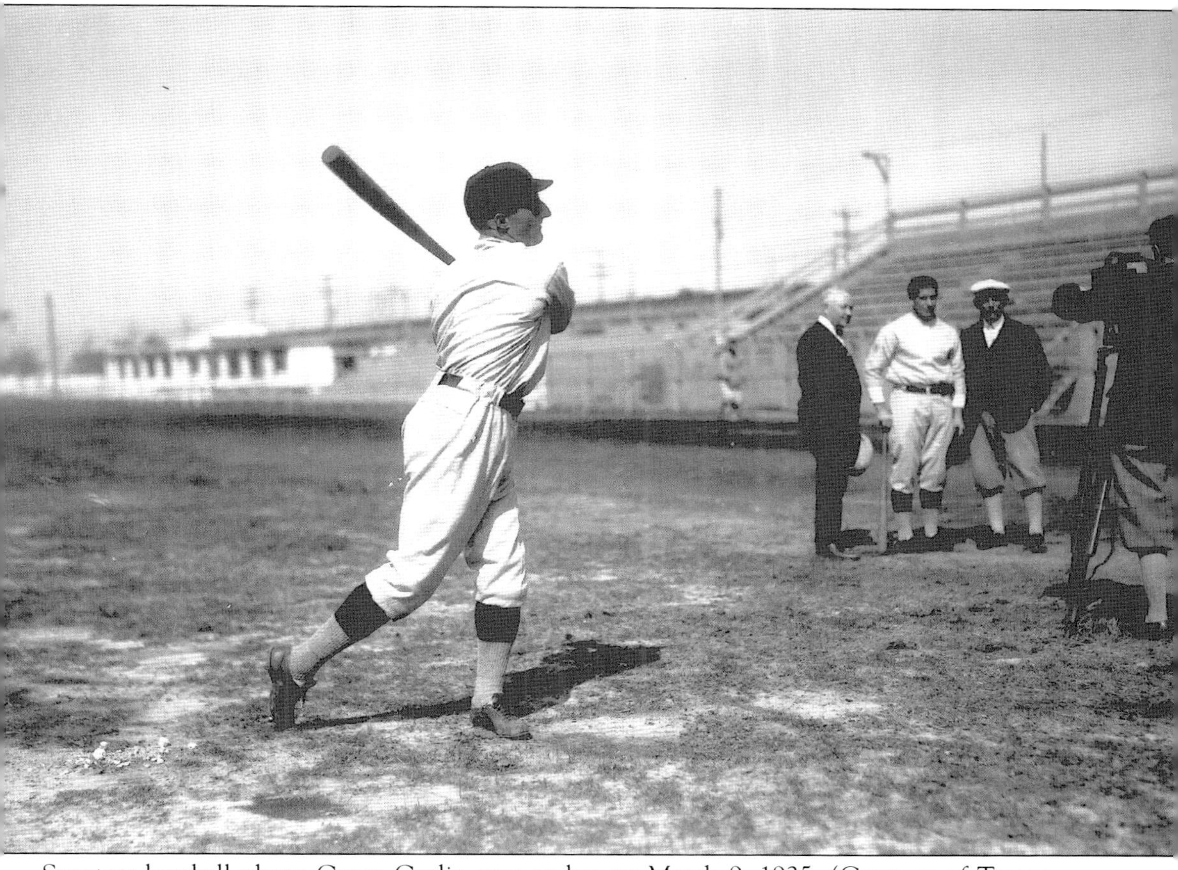

Senators baseball player Goose Goslin goes to bat on March 9, 1925. (Courtesy of Tampa-Hillsborough County Public Library System.)

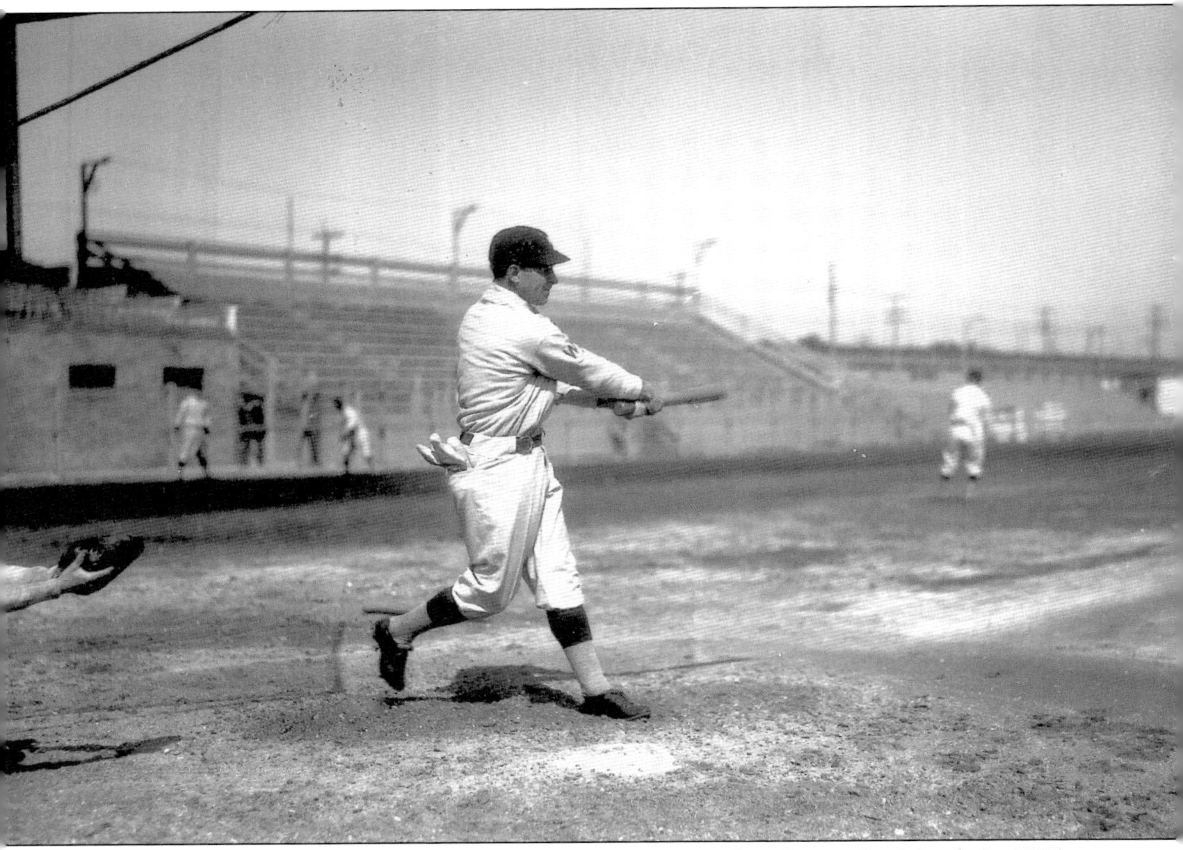

Washington Senators baseball player Bucky Harris is at bat during the March 9, 1925 game. (Courtesy of Tampa-Hillsborough County Public Library System.)

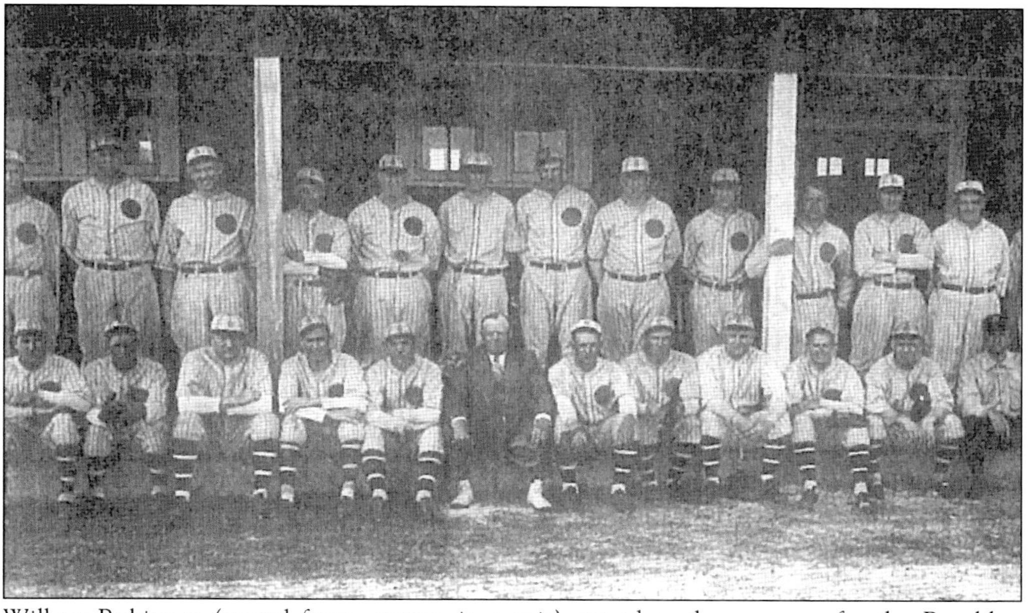

Wilbert Robinson (seated front, center, in a suit) served as the manager for the Brooklyn Dodgers. The team is pictured here in their spring training camp in Clearwater in the late 1920s. (Courtesy of Florida State Archives.)

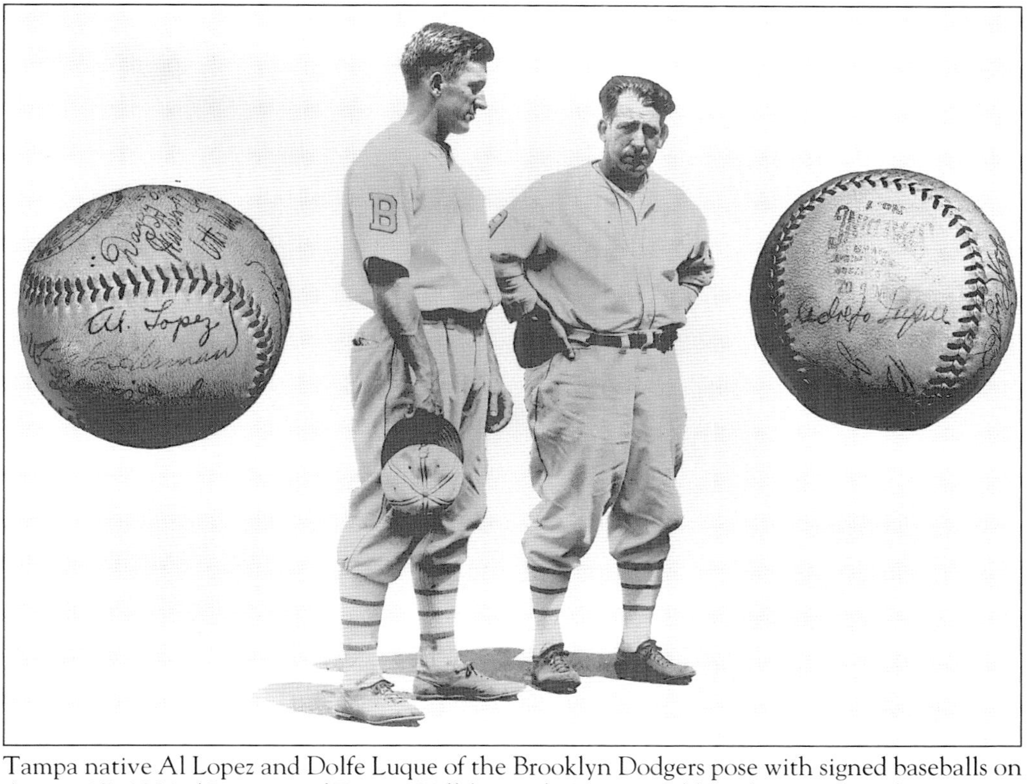

Tampa native Al Lopez and Dolfe Luque of the Brooklyn Dodgers pose with signed baseballs on August 17, 1931. (Courtesy of Tampa-Hillsborough County Public Library System.)

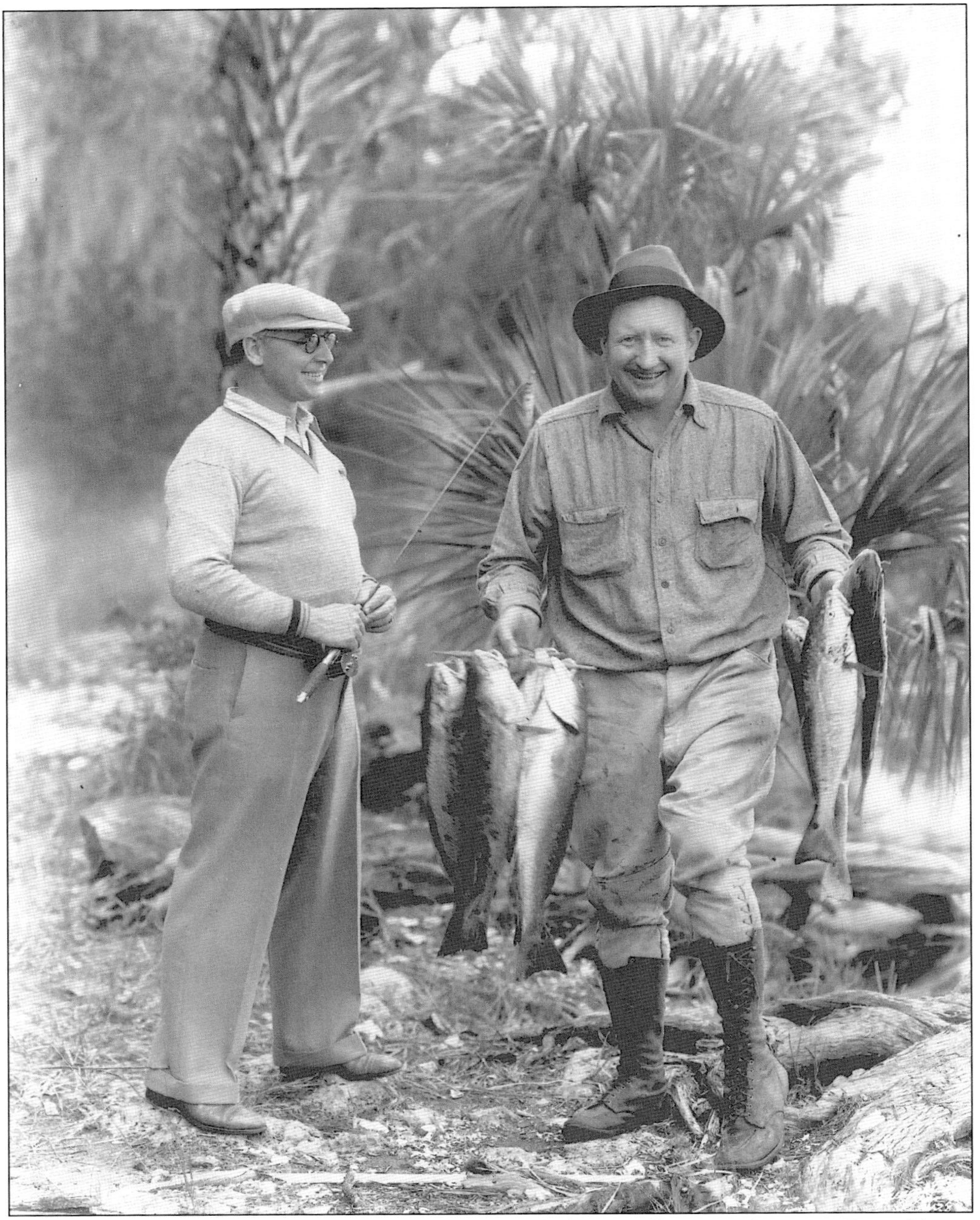

Even ball players need to rest and enjoy what Florida has to offer. Seen here are Dazzy Vance (with fish) and Edward Alexander (with fishing rod) taking a break from baseball on December 23, 1931. (Courtesy of Tampa-Hillsborough County Public Library System.)

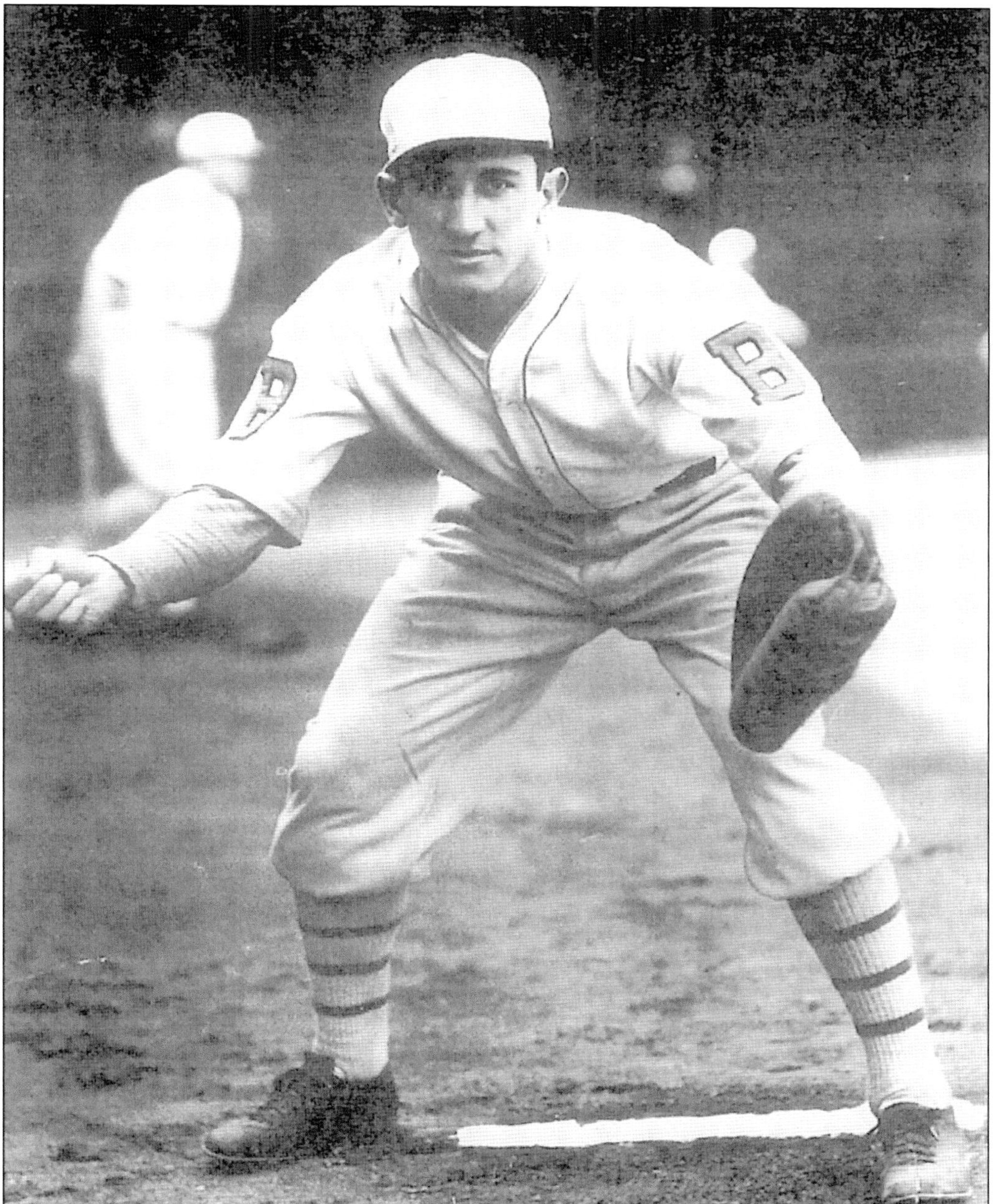

Lopez began playing for the Tampa Smokers in 1925. He was one of a few Latinos who would enter into professional baseball in the early part of the 20th century. By 1931, Lopez was playing for the Brooklyn Dodgers. (Courtesy of National Baseball Library.)

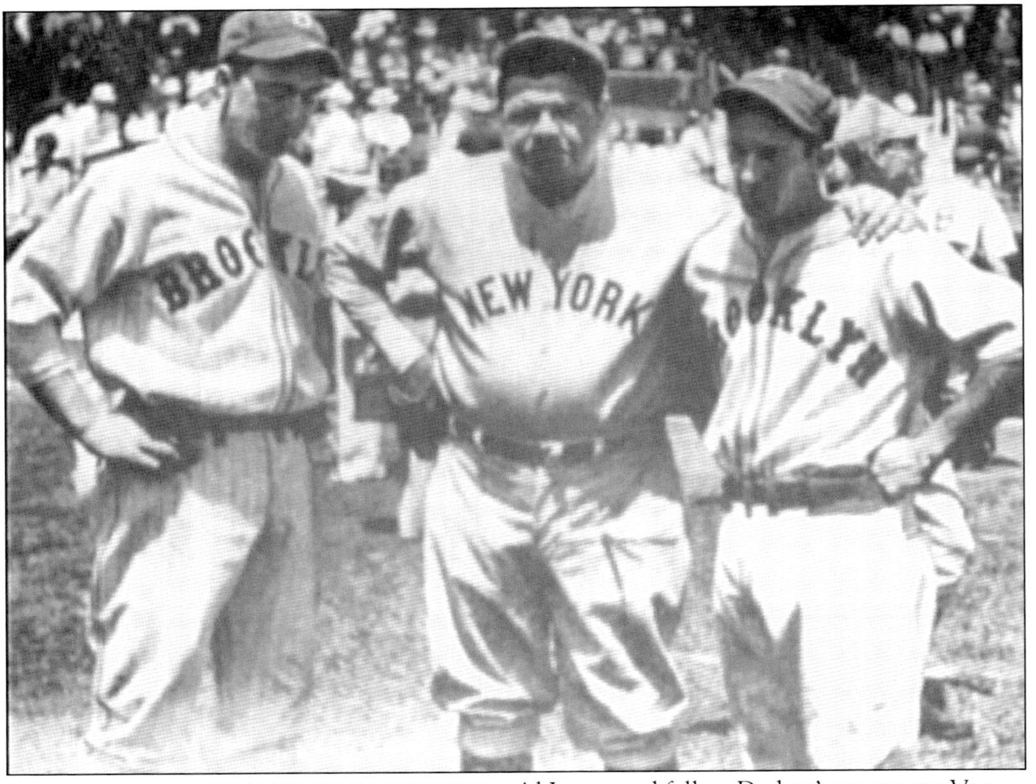

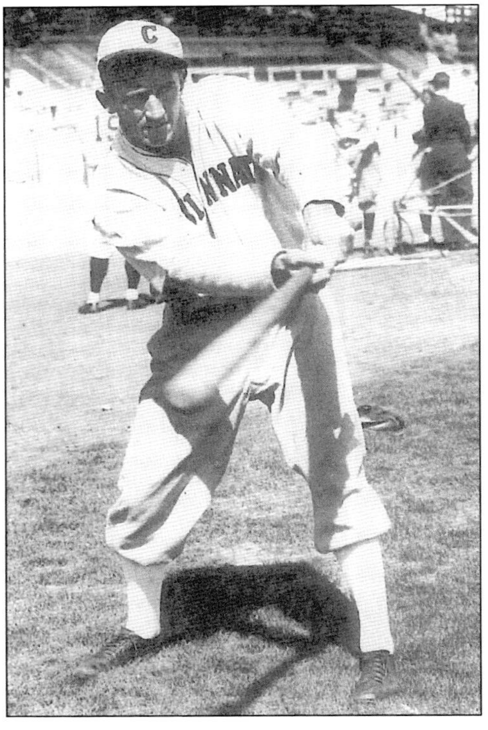

Al Lopez and fellow Dodger's teammate Van Lingle Mungo, a right-handed pitching star for the team, had their picture taken with New York Yankee great Babe Ruth, *c.* 1930s. (Courtesy of *La Gaceta.*)

Al Lopez, in a Cincinnati Reds uniform, trains in Tampa's Plant Field while holding out for a better Brooklyn Dodgers contract in 1934. The Reds used Tampa as their spring training home from 1931 to 1942 and from 1946 to 1987. (Courtesy of National Baseball Library.)

Lou Gehrig is pictured with Jennie Worden in March 1934. The New York Yankees used St. Petersburg as their spring training base from 1925 to 1942. The team also used the city during two other periods, from 1946 to 1950 and from 1952 to 1961. (Courtesy of Pinellas County Historical Museum.)

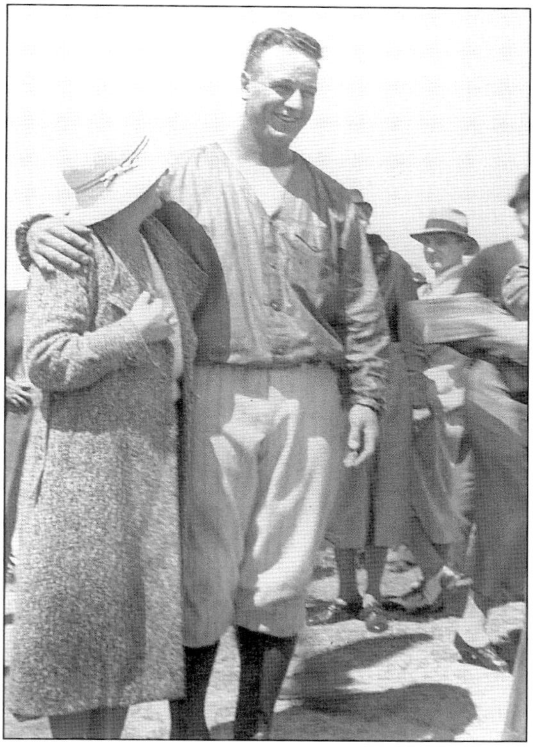

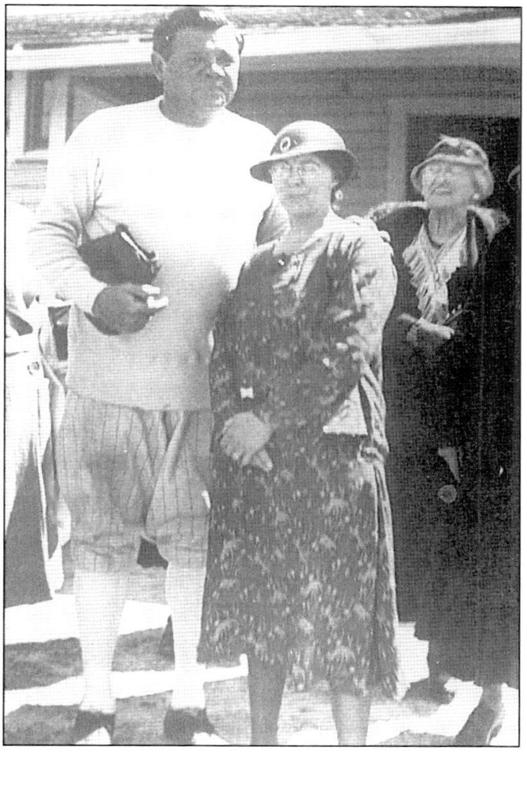

Legendary right fielder George Herman "Babe" Ruth is seen here while in St. Petersburg for spring training in March 1934. Ruth had trained in Tampa while with the Red Sox and later in St. Petersburg after being traded to the New York Yankees. There are numerous stories of Ruth's antics in Tampa Bay and, regarding his experience in St. Petersburg, he had been quoted as saying, "I ain't going out there anymore. There're alligators out there." (Courtesy of Pinellas County Historical Museum.)

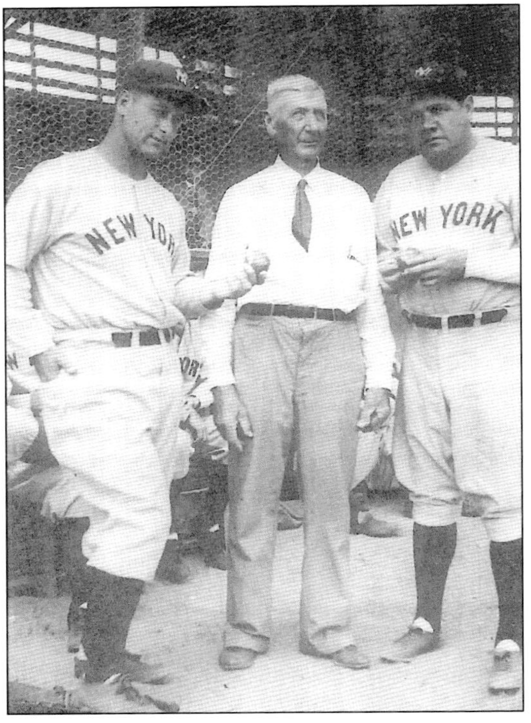

Dick Mayes, a local baseball booster from Brooksville, poses with Lou Gehrig and Babe Ruth at the Yankees spring training camp in St. Petersburg in 1934. (Courtesy of Florida State Archives.)

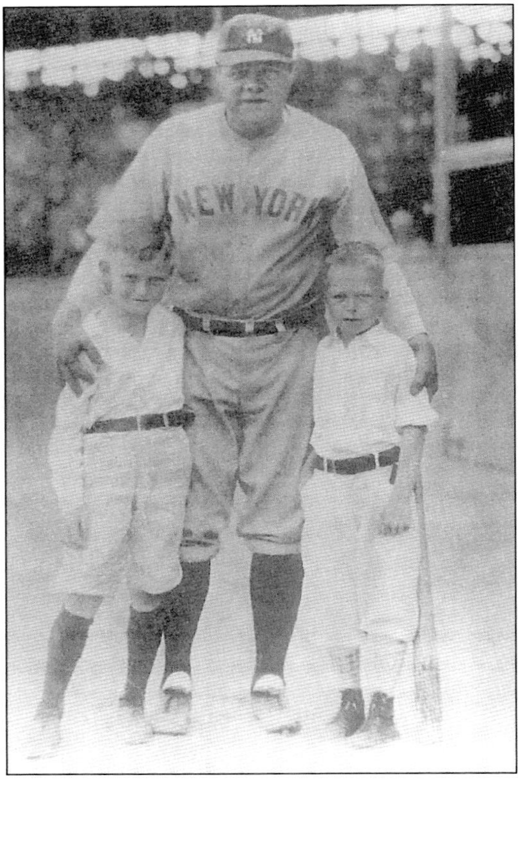

Two lucky young fans get their picture taken with their idol, Babe Ruth. (Courtesy of Pinellas County Historical Museum.)

While training in Florida, Ruth would take advantage of his free time by playing golf on nearby courses in Pinellas and Hillsborough Counties. (Courtesy of Pinellas County Historical Museum.)

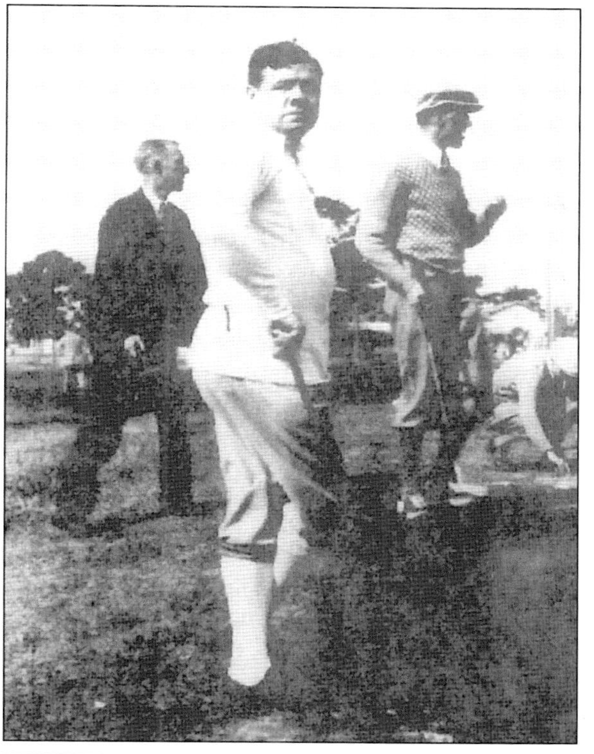

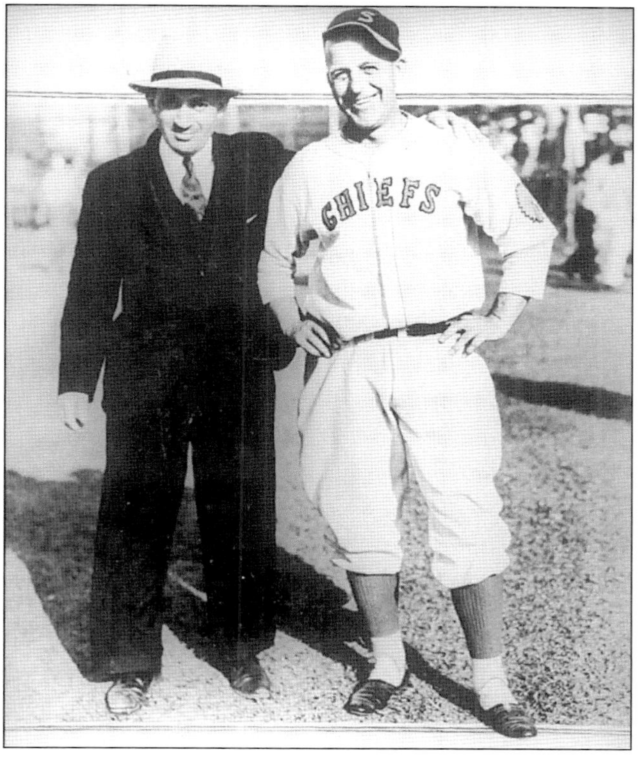

The caption on this photograph reads, "Lou Mandell, 'baseball's perpetual rookie,' with Sunny Jim Bottomley, before being tossed out of the Syracuse camp. P.S. Shortly after, he was tossed out of Hotel Tampa Terrace." The image dates from April 1938. (Courtesy of Pinellas County Historical Museum.)

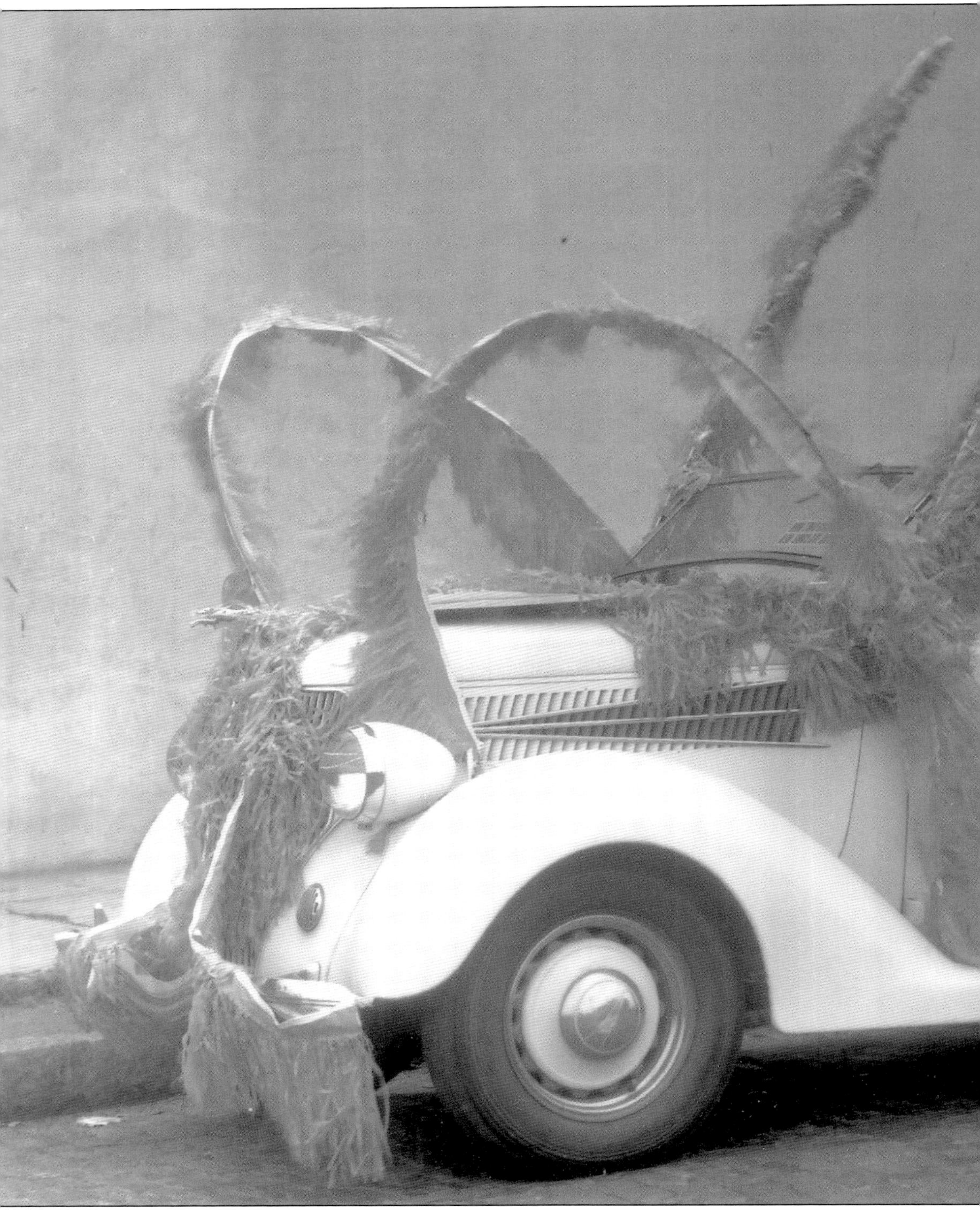

A Babe Ruth look-alike performs a promotional stunt outside of Plant Field, an area also used for the Florida State Fair—as evidenced by the livestock stables in background. The promoter in

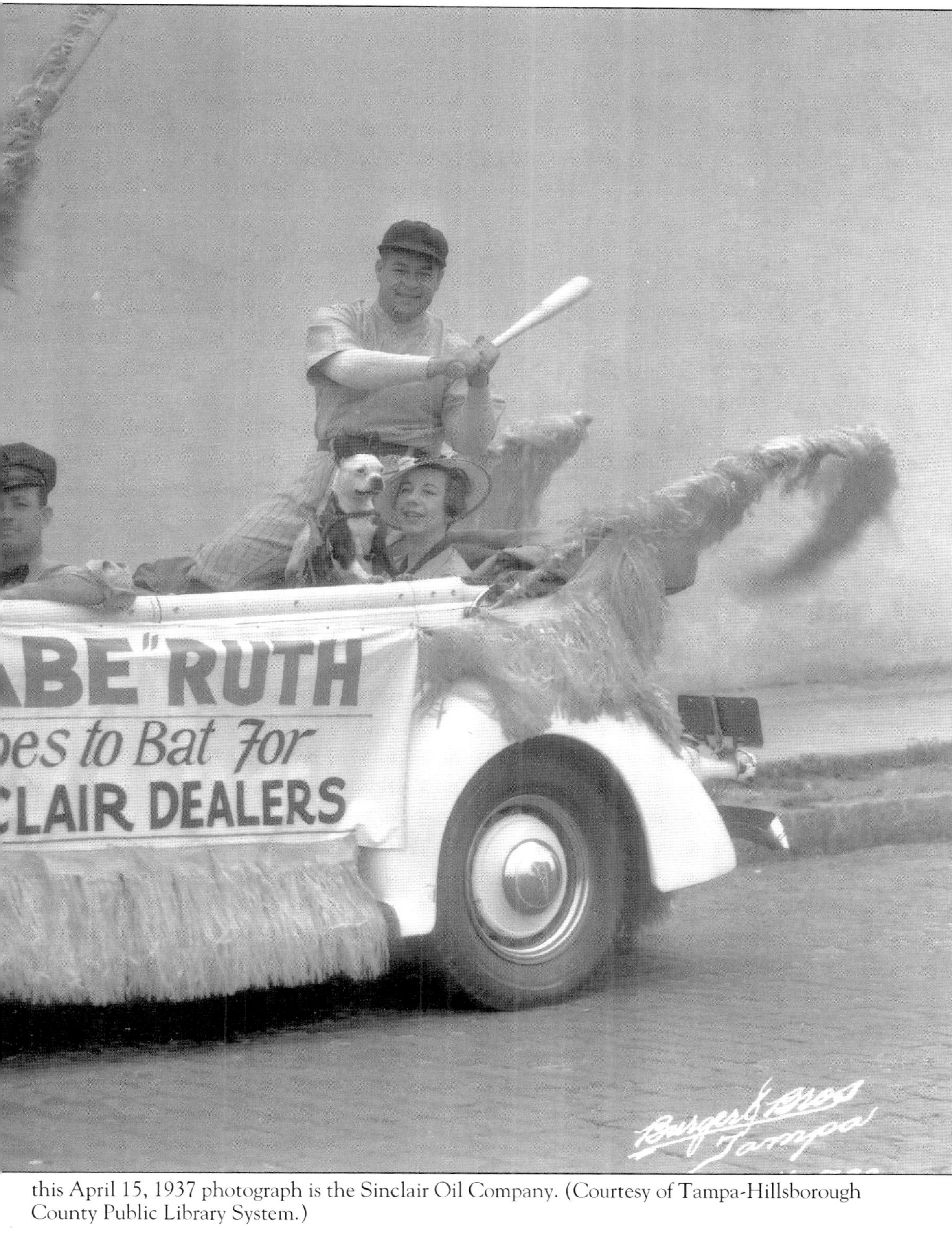

this April 15, 1937 photograph is the Sinclair Oil Company. (Courtesy of Tampa-Hillsborough County Public Library System.)

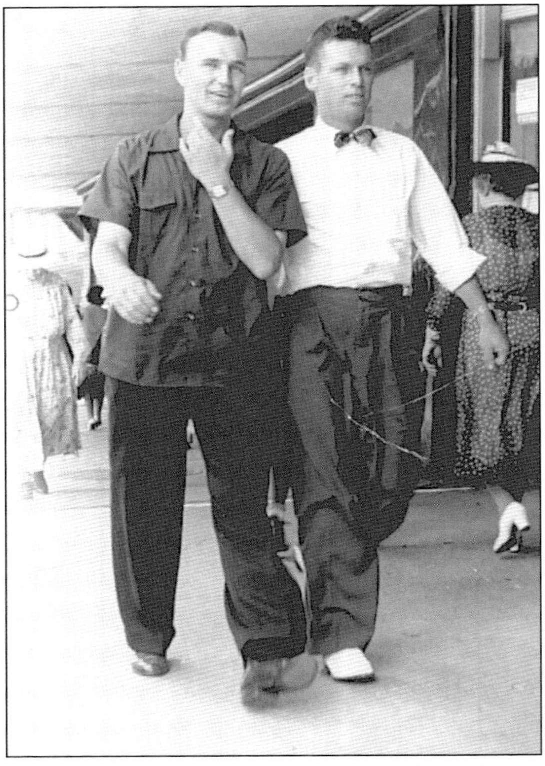

St. Louis Cardinals baseball player Edward Eilbie (right) and a teammate stroll down a street in St. Petersburg in 1938. The Cardinals used St. Petersburg as a spring training camp from 1938 to 1942 and from 1946 to 1997. (Courtesy of ADEQ Historical Resources.)

From left to right are Johnny Mize, Enos Slaughter, and Pepper Martin of the St. Louis Cardinals, watching their fellow teammates work out at the batter's cage on Al Lang Field, 1939. (Courtesy of Pinellas County Historical Museum.)

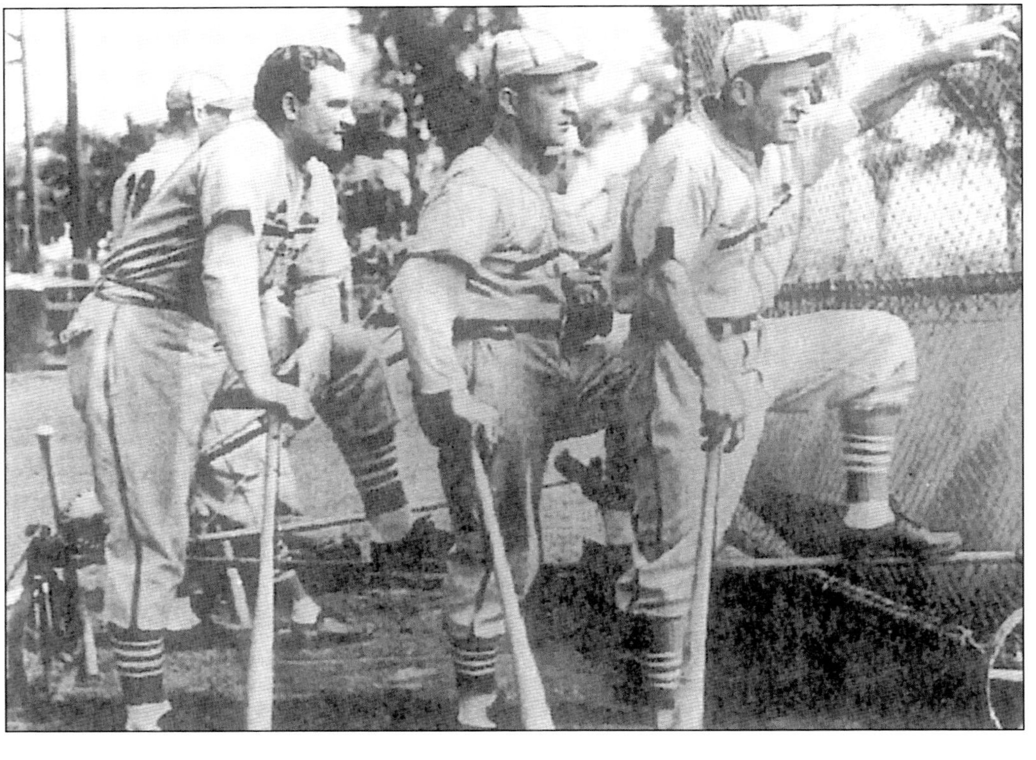

Catcher Al Lopez was with the Pittsburgh Pirates in 1941. (Courtesy of National Baseball Library.)

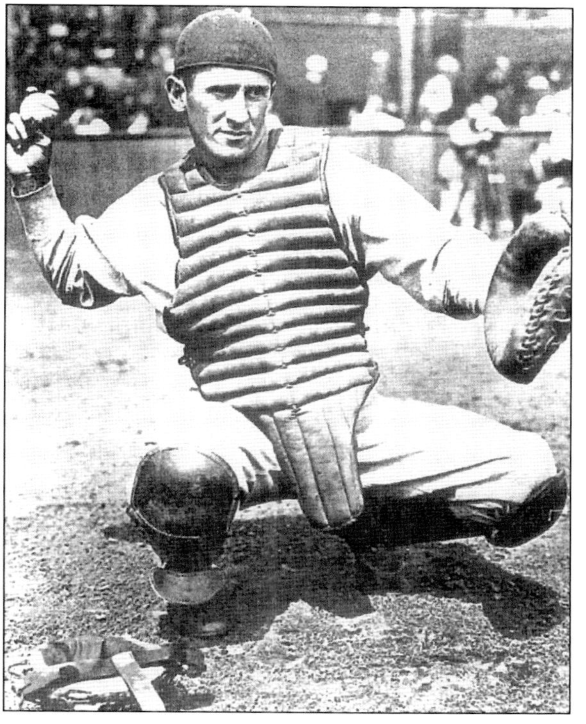

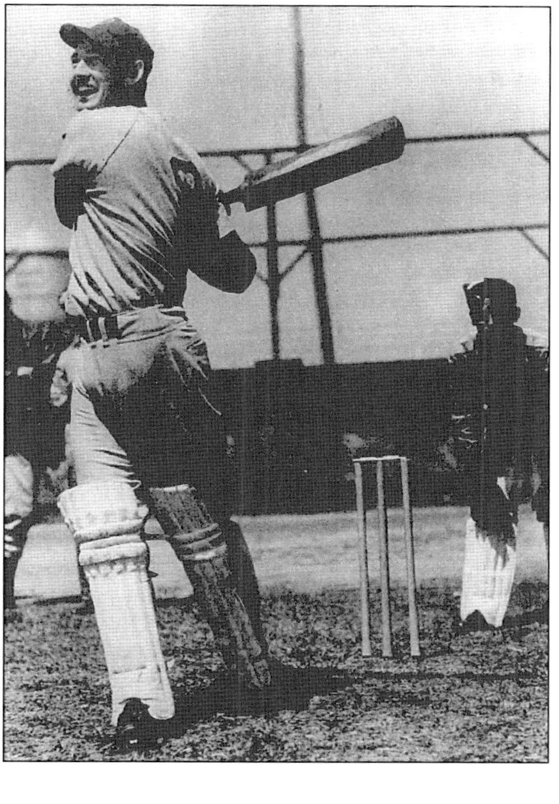

Another baseball legend, Ted Williams, plays cricket with British Royal Air Force cadets from Lakeland's Lodwick School of Aeronautics in 1941. World War II would soon put a temporary halt to spring training in Florida and to regular professional baseball games throughout the country. Many players, such as Williams and DiMaggio, served with the armed forces, draining the manpower needed to effectively run teams on a regular basis. After the war, baseball came back into the public eye. (Courtesy of Special Collections Room, Lakeland Public Library.)

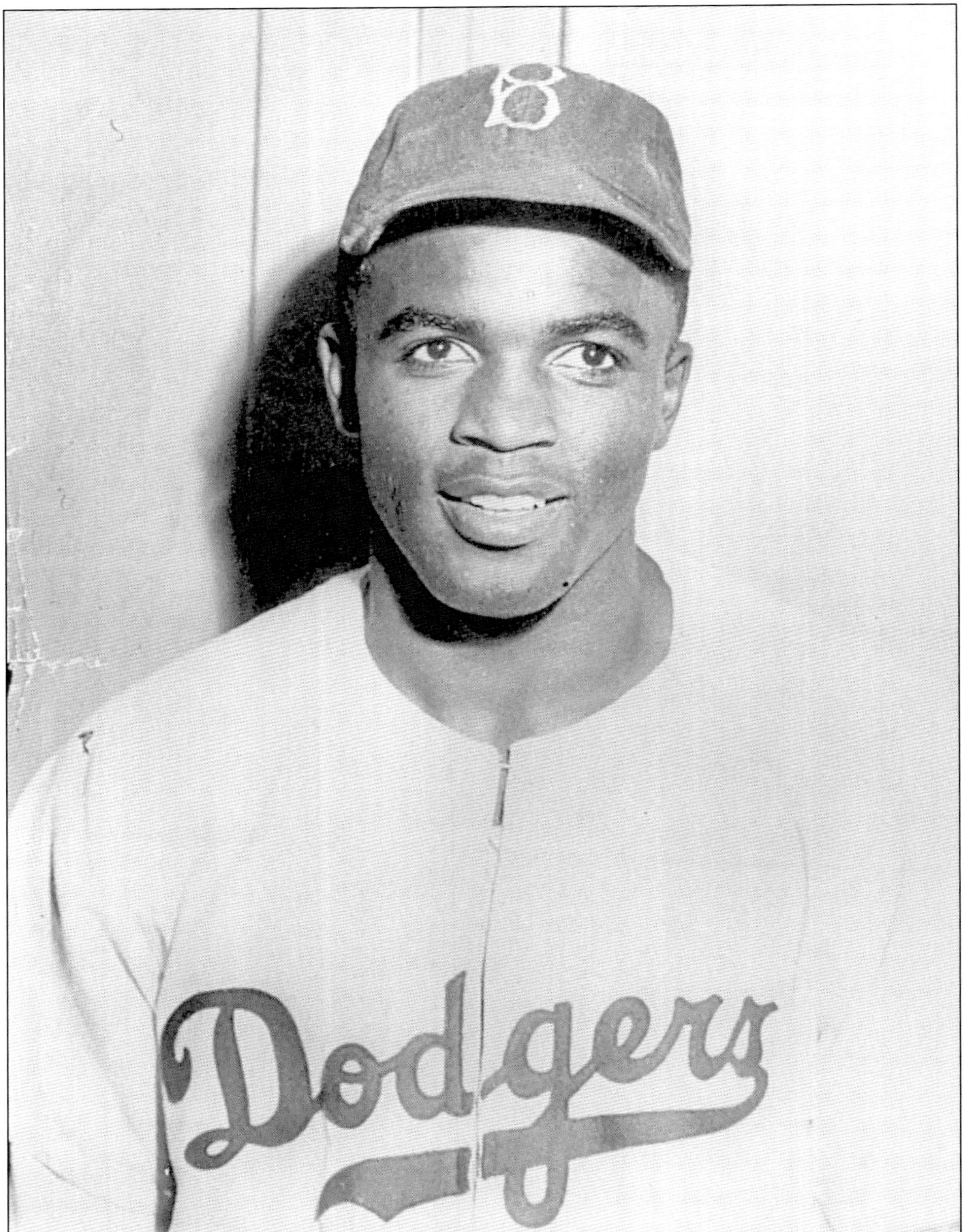

Jackie Robinson became the first African American to be signed into major league baseball, and he showed up for training with the Montreal Royals in Daytona in 1946. He is shown here in his Brooklyn Dodgers uniform during a game in St. Petersburg, 1947. (Courtesy of Pinellas County Historical Museum.)

Baseball promoter Al Lang and Stan Musial water the infield on Lang's namesake field in St. Petersburg in the late 1940s. (Courtesy of Pinellas County Historical Museum.)

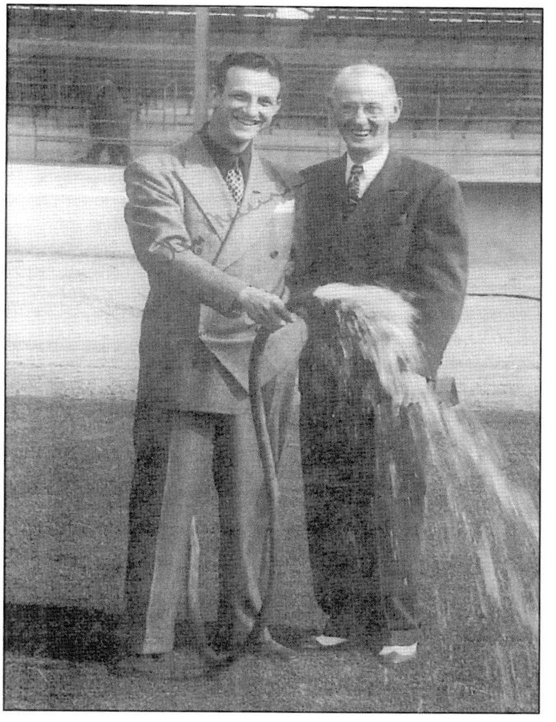

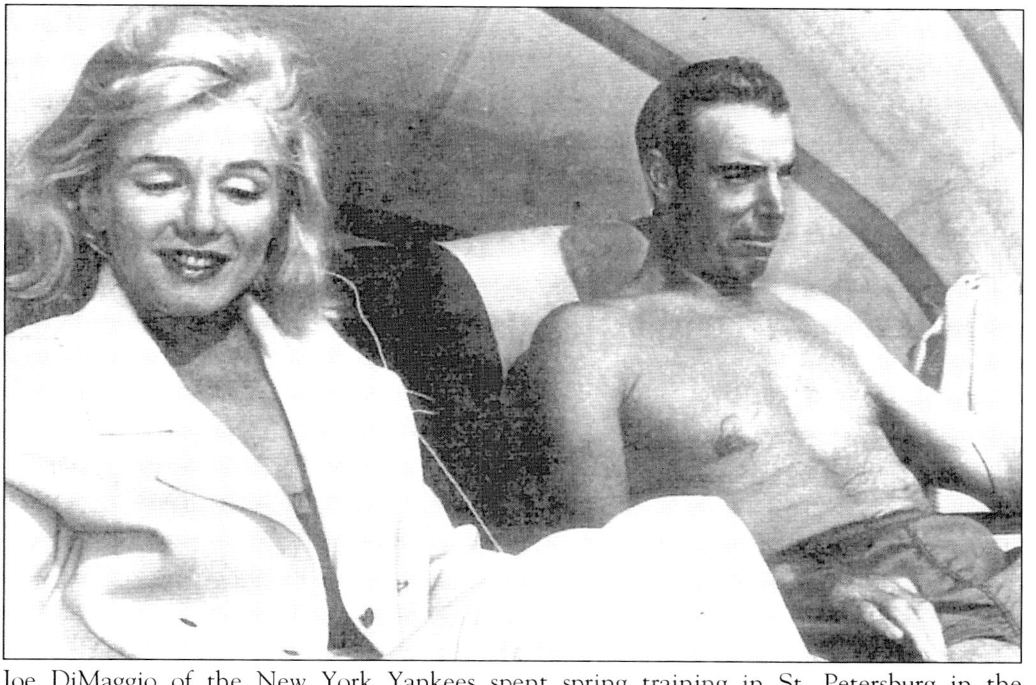

Joe DiMaggio of the New York Yankees spent spring training in St. Petersburg in the late 1930s and 1940s. He is seen here with his famous wife, Marilyn Monroe, on Madeira Beach in 1954. The marriage only lasted for nine months. (Courtesy of Pinellas County Historical Museum.)

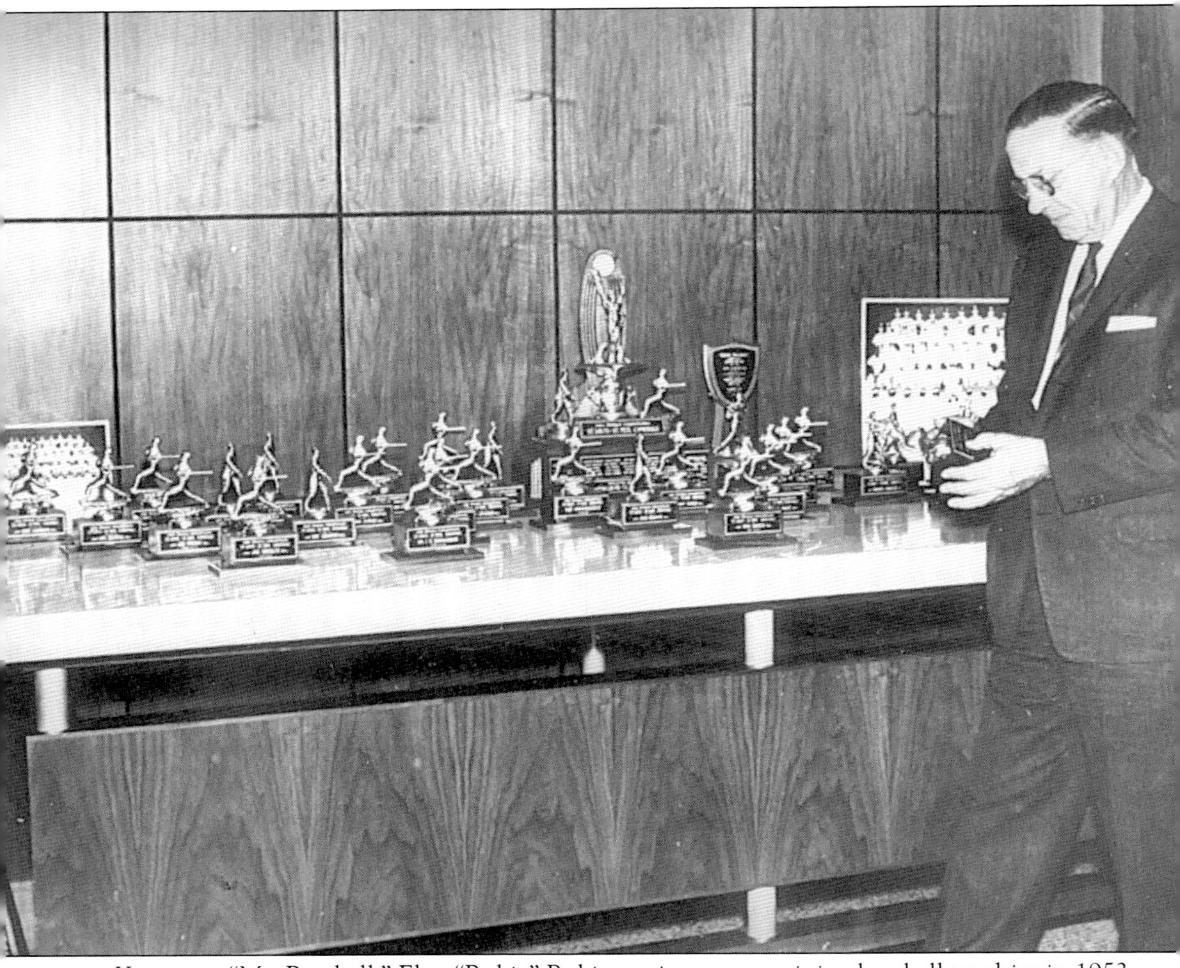

Known as "Mr. Baseball," Elan "Robie" Robinson is seen examining baseball trophies in 1953. He propelled St. Petersburg into becoming Florida's baseball capital. Robinson later became the chairman of the Baseball Committee of the Florida Chamber of Commerce. (Courtesy of Pinellas County Historical Museum.)

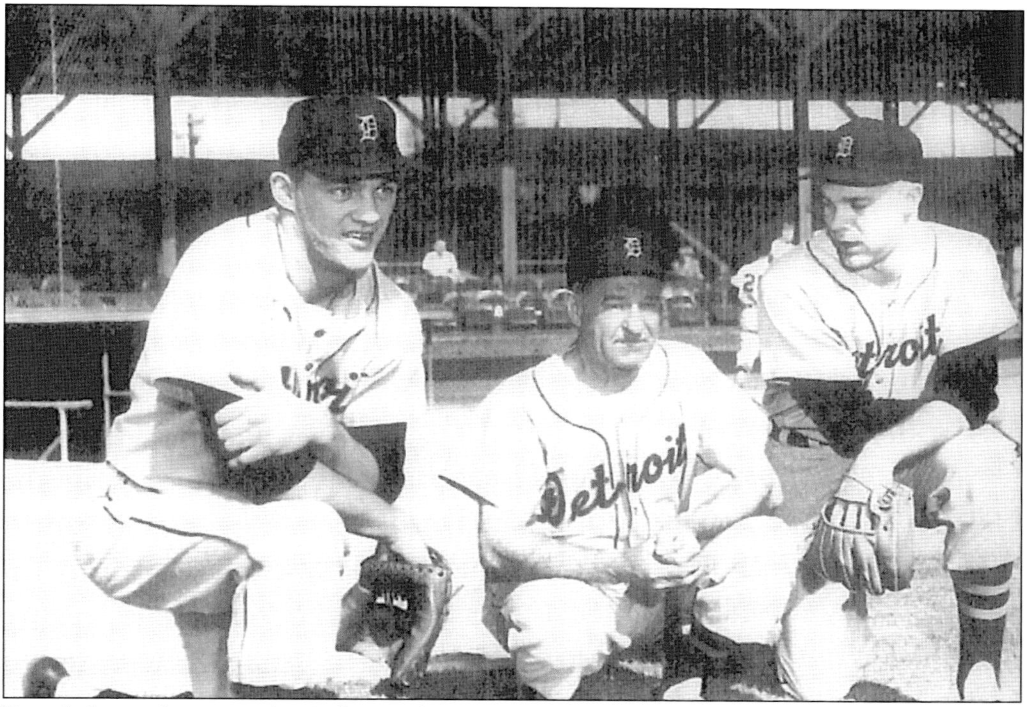

From left to right are pitcher Billy Hoeft, manager Bucky Harris, and outfielder/infielder Harvey Kuenn of the Detroit Tigers at their spring training facility in Lakeland, 1955. (Courtesy of Special Collections Room, Lakeland Public Library.)

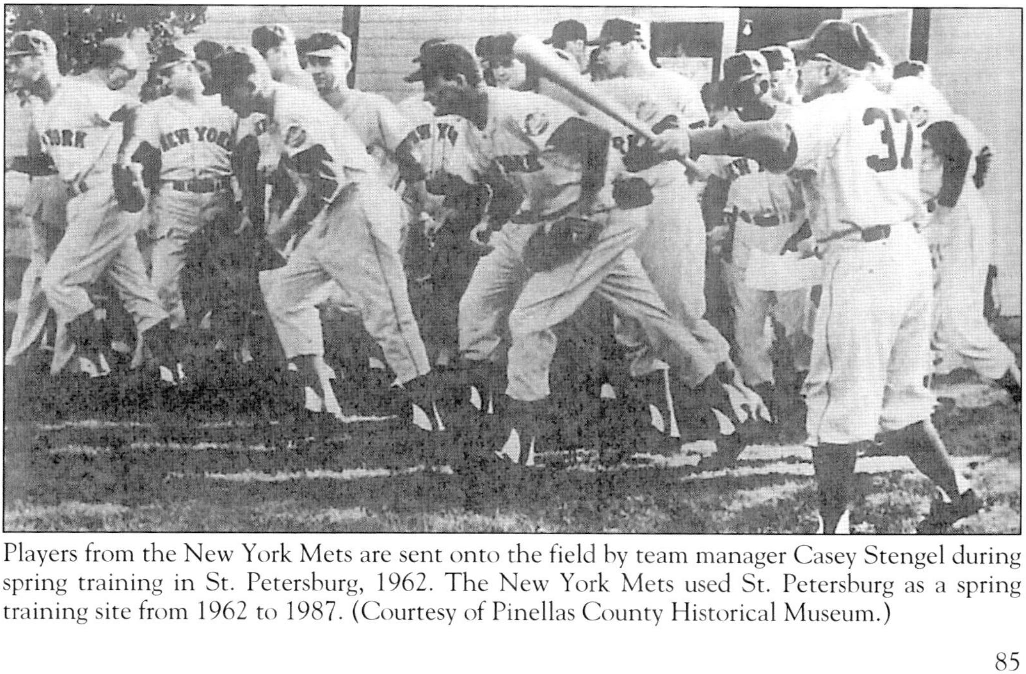

Players from the New York Mets are sent onto the field by team manager Casey Stengel during spring training in St. Petersburg, 1962. The New York Mets used St. Petersburg as a spring training site from 1962 to 1987. (Courtesy of Pinellas County Historical Museum.)

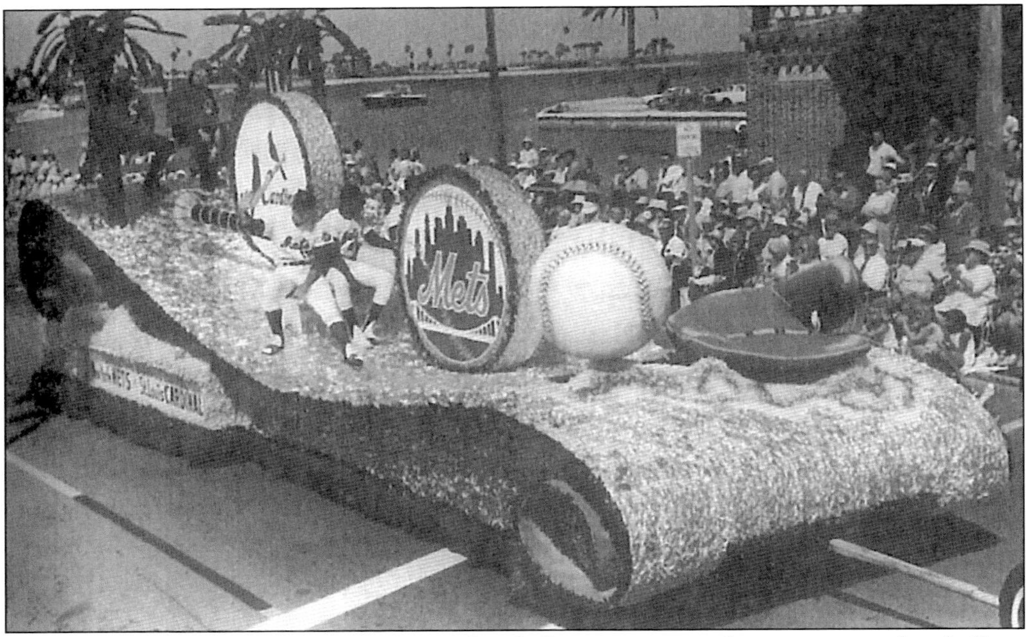

Still competing with Tampa to bring baseball to town, a float promotes baseball at St. Petersburg's Festival of States parade through town in 1966. These promotions were meant to bring more teams to the area for training as well as to secure for the town a professional team of its own. (Courtesy of Pinellas County Historical Museum.)

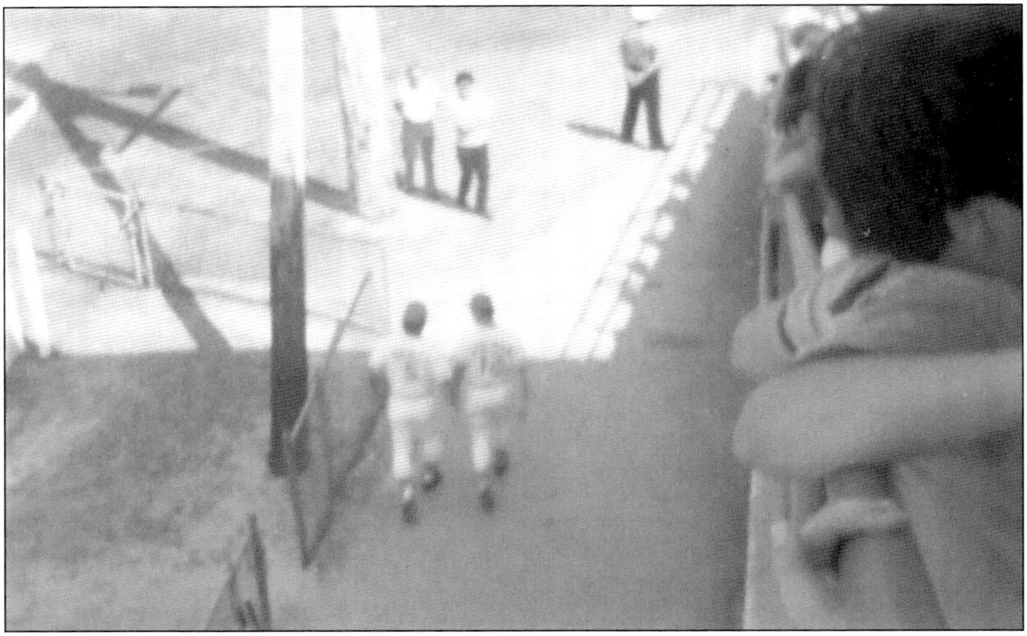

Johnny Bench (at left, #5) strolls back to the field during a game between the Cincinnati Reds and the Houston Astros at Al Lopez Field in 1977. The Reds used Tampa as their spring training home from 1931 to 1942 and from 1946 to 1987. (Courtesy of ADEQ Historical Resources.)

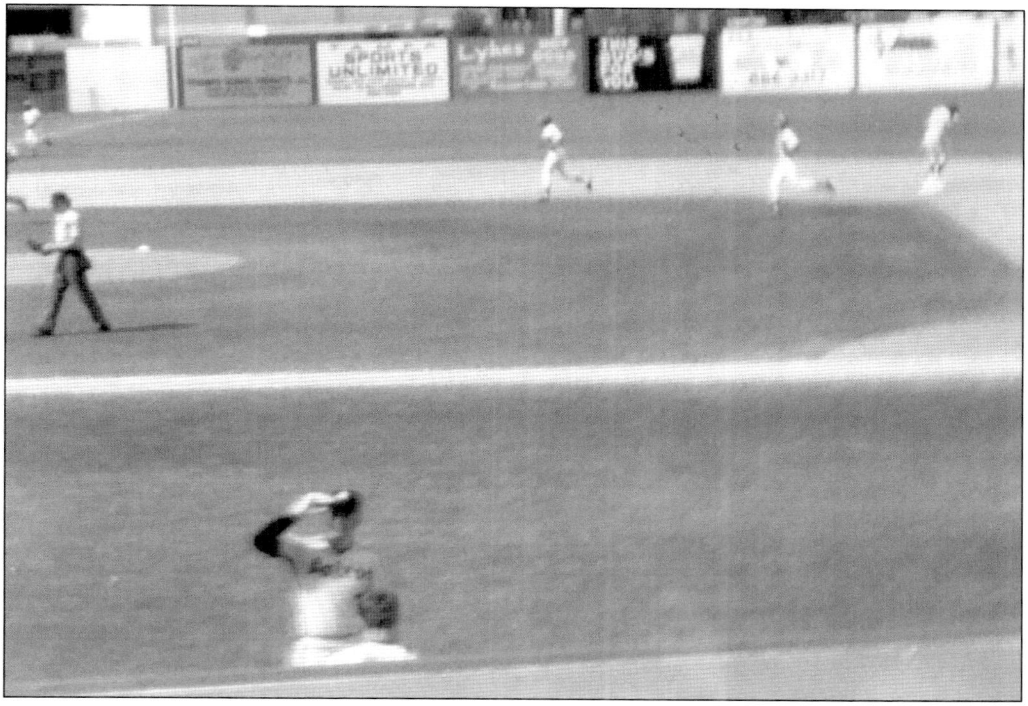

Players switch positions on the field during a game between the Astros and the Reds at Al Lopez Field. (Courtesy of ADEQ Historical Resources.)

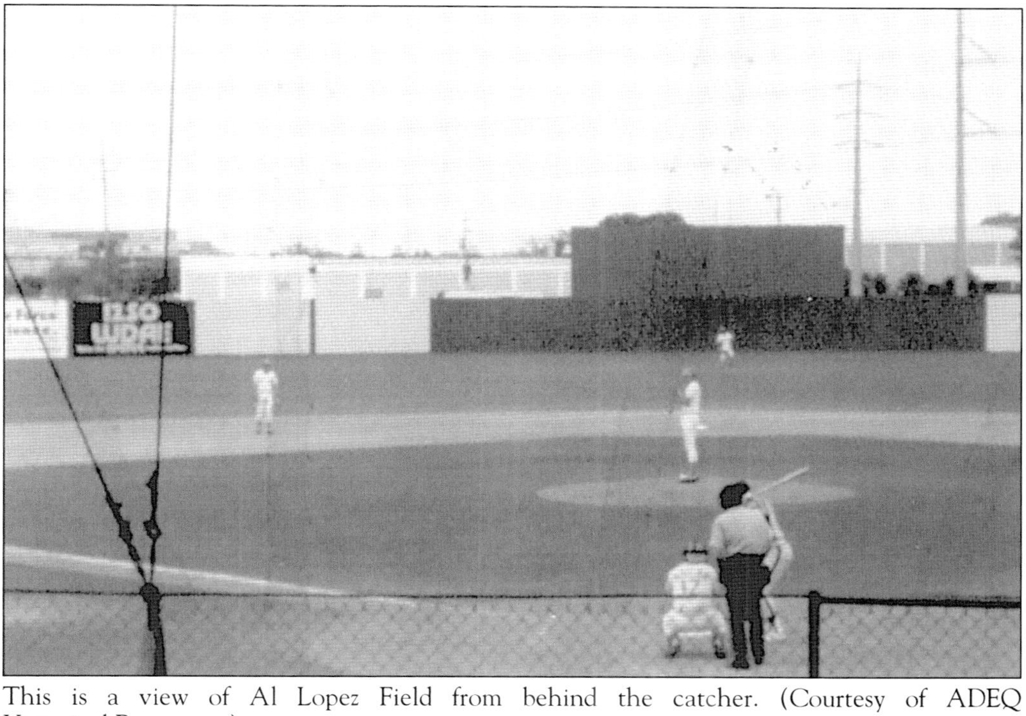

This is a view of Al Lopez Field from behind the catcher. (Courtesy of ADEQ Historical Resources.)

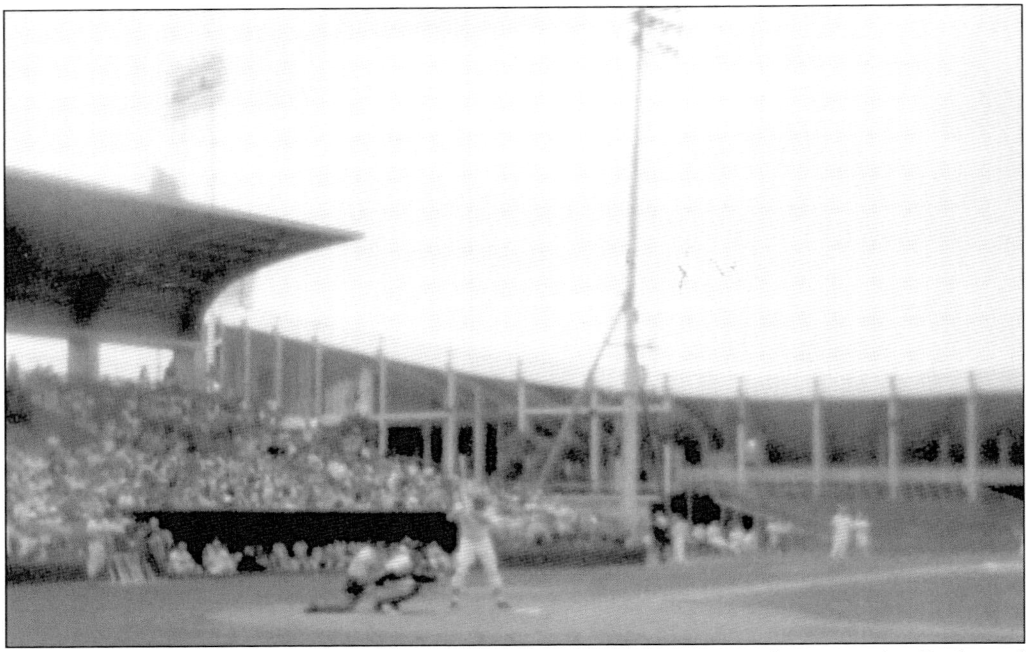

Johnny Bench is about to take a swing at the ball during a game between the Reds and the Astros. The old Tampa Bay Stadium is in the background. This football stadium hosted two Super Bowls before being torn down during the summer of 1999. (Courtesy of ADEQ Historical Resources.)

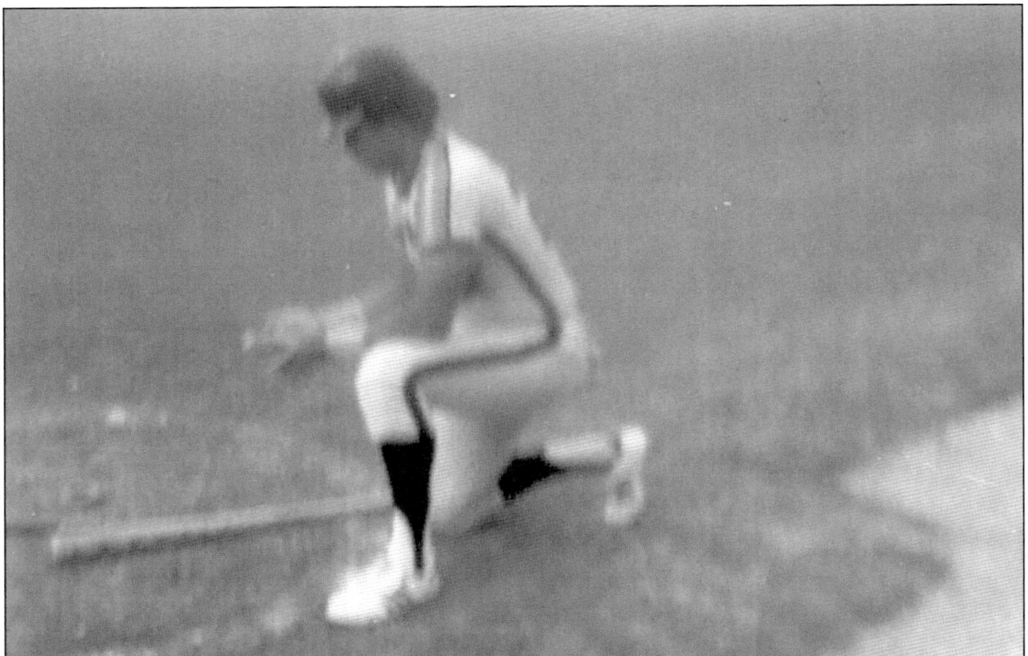

A ballplayer from the Houston Astros prepares himself before going to bat at Al Lopez Field in 1977. (Courtesy of ADEQ Historical Resources.)

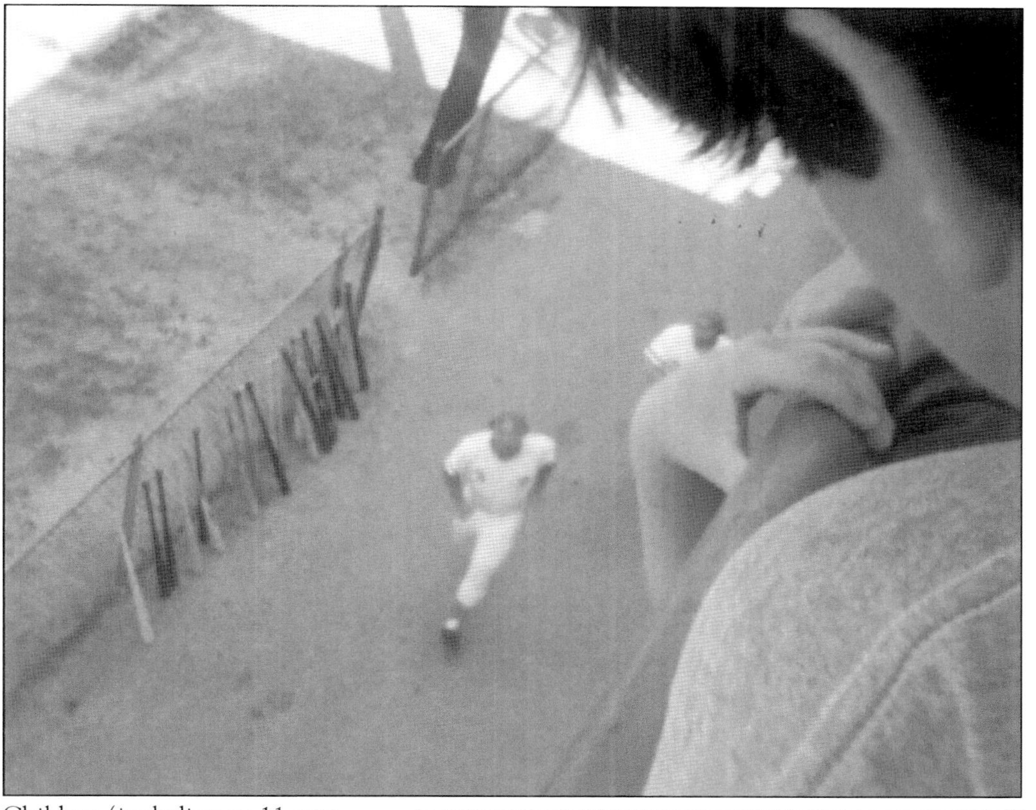

Children (including an 11-year-old author-to-be whose head nearly blocks the photo) hung from the sides of the bleachers in order to catch a glimpse of their baseball idols of the 1970s. Seen here are Johnny Bench and Pete Rose running back to their locker room after a game with the Astros. (Courtesy of ADEQ Historical Resources.)

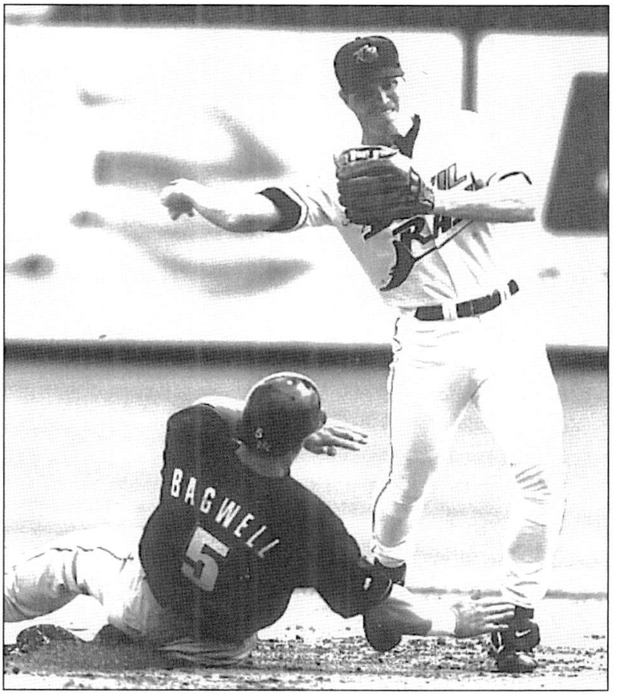

A Tampa Bay Devil Rays ball player throws the ball after taking out well-known Houston Astro Jeff Bagwell during spring training in 1997. (Courtesy of Tampa Bay Devil Rays.)

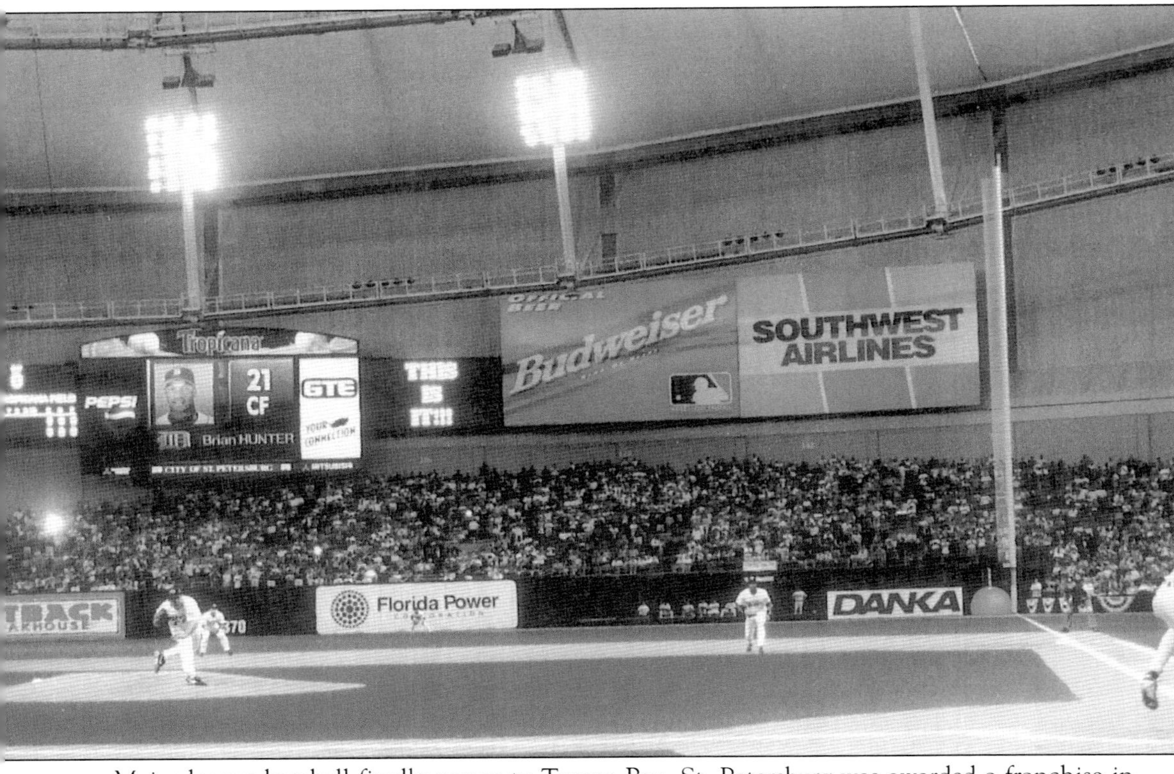

Major league baseball finally comes to Tampa Bay. St. Petersburg was awarded a franchise in 1995, and the Tampa Bay Devil Rays held their first game with the Detroit Tigers in Tropicana Field, formerly the Thunderdome, on March 31, 1998. The final score was Tigers 11, Devil Rays 6. (Courtesy of Tampa Bay Devil Rays.)

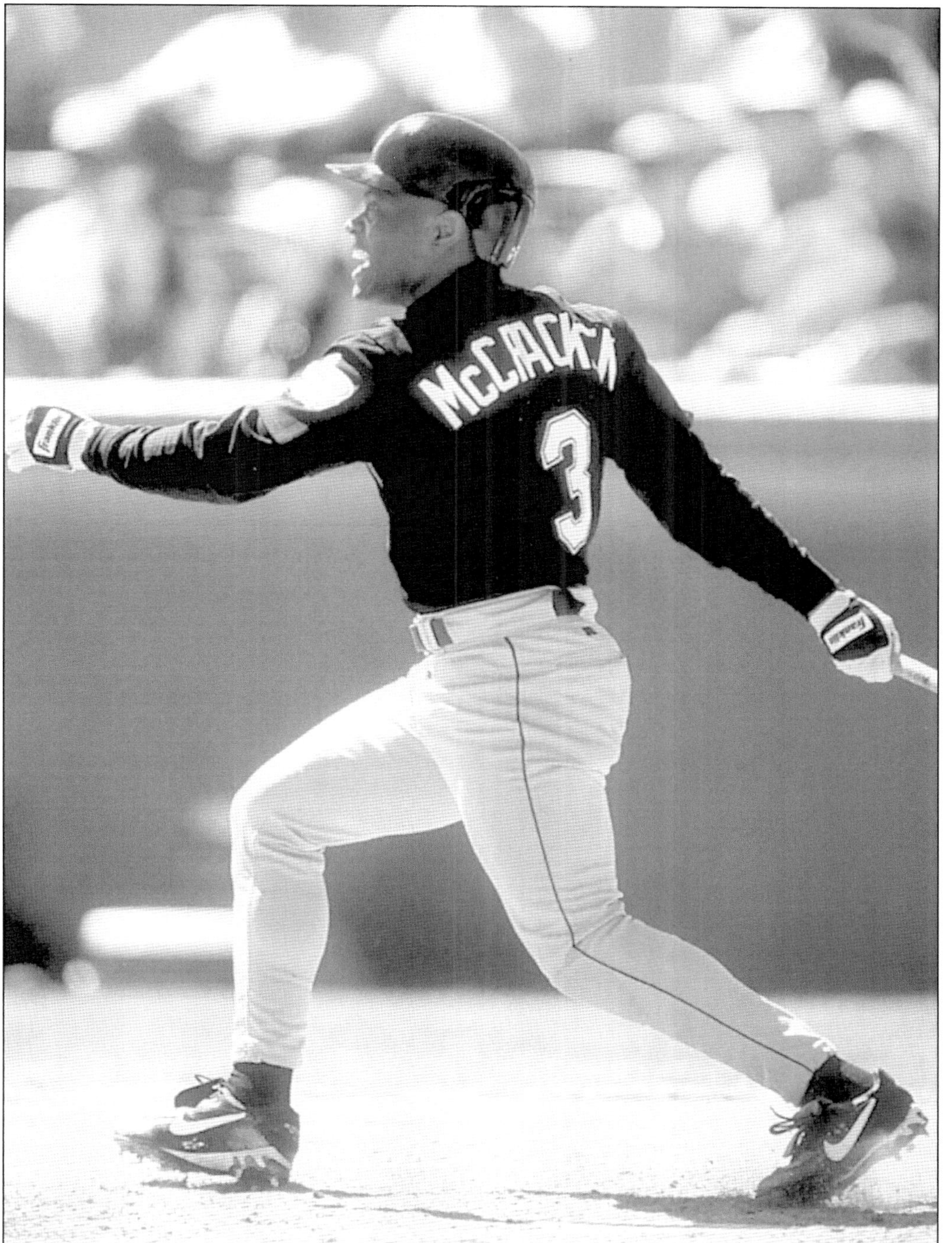

The Devil Rays were able to bring in promising new names such as outfielder Quinton McCracken, who began his career with the Colorado Rockies in the early 1990s. McCracken isn't a powerhitter, but has impressive speed and a career batting average of above .300. (Courtesy of Tampa Bay Devil Rays.)

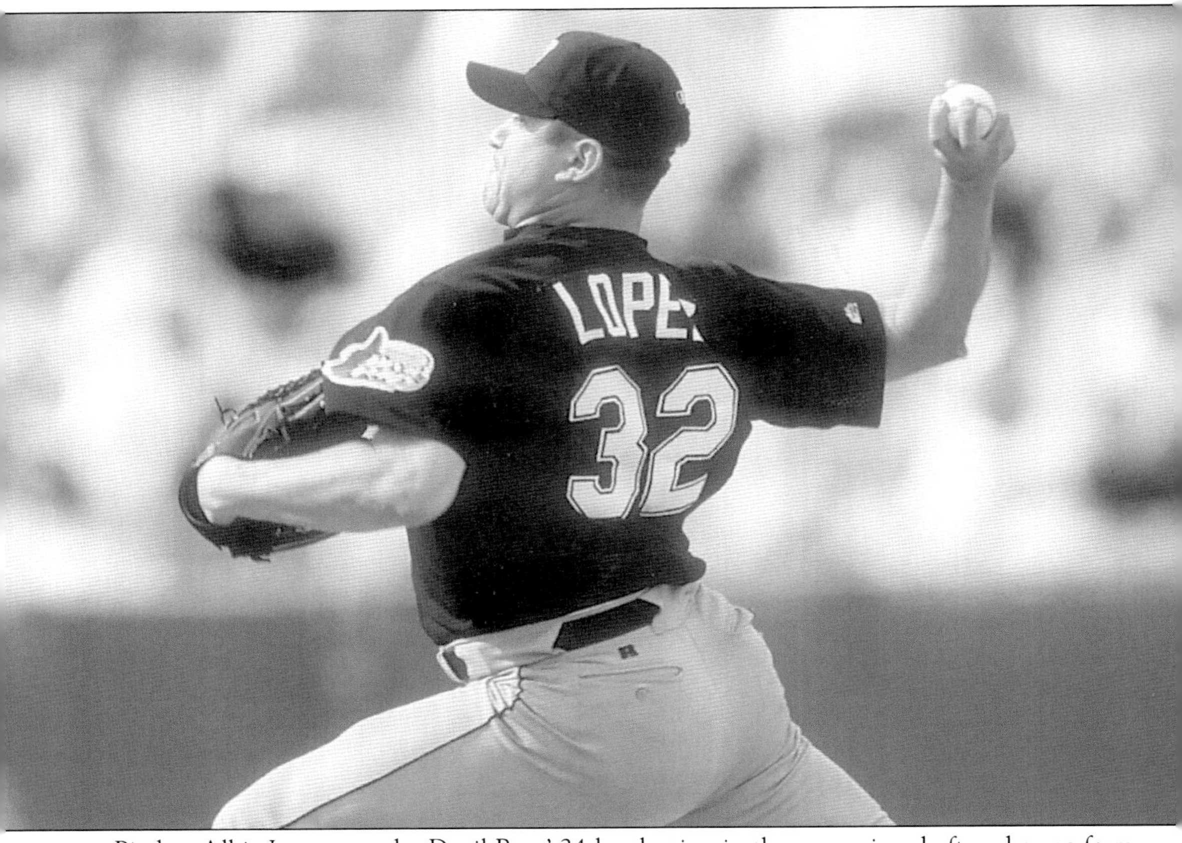

Pitcher Albie Lopez was the Devil Rays' 24th selection in the expansion draft and came from the Cleveland Indians. (Courtesy of Tampa Bay Devil Rays.)

Six

Other Baseball Leagues and Players

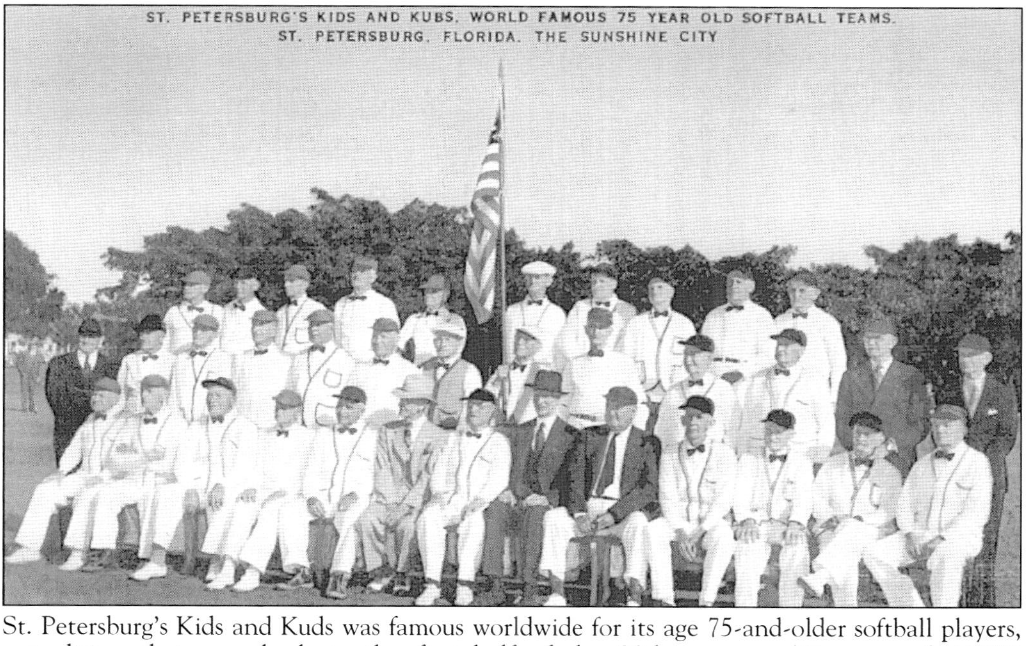

St. Petersburg's Kids and Kuds was famous worldwide for its age 75-and-older softball players, a tradition that goes back to the first half of the 20th century. (Courtesy of ADEQ Historical Resources.)

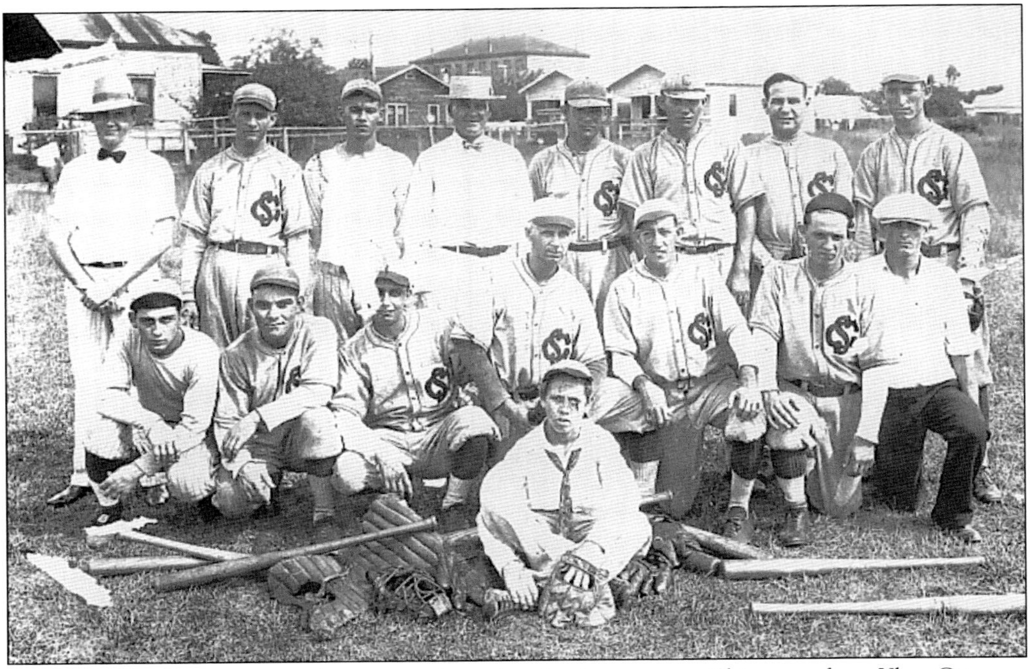

Many local businesses created teams to play other business teams. This team from Ybor City was sponsored by Spicola Cleaners. Note the cigar factory in the background, *c.* 1920. (Courtesy of Andrew Espolita.)

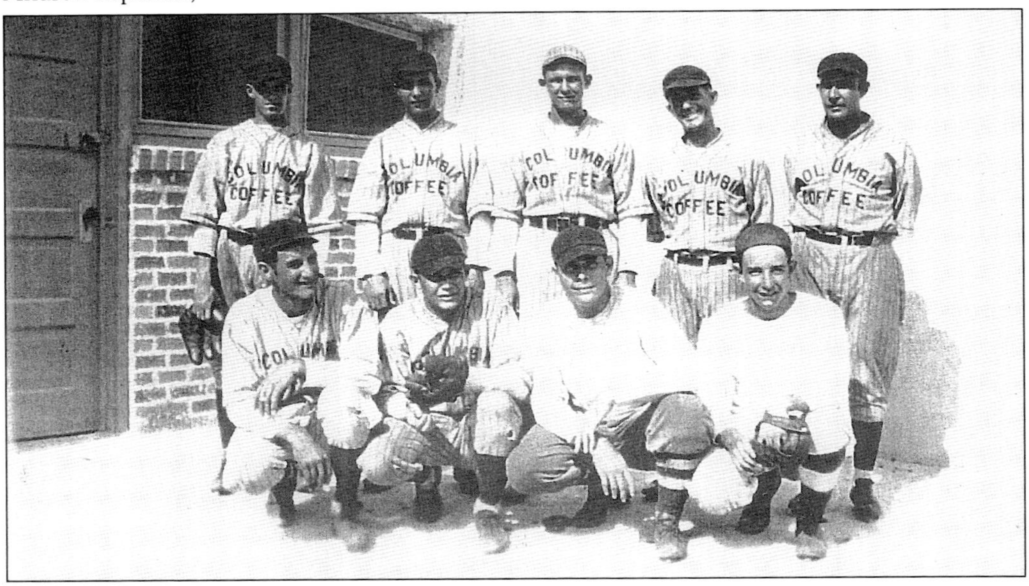

This is a group shot of the members of the Columbia Coffee Baseball Club at Plant Field in 1929. They are, from left to right, as follows: (front row) pitcher Pedro Hevia, third baseman Andrew Espolita, catcher/captain Rosendo Duran, and right fielder/catcher Severino Peña; (back row) pitcher Robert "Machito" Jerez, shortstop Lumino Valdes, left fielder Jackie Jordan, second baseman Mario Mira, and pitcher/manager Emiliano "Nano" Fernandez. (Courtesy of Andrew Espolita.)

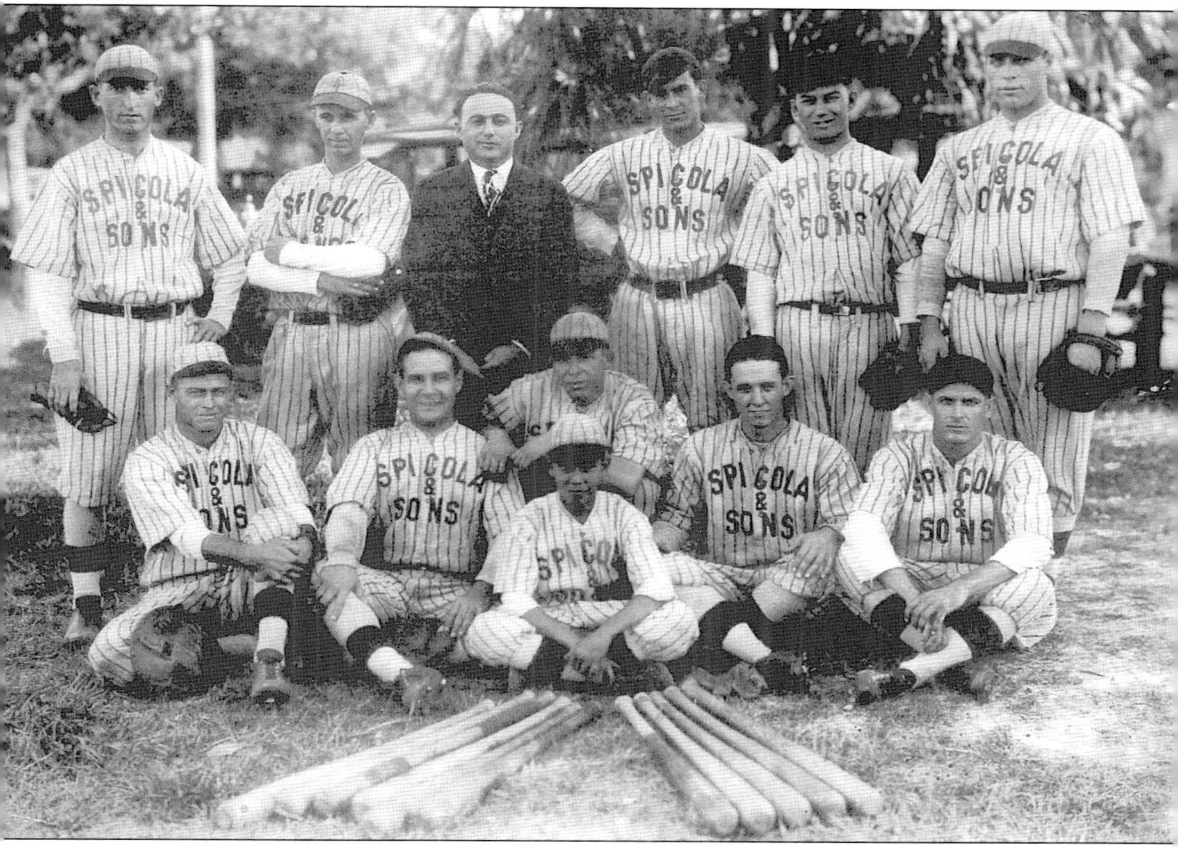

Here is another photograph of the Spicola & Sons baseball team as they appeared in the late 1920s. (Courtesy of Andrew Espolita.)

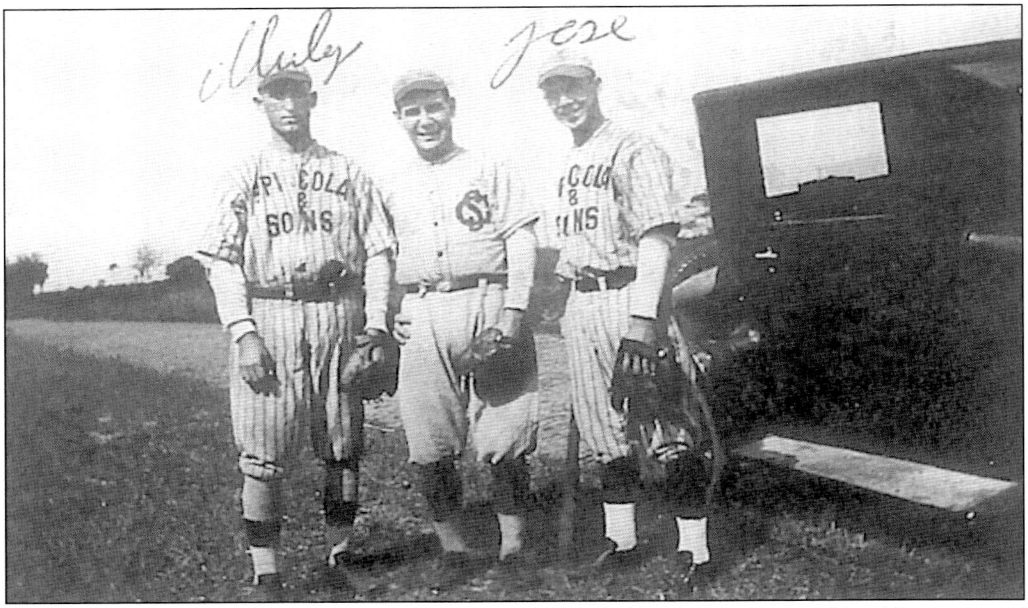

Andrew Espolita (center) poses with fellow baseball players in 1930. (Courtesy of Andrew Espolita.)

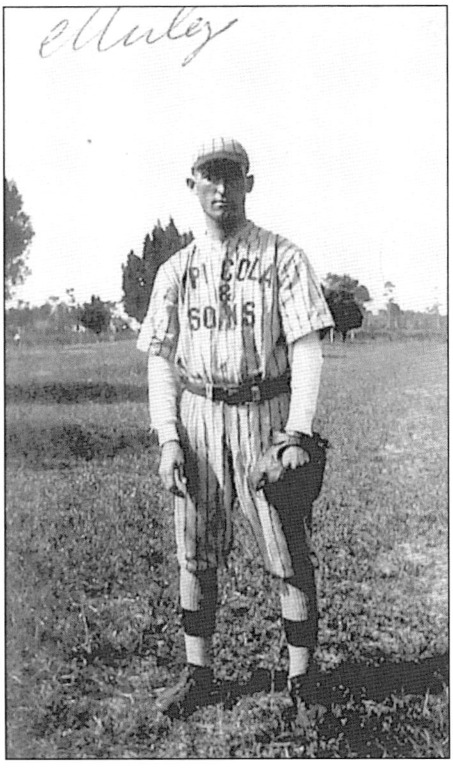

"Muly" of the Spicola & Sons baseball club poses in Ybor City, Florida, in 1930. (Courtesy of Andrew Espolita.)

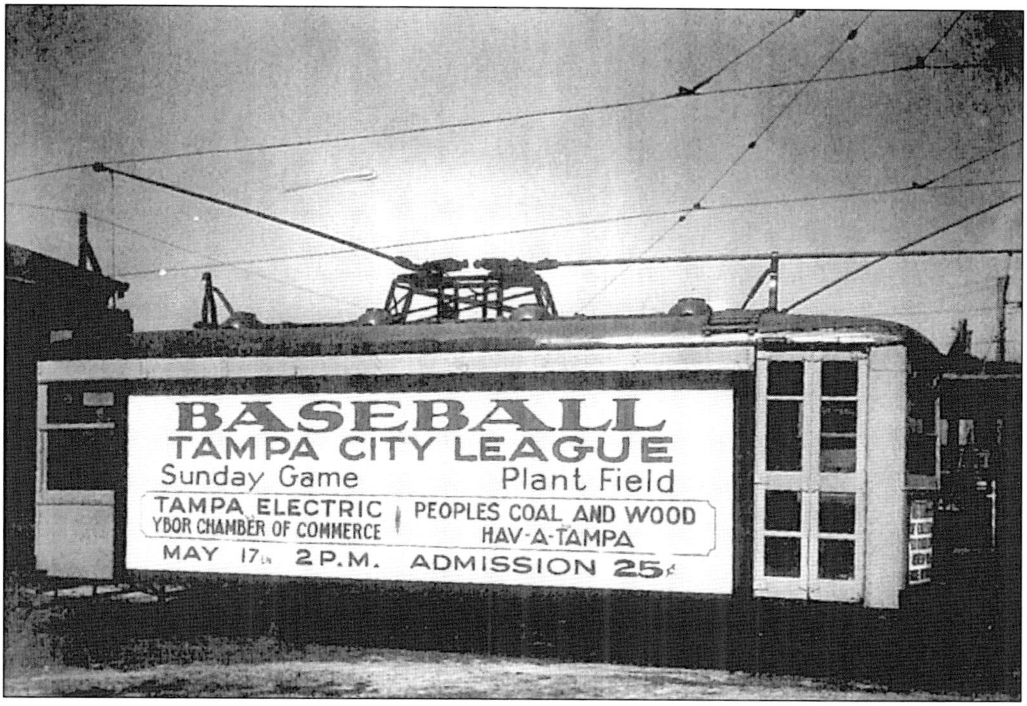

A streetcar advertises a baseball game of the Tampa City League in 1940. (Courtesy of Florida State Archives.)

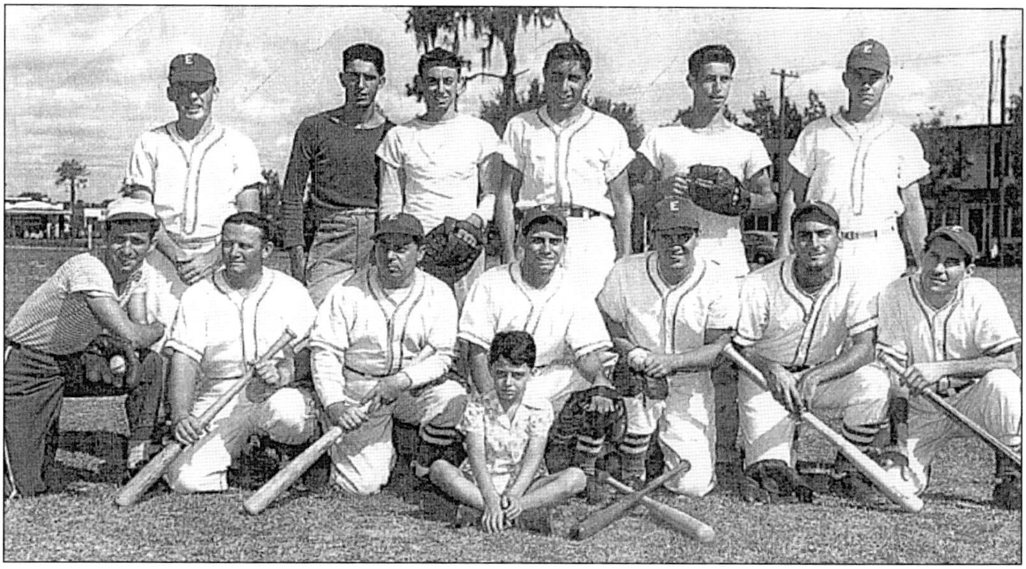

This photograph, taken June 20, 1948, at Ragen Park by Art Thomas, shows the Empire Body Shop team, which won the Municipal Baseball League championship that year. From left to right are as follows: (front row) Tom Woods, P.M. Gonzalez, Tinky Carrera, Joe Lopez, Robert Martinez, Emilio Rodriguez, and Tony Villar; (back row) manager and league founder Jerome Sierra Jr., George Martinez, Joe Diaz, Andy Prieto, Bernard Freeman, and Manuel Tuero Jr. (Courtesy of *La Gaceta.*)

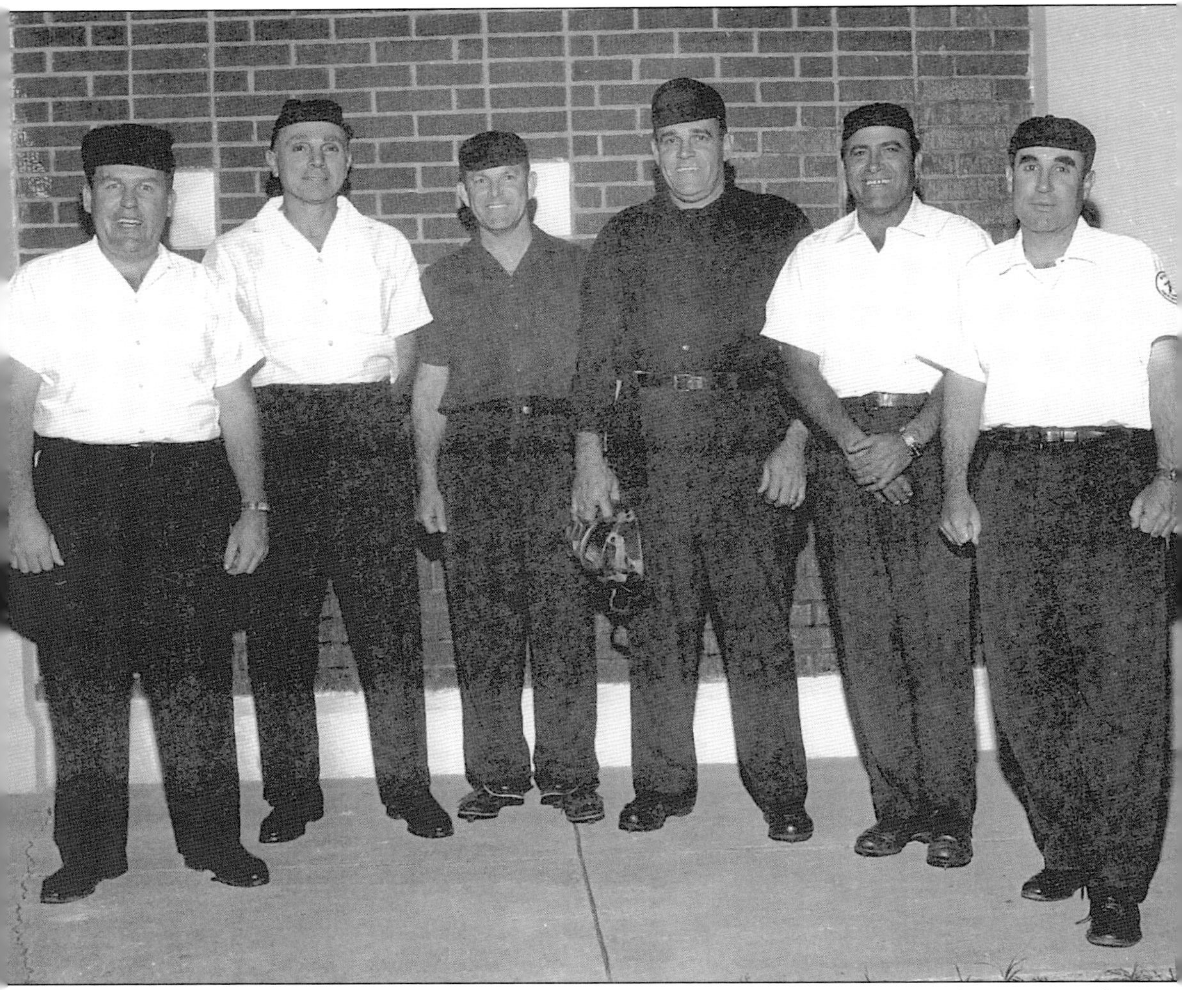

The West Coast Umpire Baseball Group takes time out to have their picture taken at Cascaden Park in 1955. From left to right are Jerome Sierra Jr., Joe Greco Sr., Al Jiminez, Luis "Moose" Vigil, Angel Falcon, and Pell Mann. (Courtesy of *La Gaceta*.)

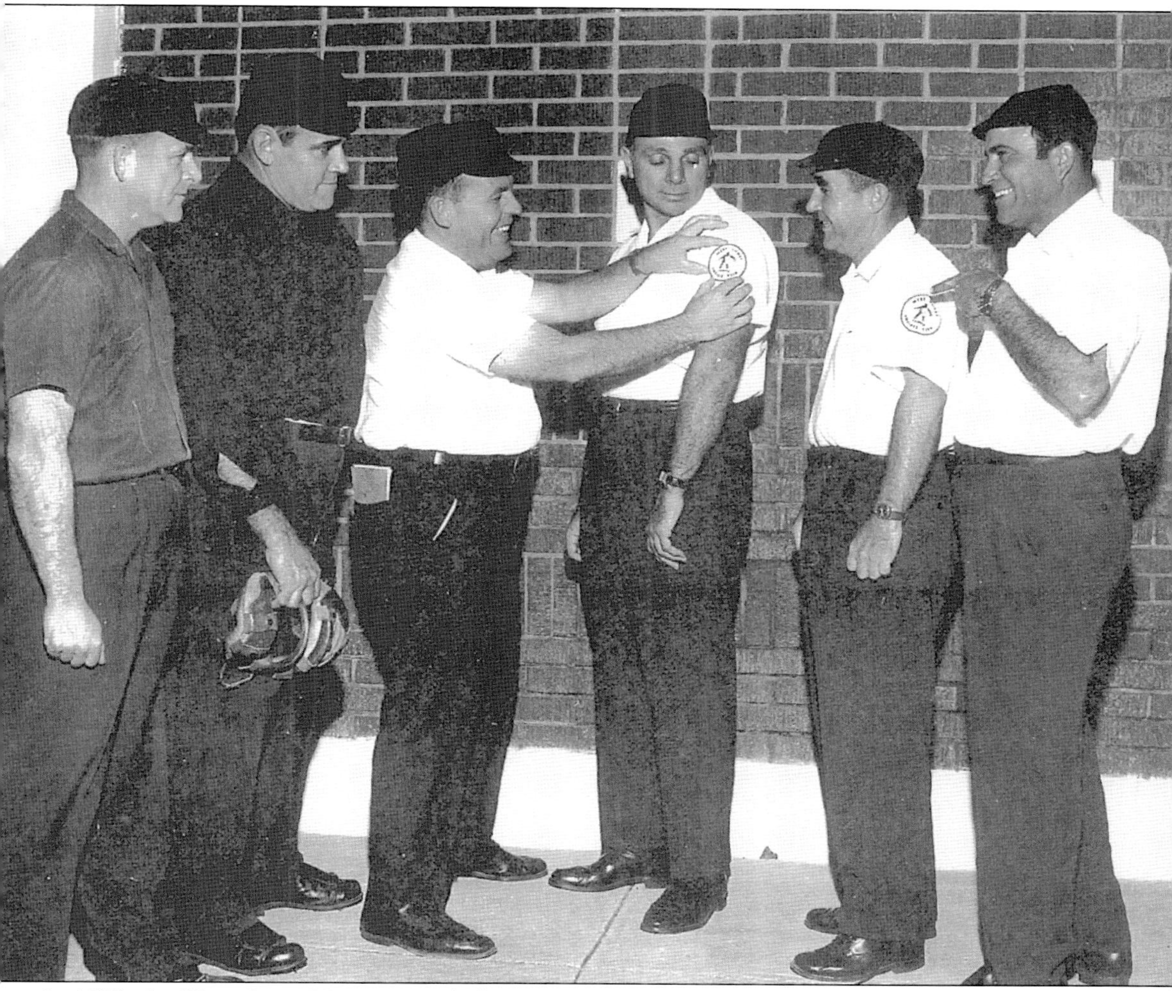

In 1955, the West Coast Umpire Baseball Group had 15 members. By 1992, the group had well over 130 members under President Bill DeCosta. (Courtesy of *La Gaceta*.)

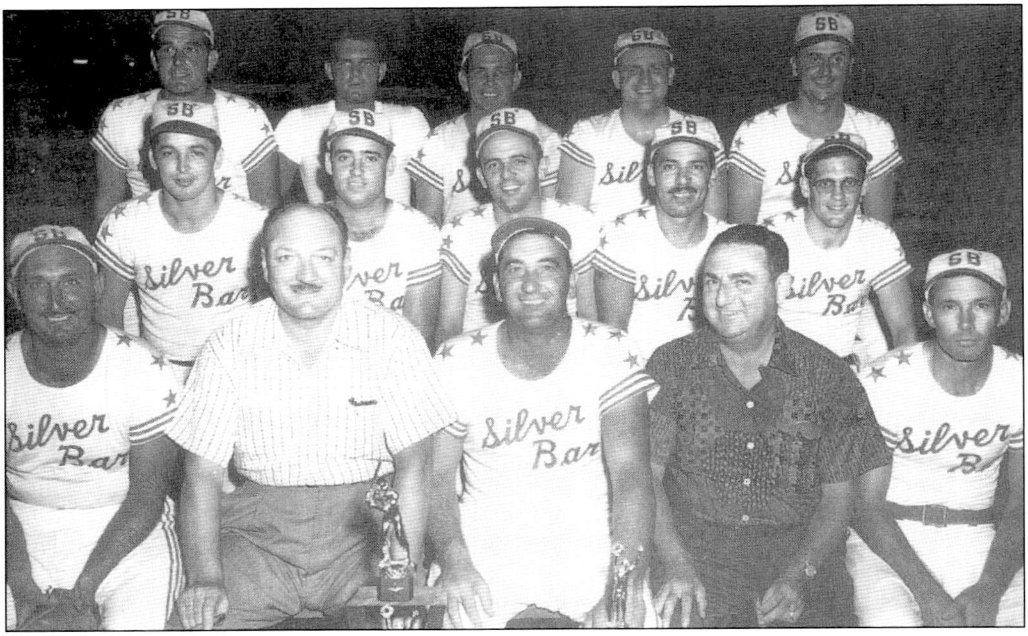

This team, representing Tampa's Silver Bar Brewing Company, posed for a photo after winning the Florida Men's Fast Pitch Softball championship in 1954. From left to right are as follows: (front row) Albert De La Torre, Silver Bar Brewery president Gene Warenstead, player-manager Reggie Fernandez, brewery vice president Tom Spicola, and Harold Beasley; (middle row) Raymond Gonzalez, Eloy Fernandez, John Rañon, Victor Collazo, and Bob Hutchson; (back row) Benny Fernandez, Tommy Bell, Pete Fernandez, Stacy Stephans, and Leon Senk. (Courtesy of *La Gaceta.*)

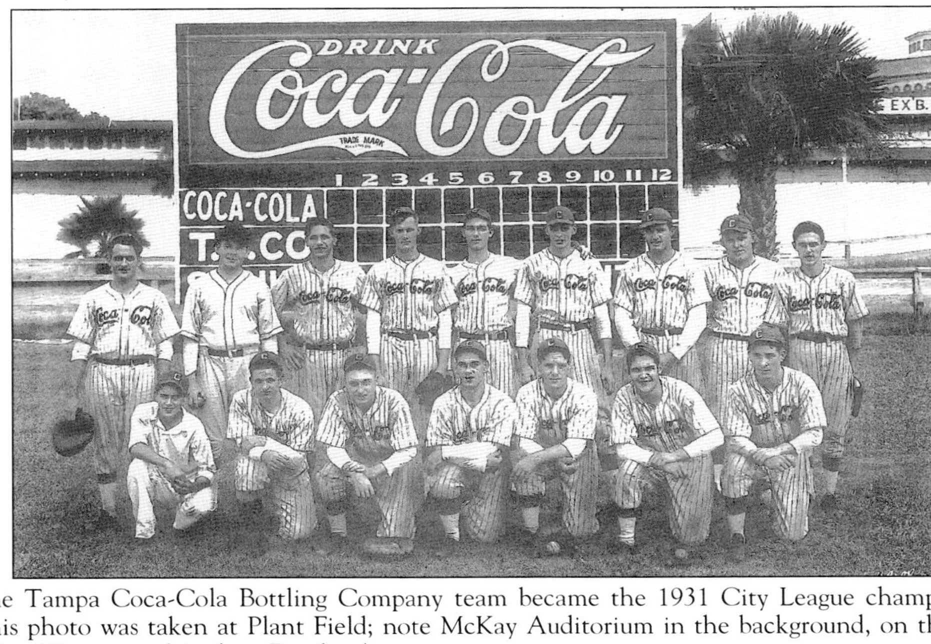

The Tampa Coca-Cola Bottling Company team became the 1931 City League champions. This photo was taken at Plant Field; note McKay Auditorium in the background, on the far right. (Courtesy of Andrew Espolita.)

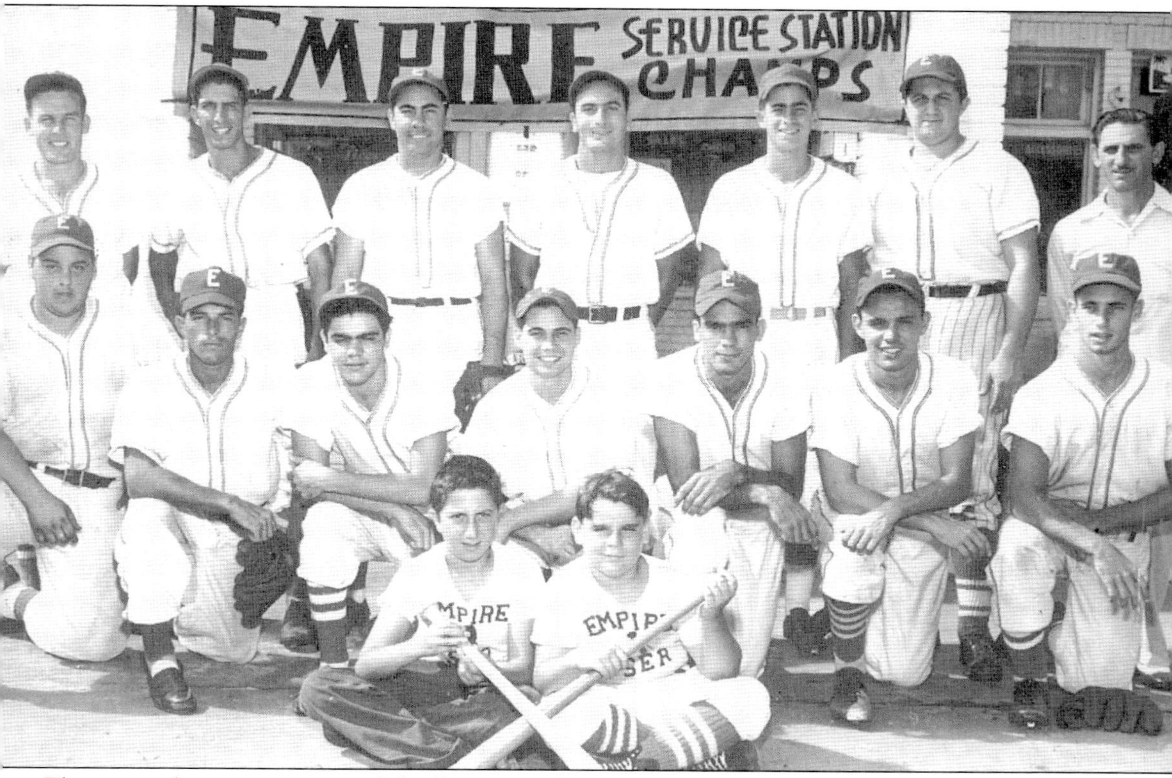

This is another team picture of the Empire Body Shop "Sluggers" baseball team of Ybor City. The team was the champion for three straight years (1952, 1953, and 1954) in the Municipal Baseball League. The Empire Body Shop was located on Seventh Avenue in Ybor City for over 25 years and then moved to Second Avenue and Fifteenth Street to make room for apartment housing. The batboys are Joe Vizzi and Roy Thomas. The others are, from left to right, as follows: (front row) Leo Alfonso, Steve Alfonso, C.M. Martinez, Joe Lopez, Raymond Rodriguez, Manuel Tuero, and Bernard Friedman; (back row) manager and league founder Jerome Sierra Jr., George Martinez, Angelo Loredo, Emilio Rodriguez, Arnold Martinez, Fernando A. Vizzi, and general manager Angelo Comparetto. Also on the team but not pictured are treasurer Sam Comparetto and business manager Bobby Comparetto. Arnold Martinez is now an artist with a studio on Seventh Avenue, and Fernando Vizz is a former director of the Ybor City Boys' Club. (Courtesy of *La Gaceta*.)

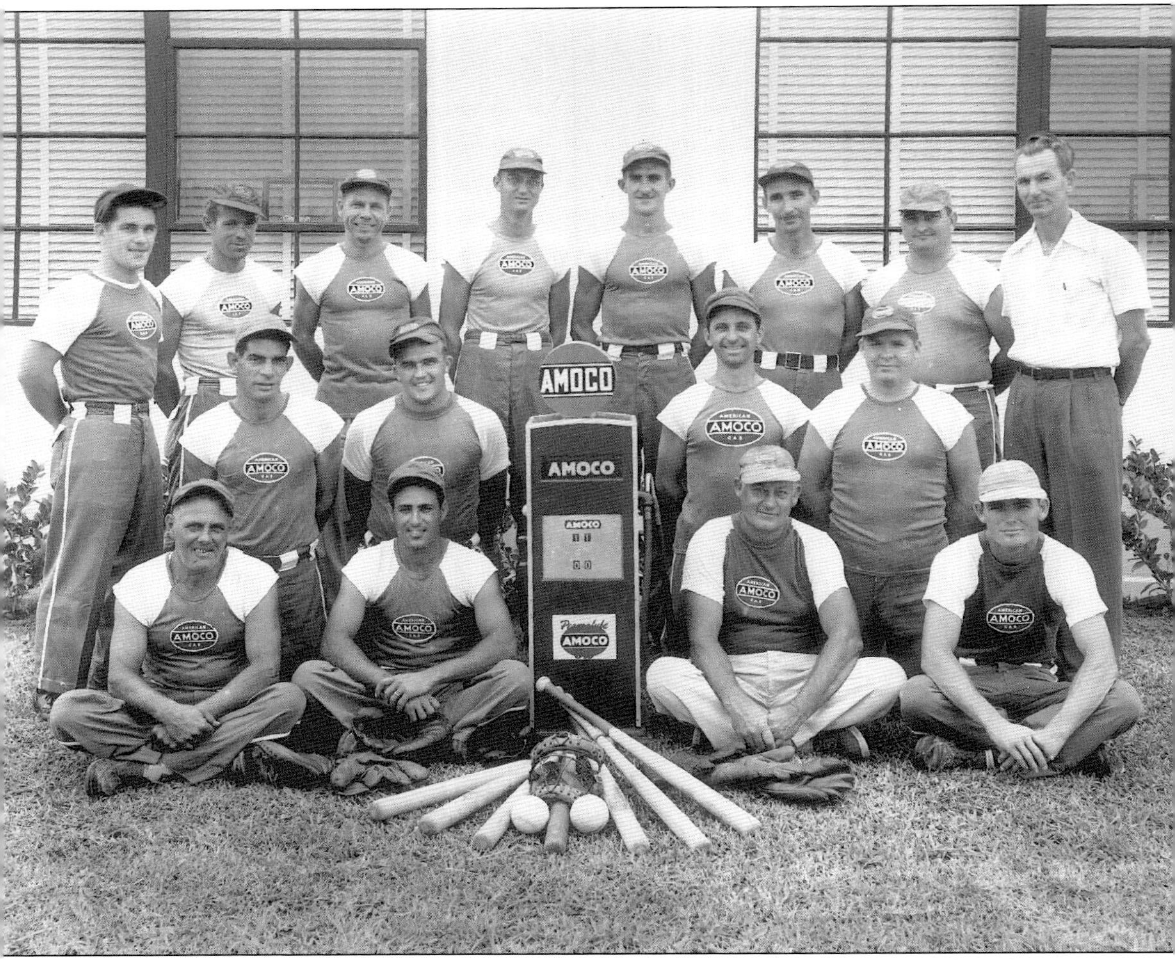

The individuals in this photograph are identified as members of the Tampa-based American Motor Oil Company (AMOCO) baseball team, *c.* 1950; however, note the softballs in the foreground. (Courtesy of Tampa-Hillsborough County Public Library System.)

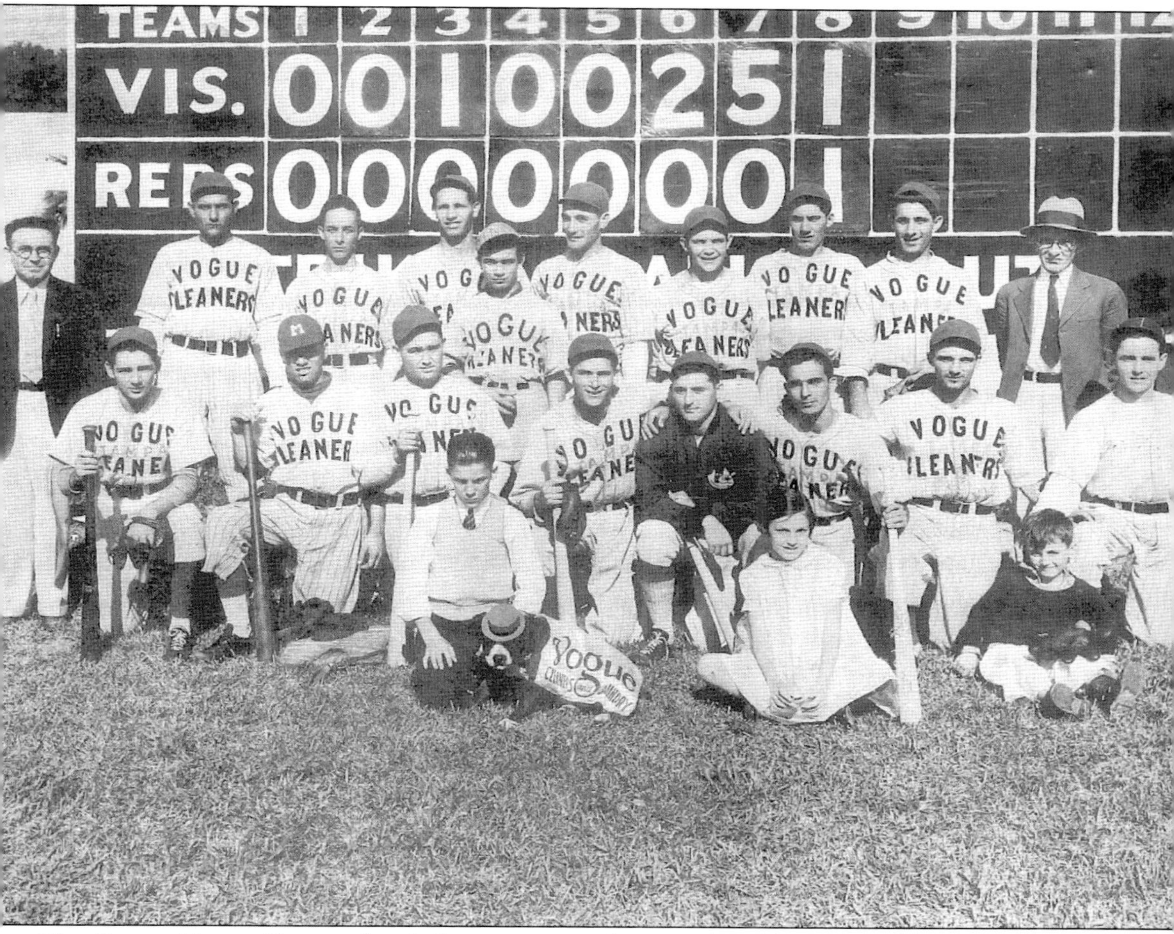

The Tampa Vogue Cleaners baseball team appears here in the 1930s. Note that the Boston bull terrier was the team's mascot and his image is on a team patch on the jacket of one of the kneeling players. (Courtesy of Andrew Espolita.)

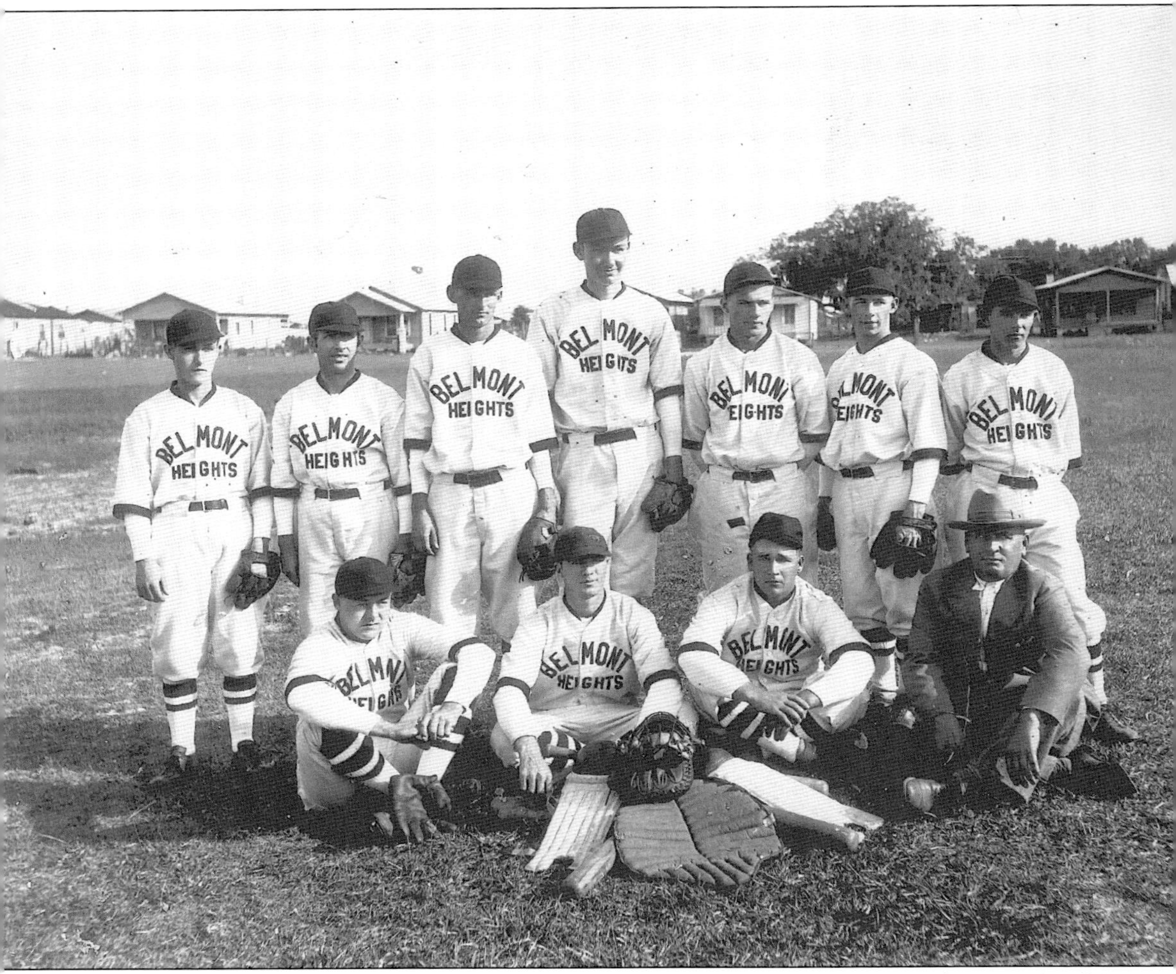

Another team based in Tampa was the Belmont Heights baseball team, seen here on April 21, 1950. (Courtesy of Tampa-Hillsborough County Public Library System.)

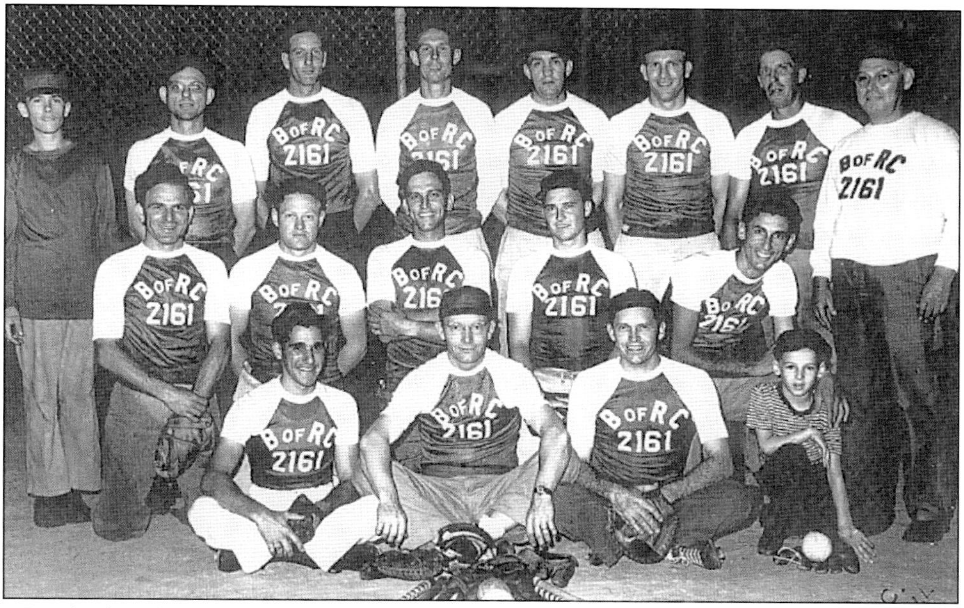

The Brotherhood of Railroad Clerks softball team played in the Ybor City Merchants League at Cuscaden Park. They were the champions in 1946, the year that this photo was taken. From left to right, they are as follows: (seated) Ricardo Silver, Russell Cawthon, Bill White, and batboy Rick Perez; (middle row) J.T. Landrum, Bill Smith, Elmer Propper, Gene Brown, and Marcy Perez; (standing) Sonny Guerra, Harry Grimes, Louis Valdez, Gene York, Tony Kolka, J.D. Carpenter, Sam King, and manager Joe Guerra. (Courtesy of *La Gaceta*.)

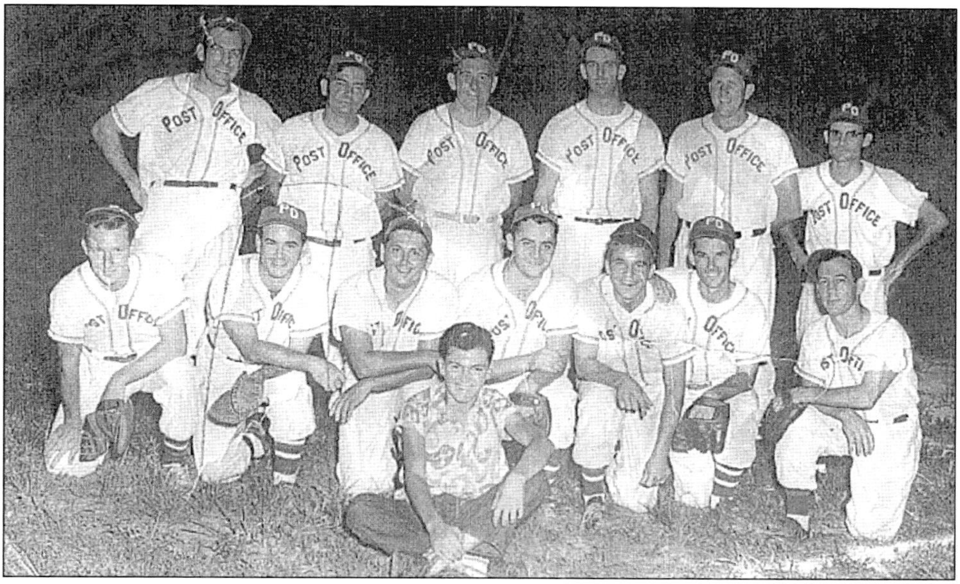

This 1960 photograph shows the postal workers who played on the local post office baseball team. From left to right are as follows: (seated) Carmelo Monteleone Jr. (in front), Virgil Howell, Herbert Tornero, Braulio Ramil, Ruben Ares, Vernon Taylor, Frank Rodriguez, and Henry Orihuela; (standing) Mario Vigil, Peter Monteleone Sr., coach and manager Peter D. Leto, Ralph Davidson, Robert Joyce, and Nelson Lodato. (Courtesy of *La Gaceta*.)

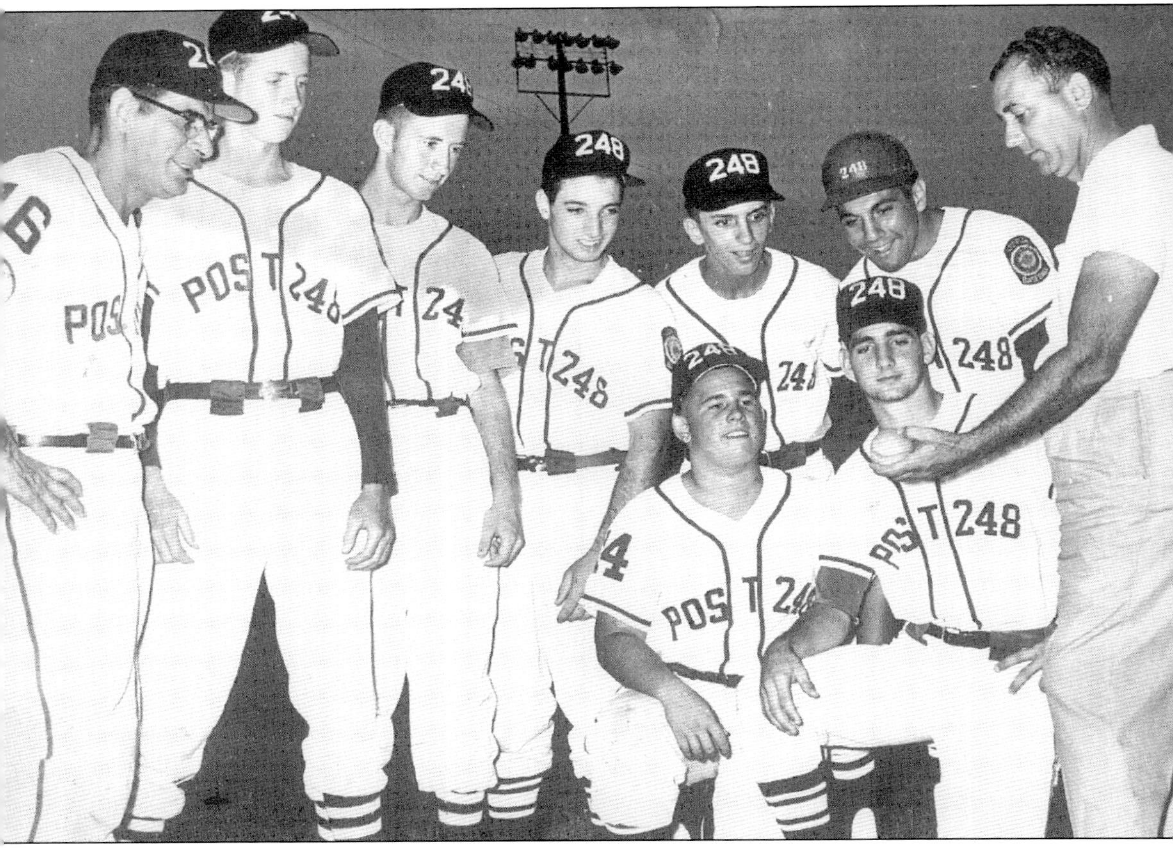

Coach Joe Yglesias gave a few pointers to his talented West Tampa American Legion Post 248 mound staff before they departed for the state American Legion baseball tournament in Miami in August 1961. From left to right are the following: (kneeling) Bob Jordan and Ray Carrasco; (standing) coach Lingo Rodriguez, Wayne Bright, Leon Stephens, Ron Sanchez, Fred Tomasello, Nick Bruno, and coach Joe Yglesias. (Courtesy of *La Gaceta*.)

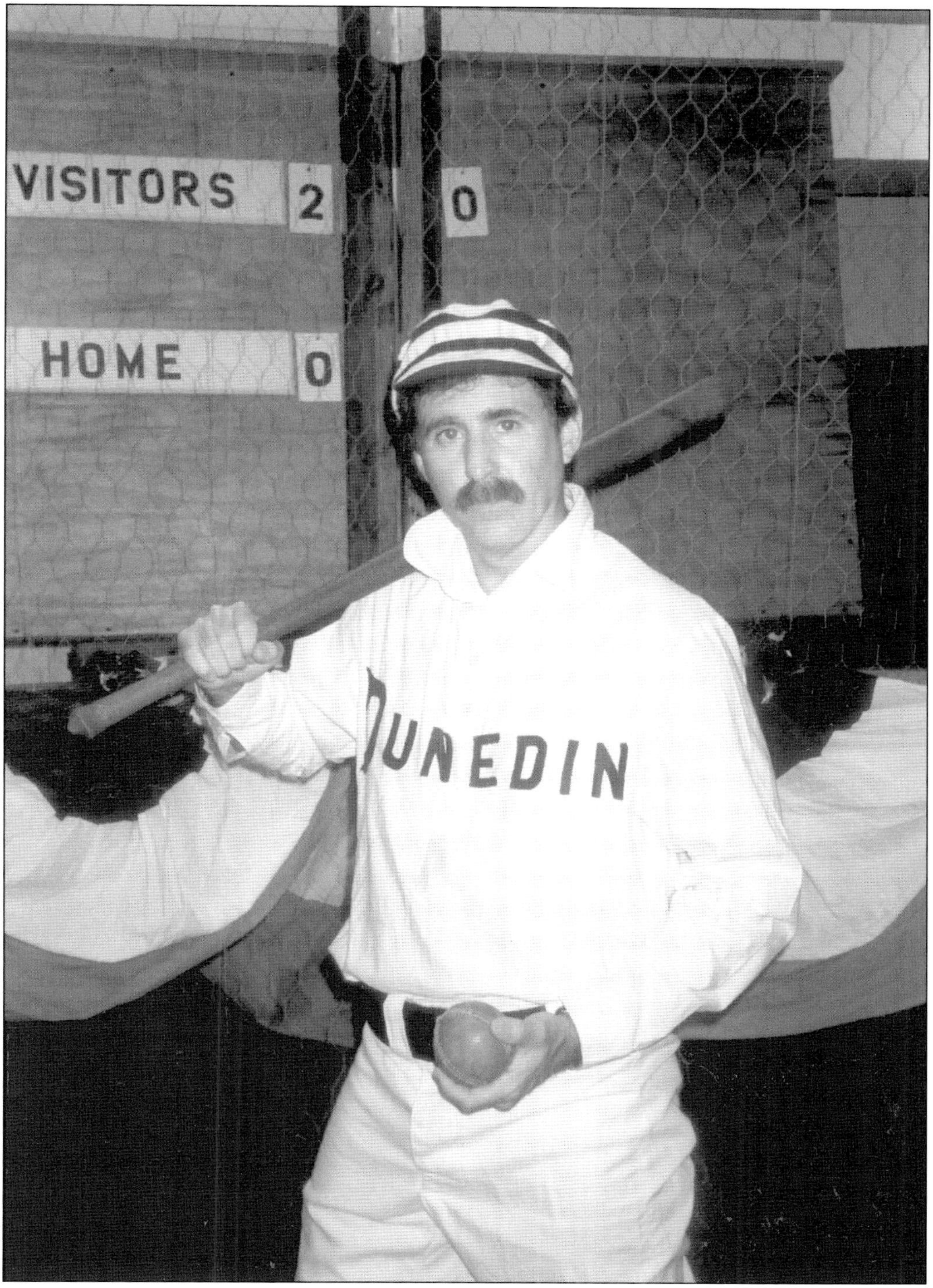

As the centennial of the Spanish-American War approached in 1998, many local baseball enthusiasts created a vintage baseball league. Teams from the turn of the century were recreated; here is a member of the Dunedin Railers. (Photo by the author.)

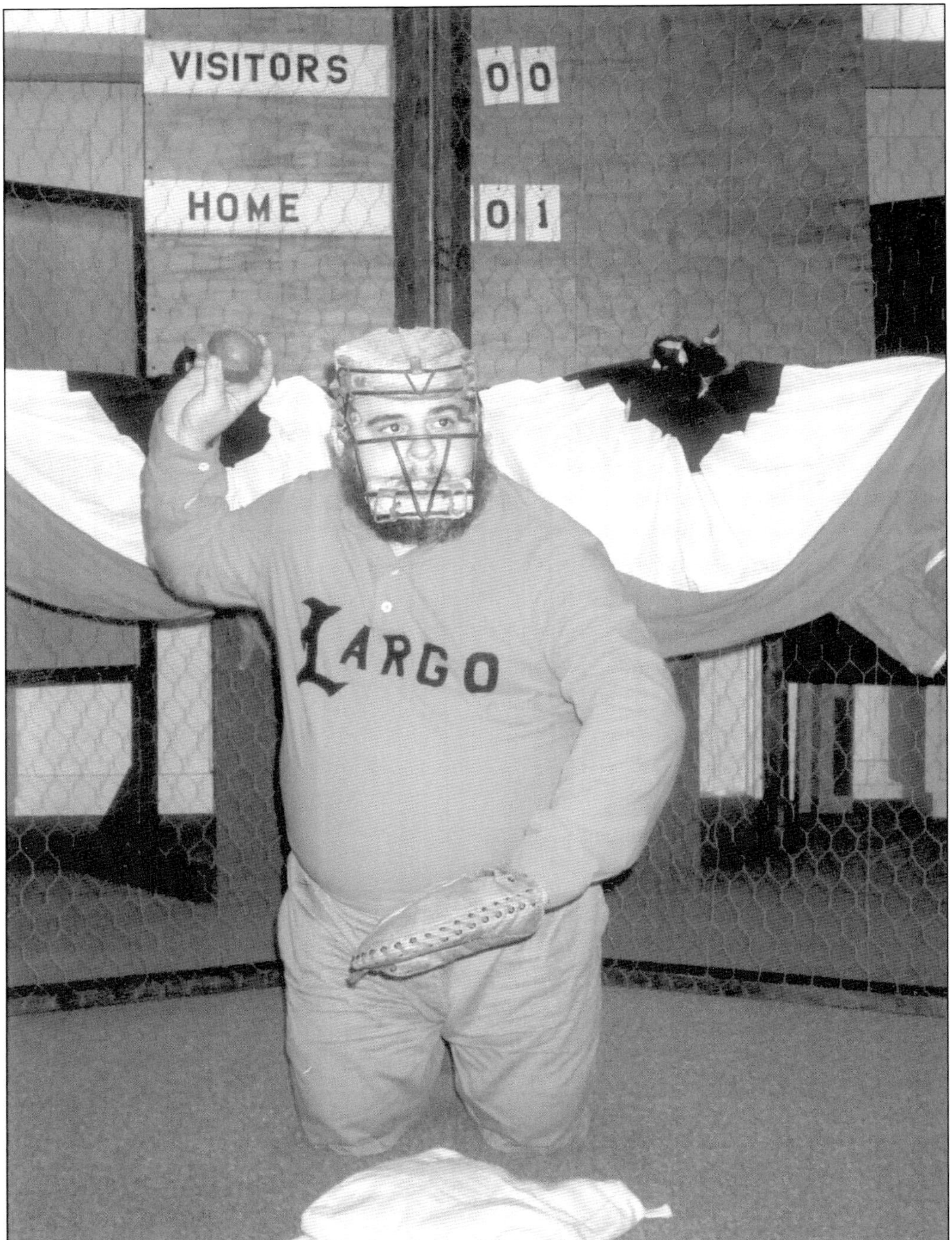

Many 19th-century baseball rules were reinstated in the game, such as the rule that a ball could bounce before home plate and still be called a strike and that there was no leading off the base, so stealing head first was standard. Other peculiar rules included ones that said that a batter could request a special pitch and that spitballs, dirtballs, and others were legal! Here, a member of the Largo Crackers throws a ball. (Photo by the author.)

Seven

BALL PARKS

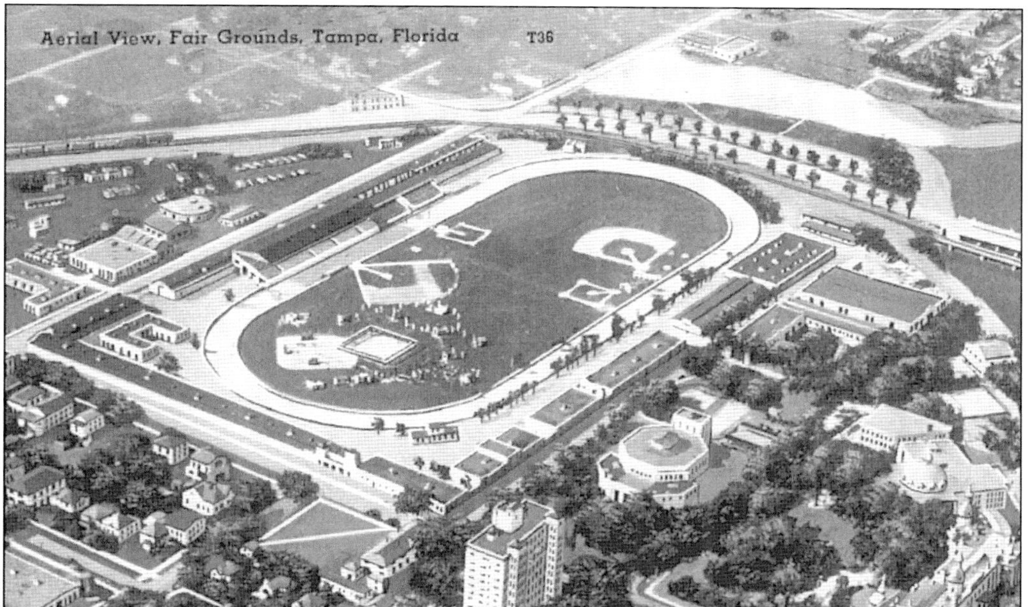

This is an aerial view of Plant Field as it appeared in the 1940s. Until the late 1970s, the field and surrounding buildings were the site for the Florida State Fair. After 1932, the nearby old Tampa Bay Hotel was converted into a college—The University of Tampa. (Courtesy of ADEQ Historical Resources.)

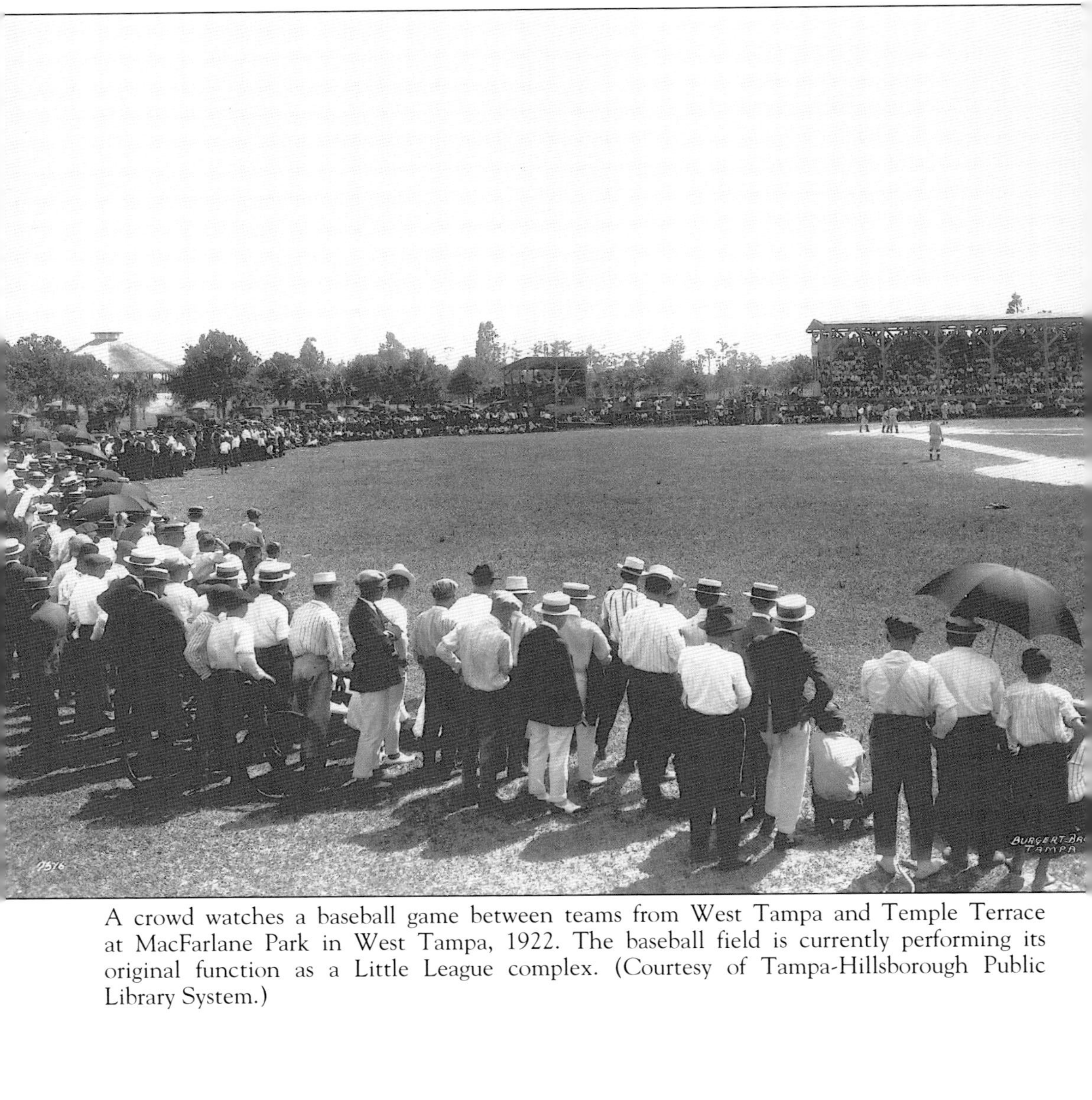

A crowd watches a baseball game between teams from West Tampa and Temple Terrace at MacFarlane Park in West Tampa, 1922. The baseball field is currently performing its original function as a Little League complex. (Courtesy of Tampa-Hillsborough Public Library System.)

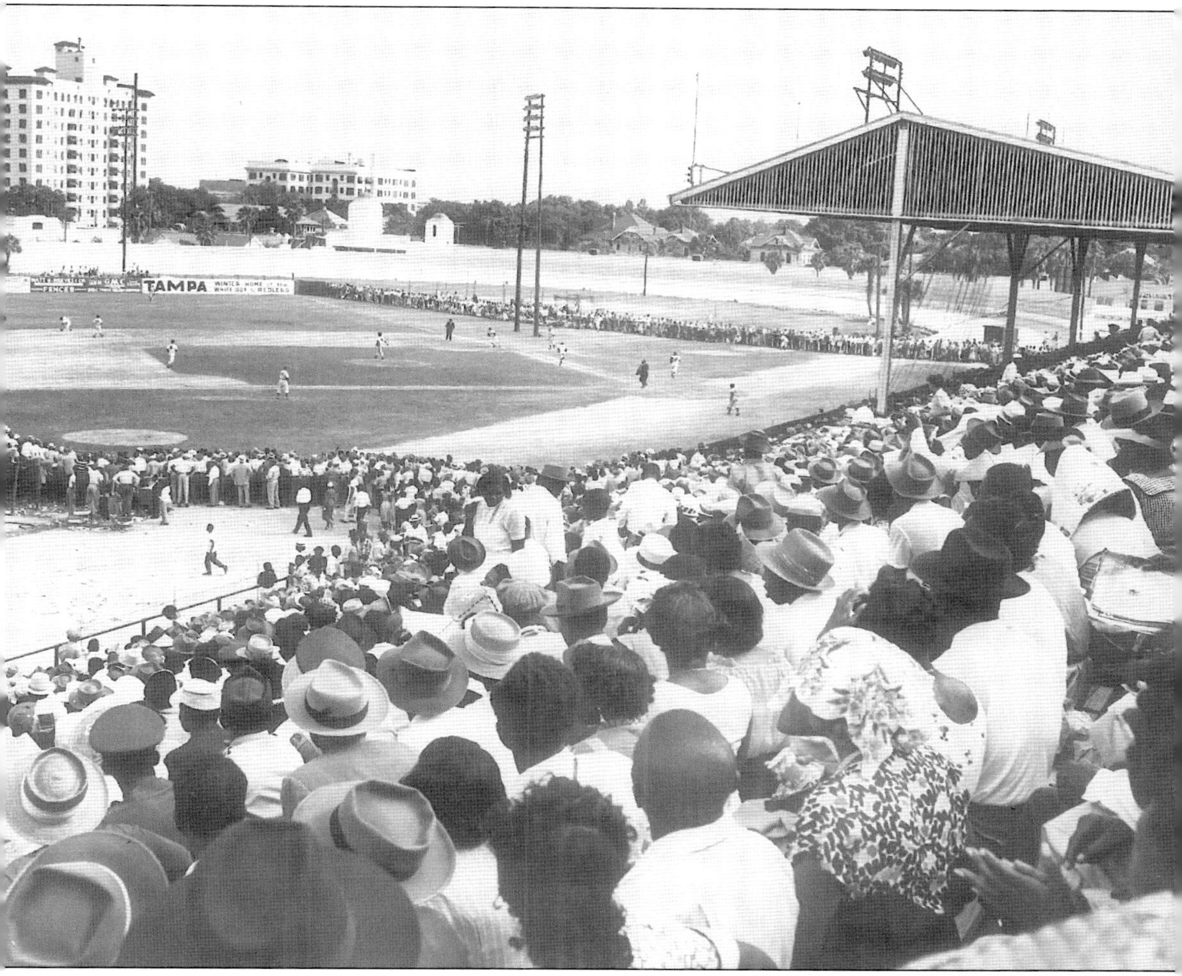

Crowds watch a game between the Dodgers and the Chicago White Sox at Plant Field on March 28, 1954. Note that the uncovered stands were reserved for African Americans and were referred as the "Colored Section." These fans' white counterparts were in the covered section, where they were protected from the elements, including the harsh Florida sun and rainstorms. In the days before desegregation and equal rights, many African Americans had to make do with what was provided. (Courtesy of Tampa-Hillsborough Public Library System.)

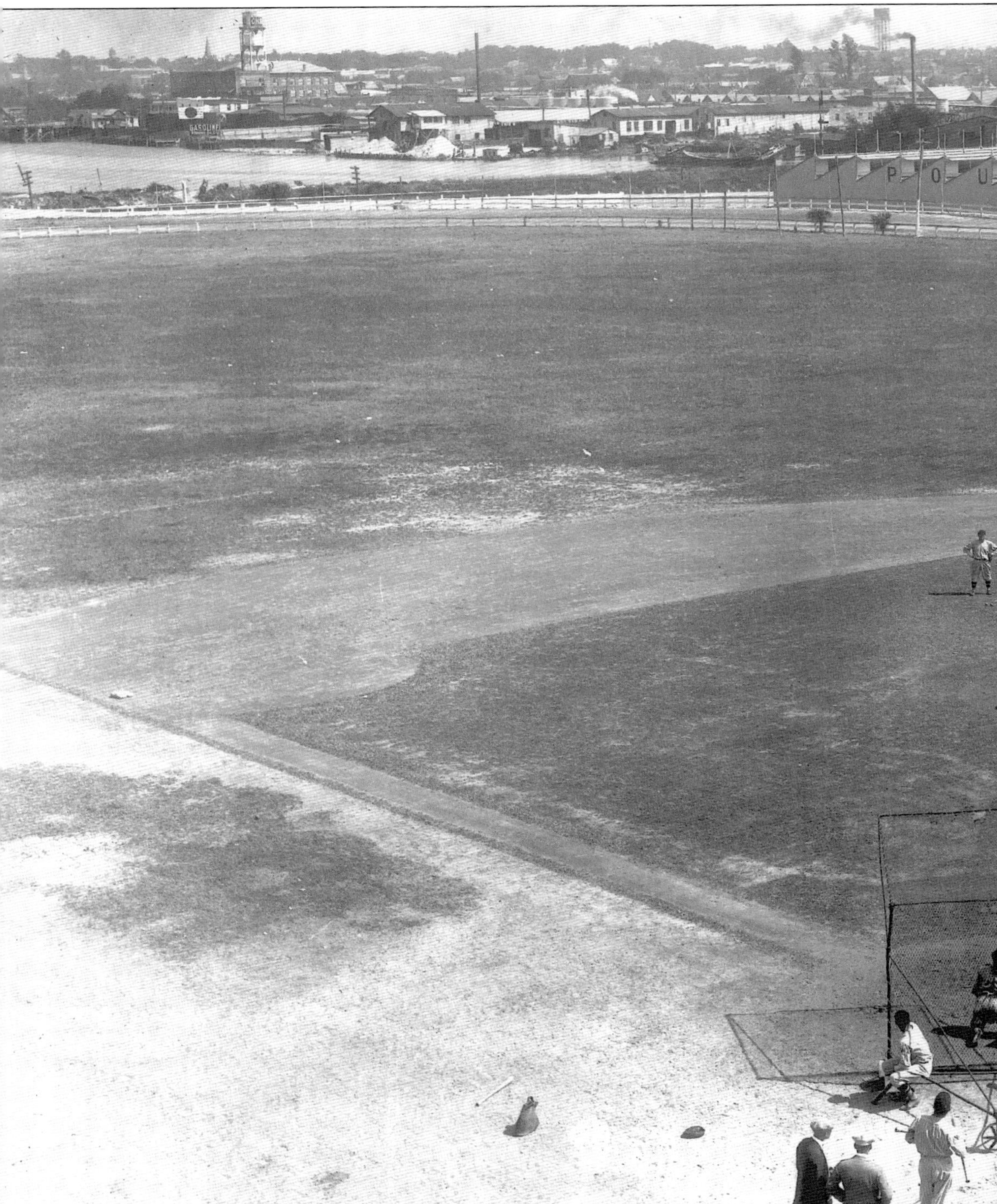

Plant Field is one of the oldest fields in Tampa. Major league teams began using the site as early as 1913 with the arrival of the Reds and, later, with the arrival of the Senators in 1920. Here,

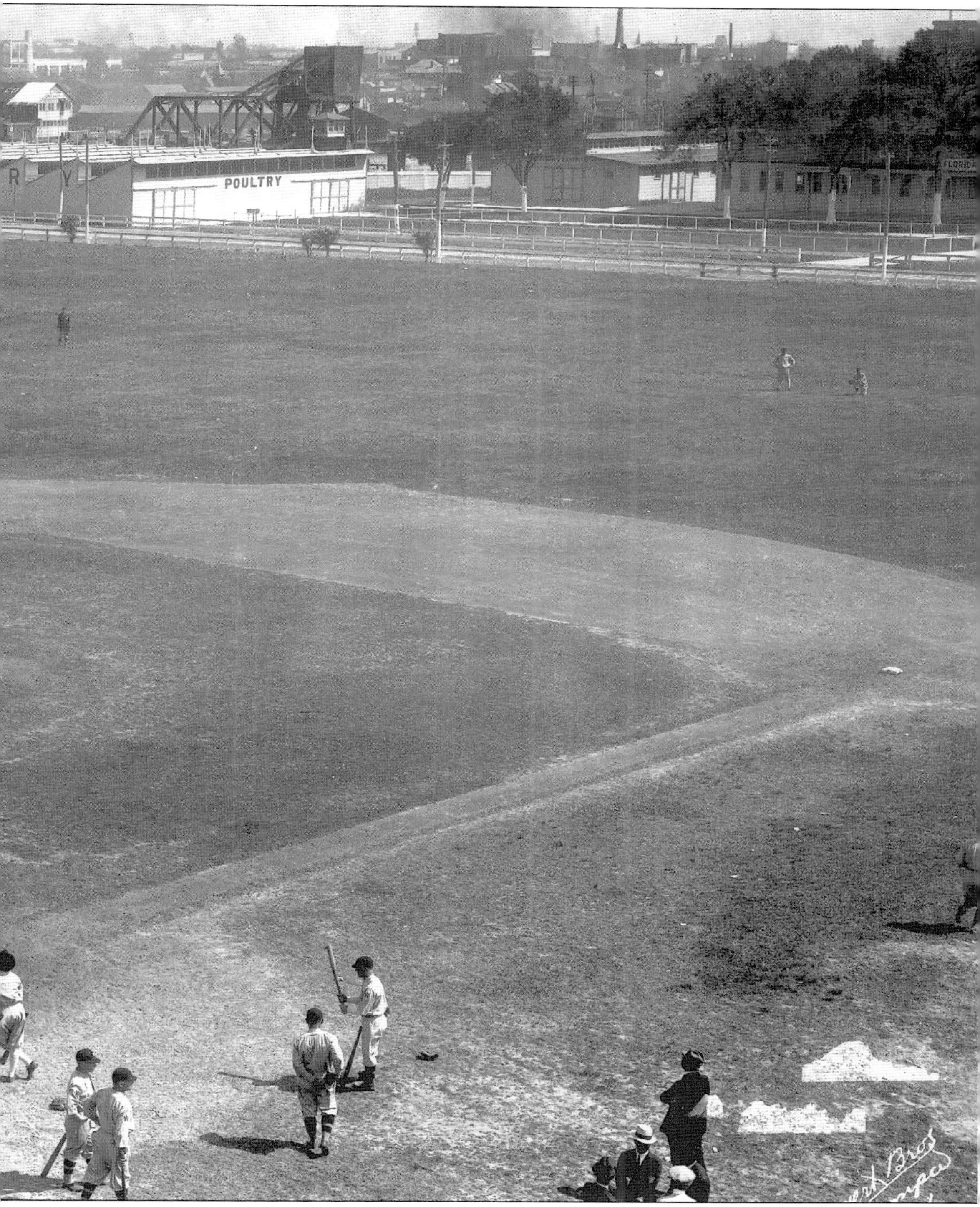

the Washington Senators are seen playing a game during spring training on March 18, 1923. (Courtesy of Tampa-Hillsborough Public Library System)

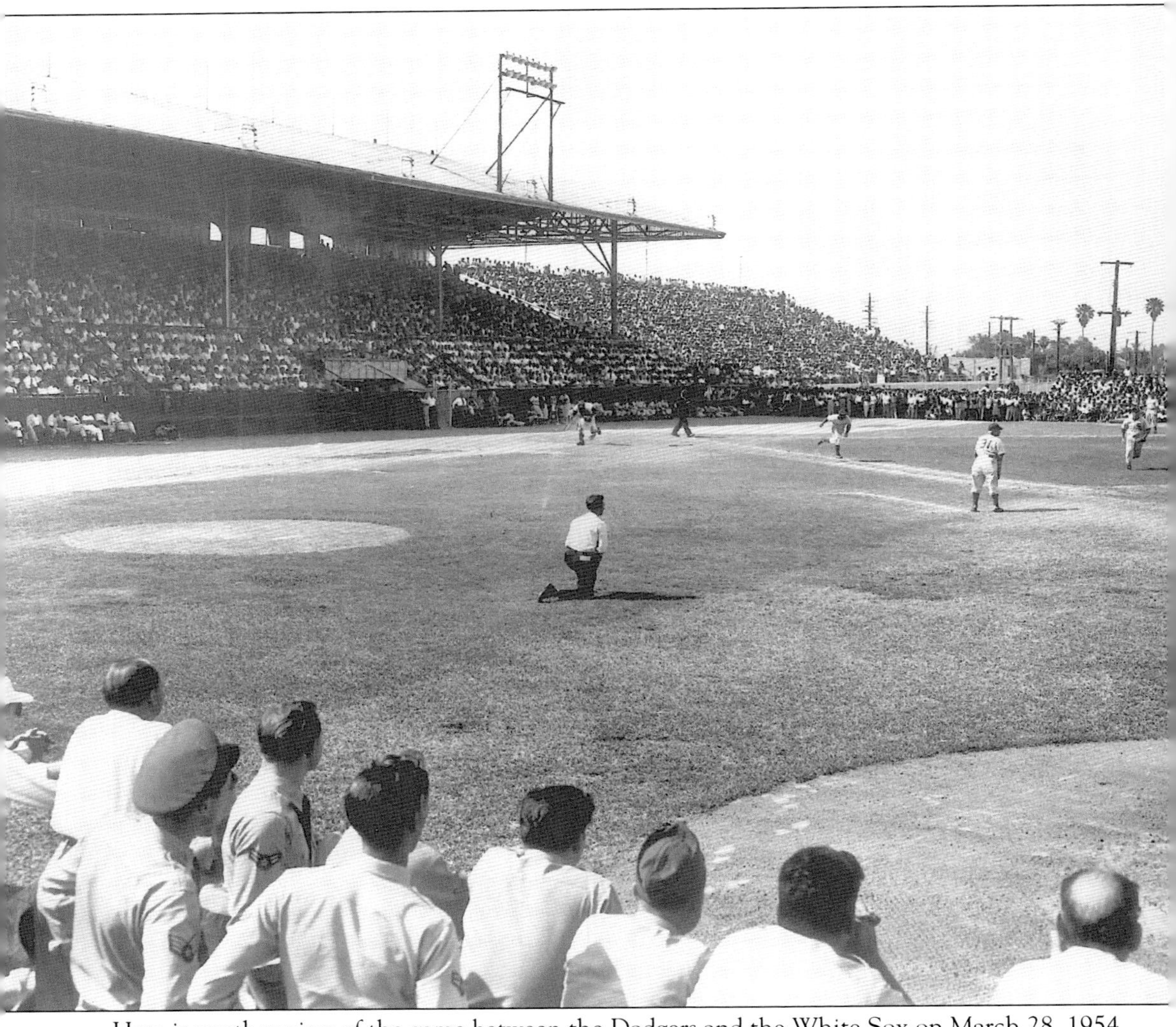

Here is another view of the game between the Dodgers and the White Sox on March 28, 1954. Note the difference between the white and "colored" sections on the stands at Plant Field. The best view of the game was definitely reserved for the privileged white spectators. (Courtesy of Tampa-Hillsborough Public Library System.)

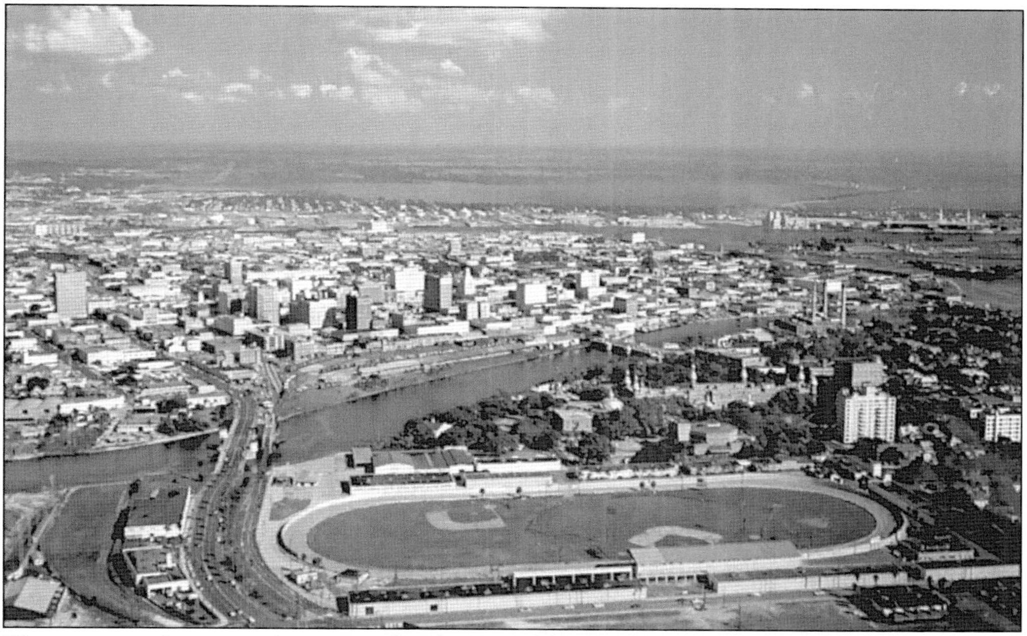

This is another aerial view of Plant Field in the 1960s. (Courtesy of ADEQ Historical Resources.)

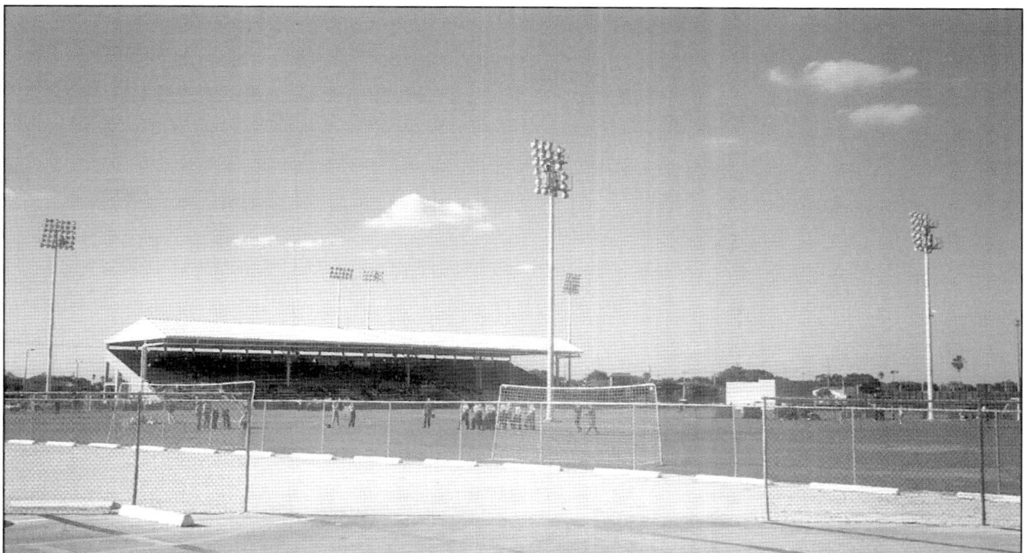

Plant Field is seen here as it appeared in 1999. The area is now known as Pepin-Rude Stadium and is a part of the University of Tampa. (Photo by the author.)

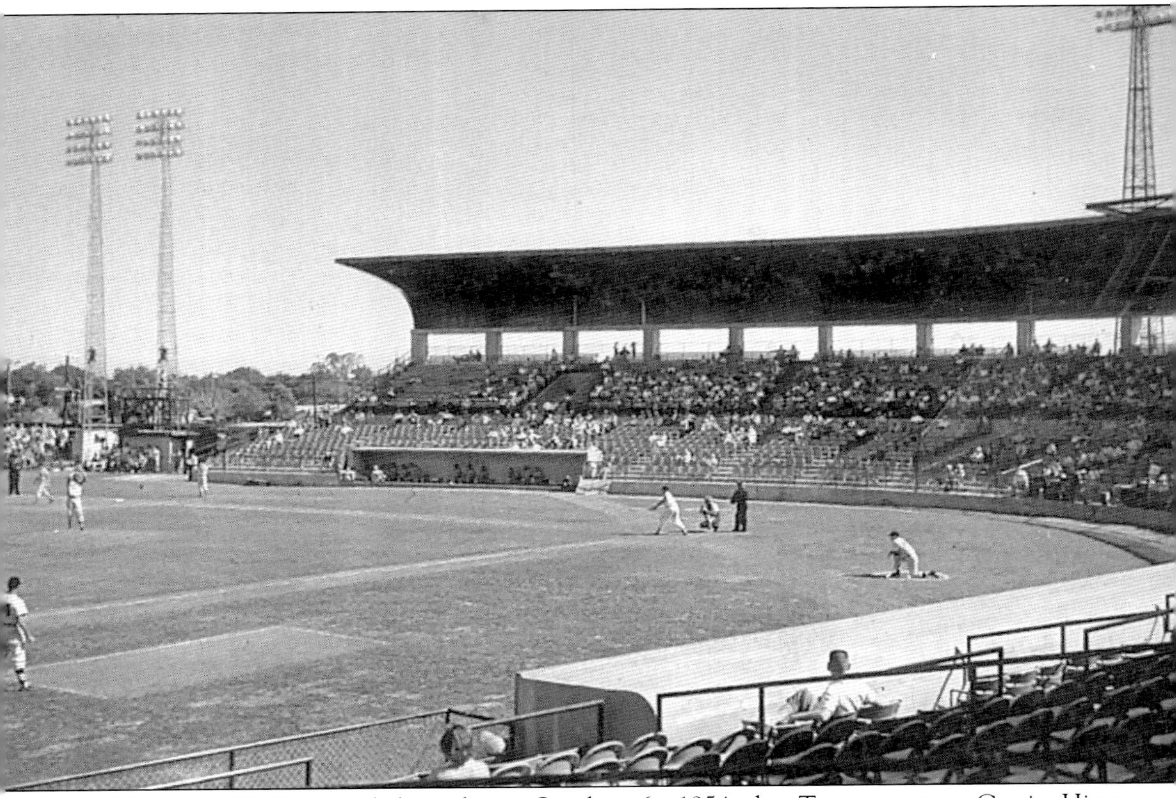

Al Lopez Field was dedicated on October 6, 1954, by Tampa mayor Curtis Hixon in honor of Lopez's baseball feats. The stadium was the spring training home of the Cincinnati Reds and their minor league affiliate, the Tampa Tarpons, until 1987. (Courtesy of ADEQ Historical Resources.)

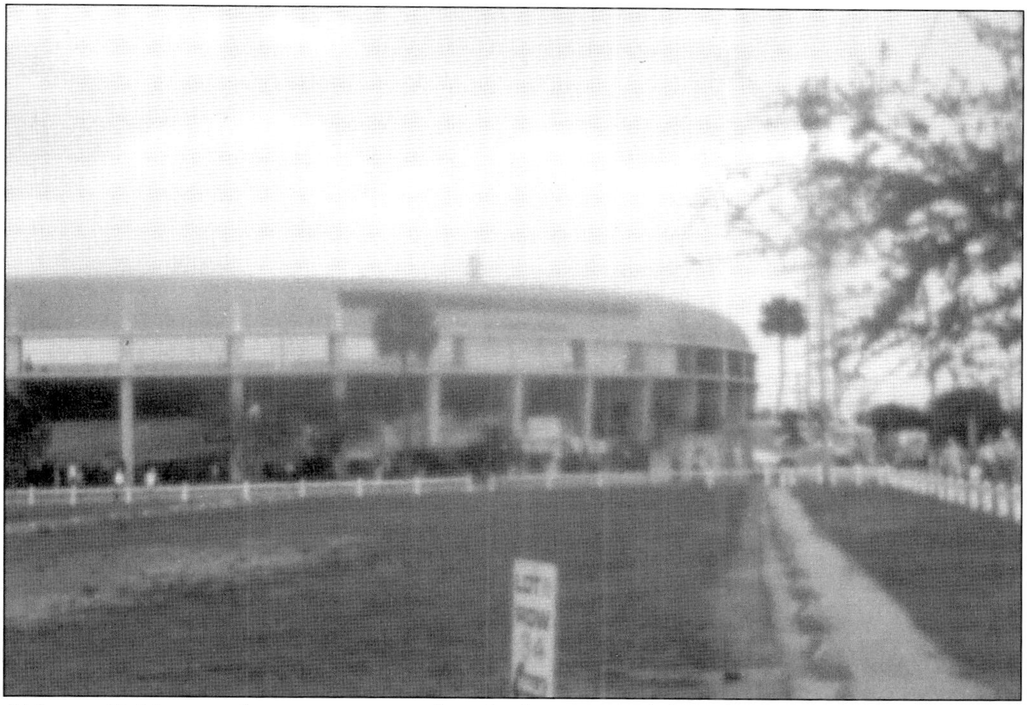

Al Lopez Field is seen here as it appeared in the late 1970s. (Photo by the author.)

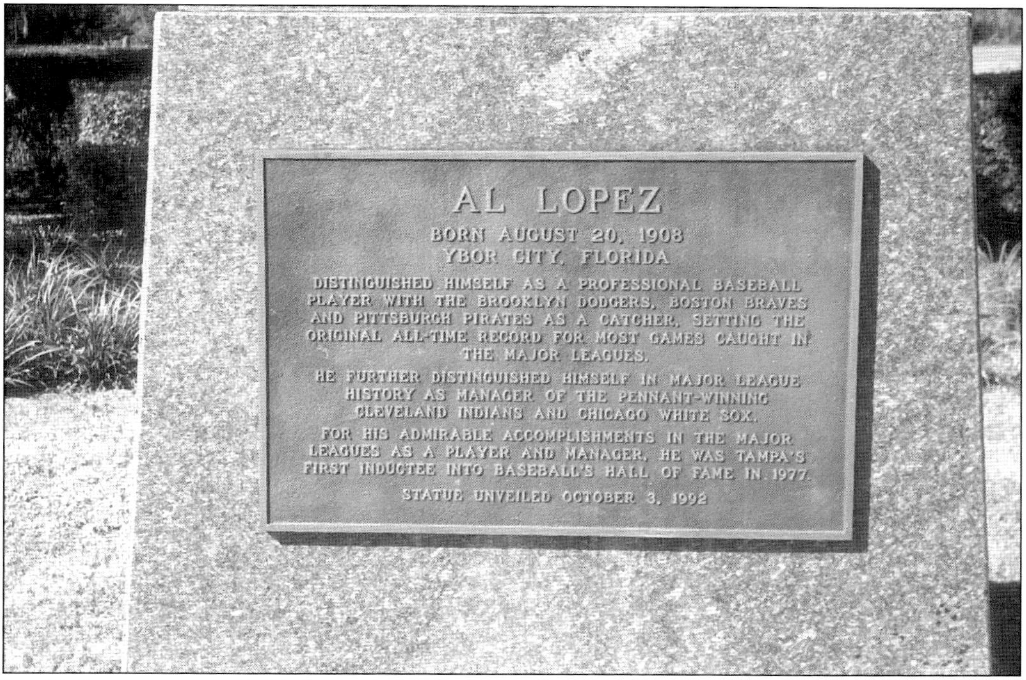

In 1992, a statue of Al Lopez was unveiled not far from the old ballpark that once bore his name. This is a close-up view of the dedication plaque of the Al Lopez statue. (Photo by the author.)

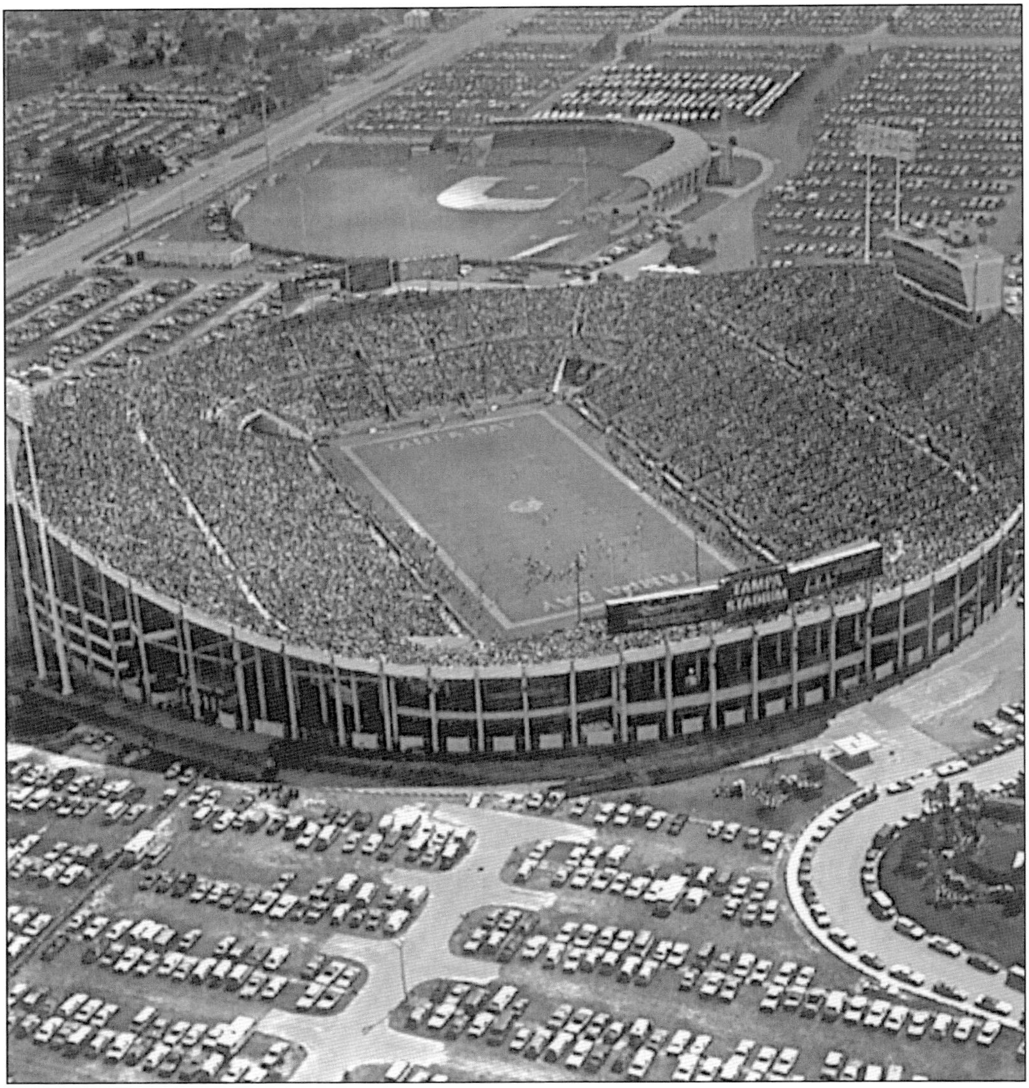

Tampa Stadium was later built next to Al Lopez Field. When the Reds departed Tampa for Plant City in 1987, the baseball field was razed to the ground two years later. Tampa Stadium also shared a similar fate; after hosting two Super Bowls, the stadium was razed in 1999. This aerial photograph dates to about 1980. (Courtesy of ADEQ Historical Resources.)

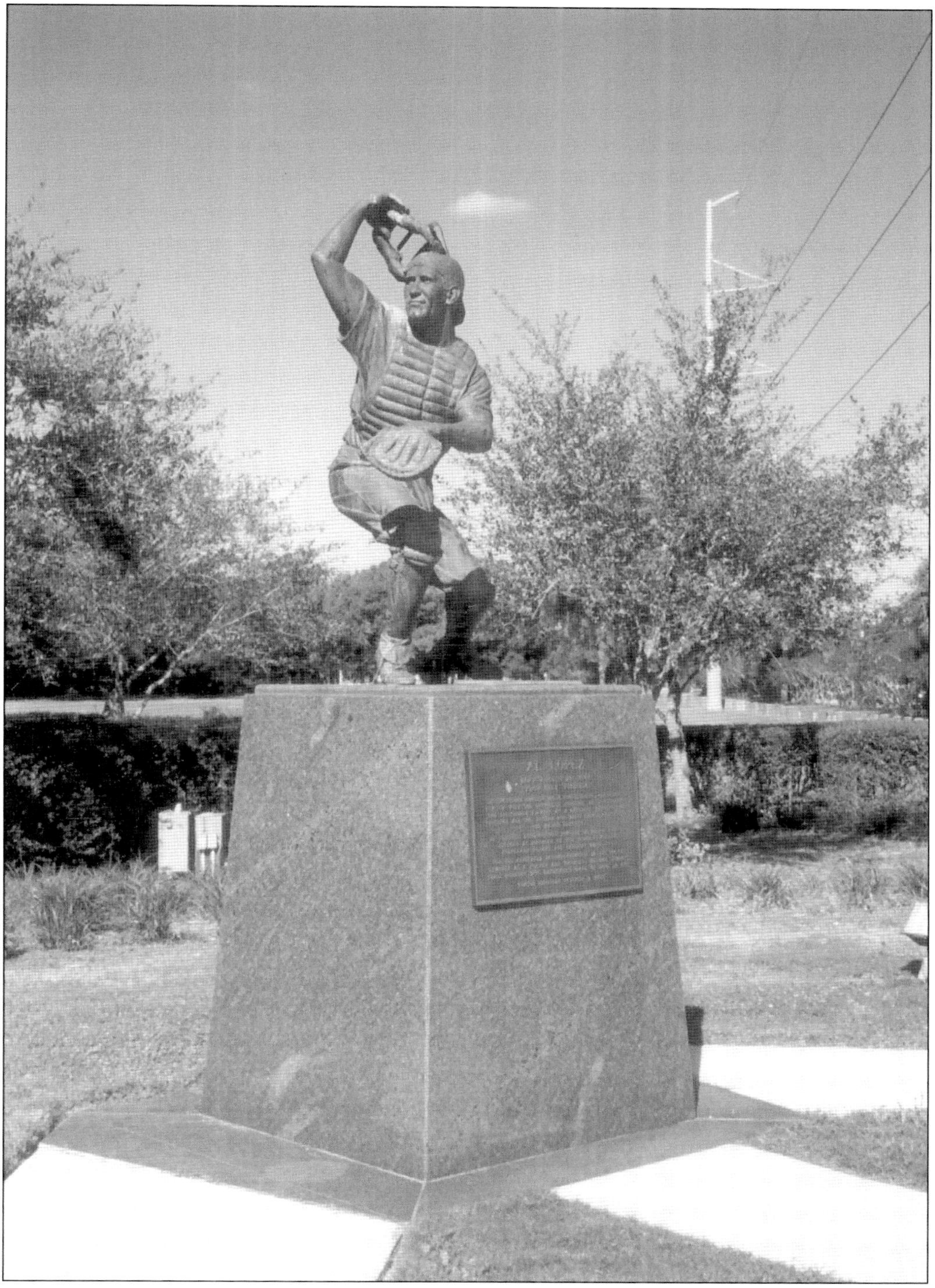

In 1992, a statue of Al Lopez was unveiled not far from the old ballpark that once bore his name. A nearby city park off Himes Avenue was renamed Al Lopez Park in his honor. (Photo by the author.)

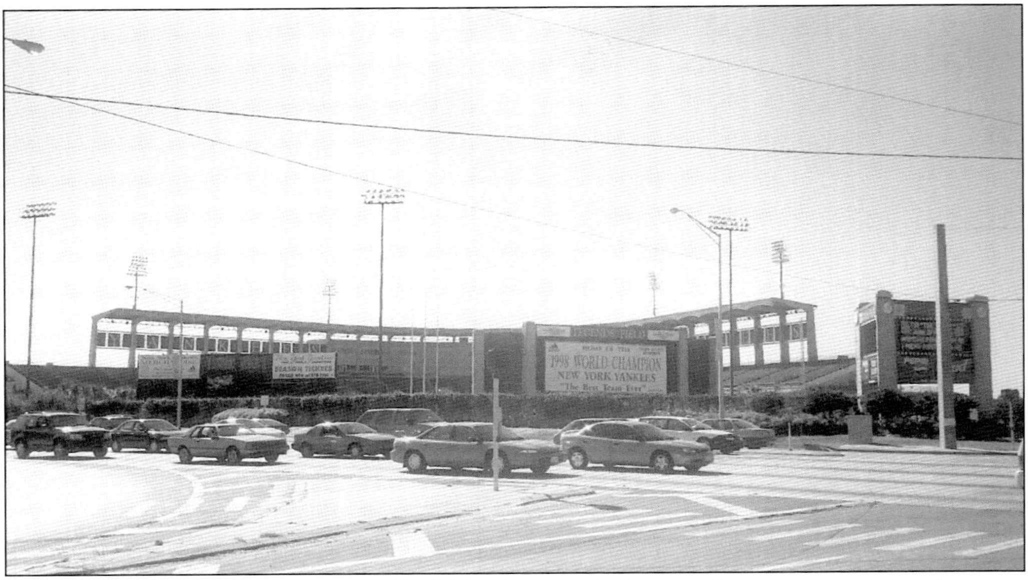

When George Steinbrenner's New York Yankees made Tampa their spring training home in 1996, Legends Field was constructed to fit their needs. Located across the street from where Al Lopez Field once stood on Dale Mabry Highway, the stadium is also home to the Tampa Yankees. (Photo by the author.)

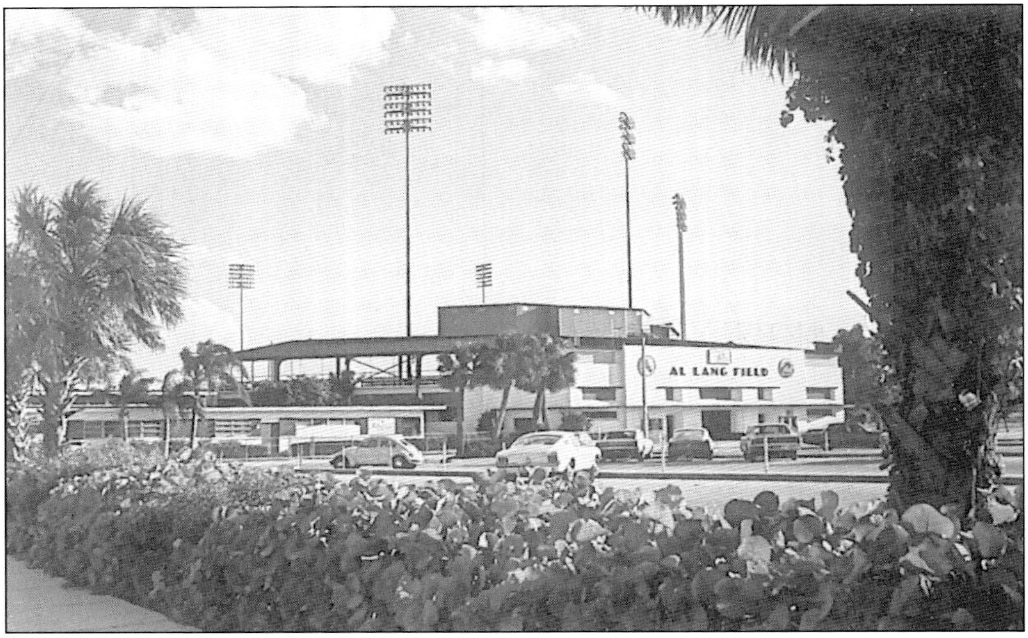

In St. Petersburg, Al Lang Field was the spring training home for the St. Louis Cardinals (1946–1997) and the New York Mets (1962–1987). When the city received a new baseball franchise, the Cardinals vacated to make room for the St. Petersburg Devil Rays, a minor league farm team of the Tampa Bay Devil Rays in 1997. (Courtesy of ADEQ Historical Resources.)

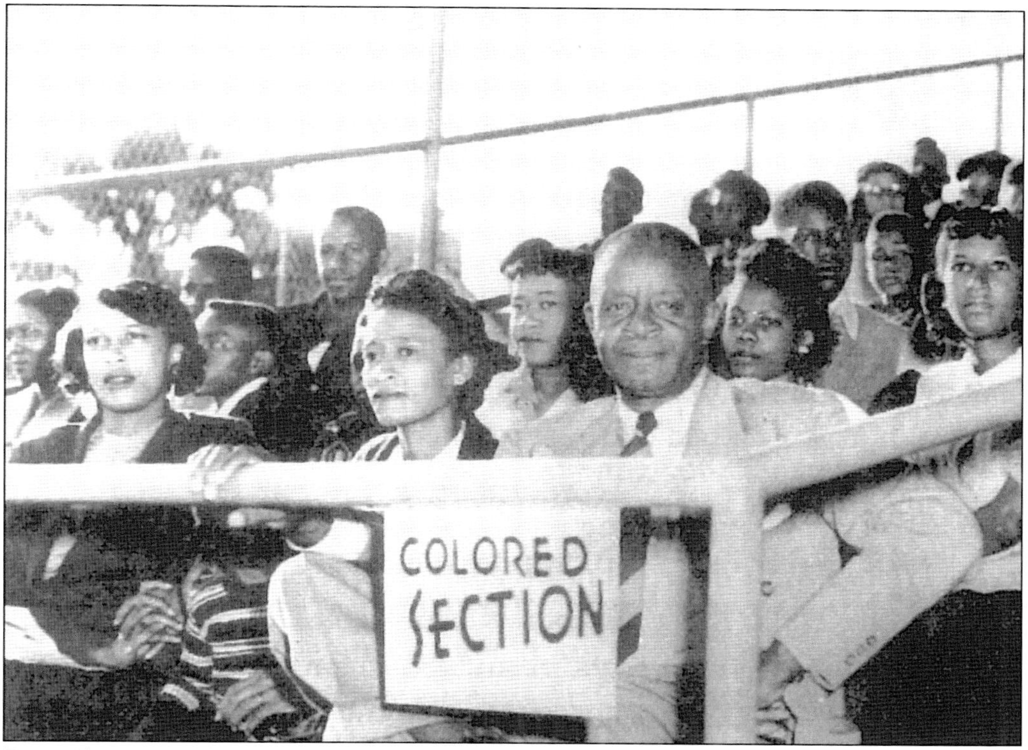

Even Al Lang Field was fitted with a segregated section for "colored" fans, as evidenced in this 1953 photograph. (Courtesy of Pinellas County Historical Museum.)

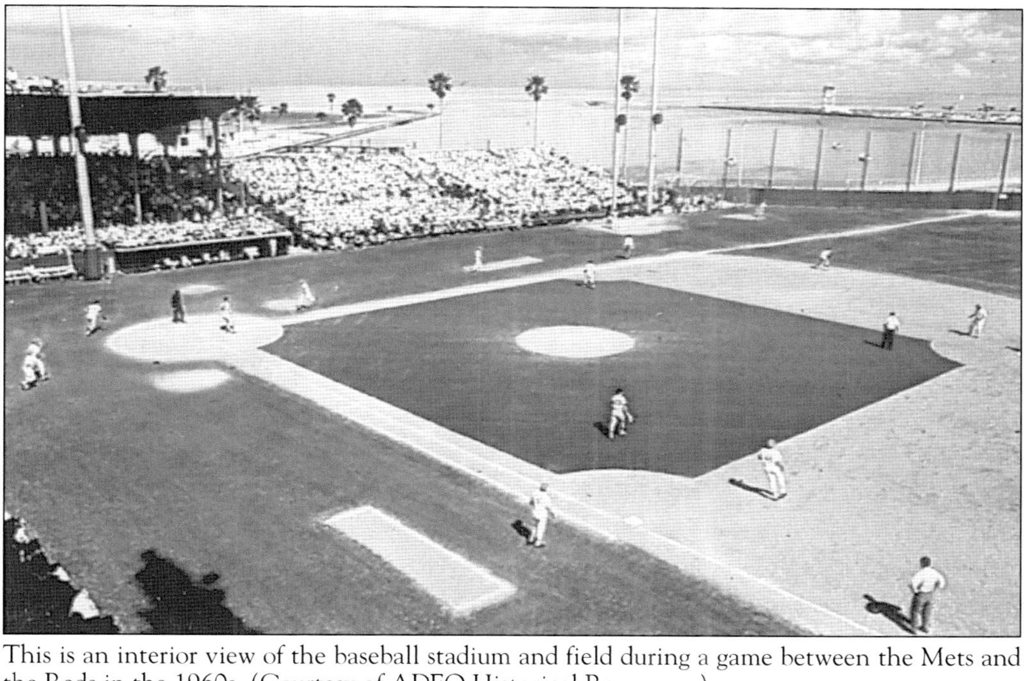

This is an interior view of the baseball stadium and field during a game between the Mets and the Reds in the 1960s. (Courtesy of ADEQ Historical Resources.)

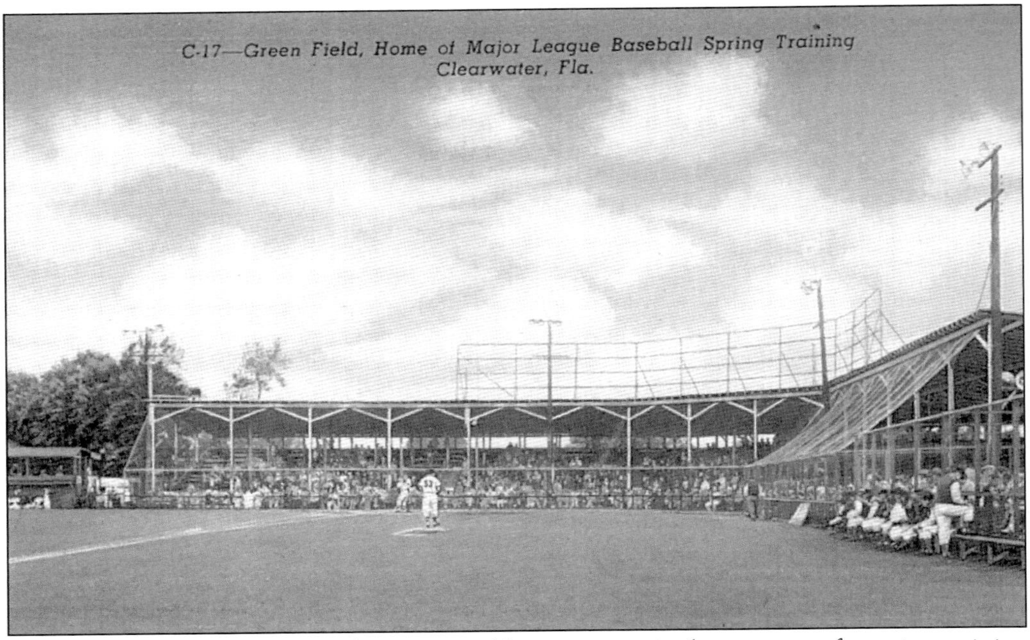

Green Field in Clearwater was also a site used by various major league teams for spring training in the 1930s and 1940s. Clearwater was home to such teams as the Dodgers (1923–1932, 1936–1940), the Indians (1942, 1946), and the Phillies (1947–present). (Courtesy of ADEQ Historical Resources.)

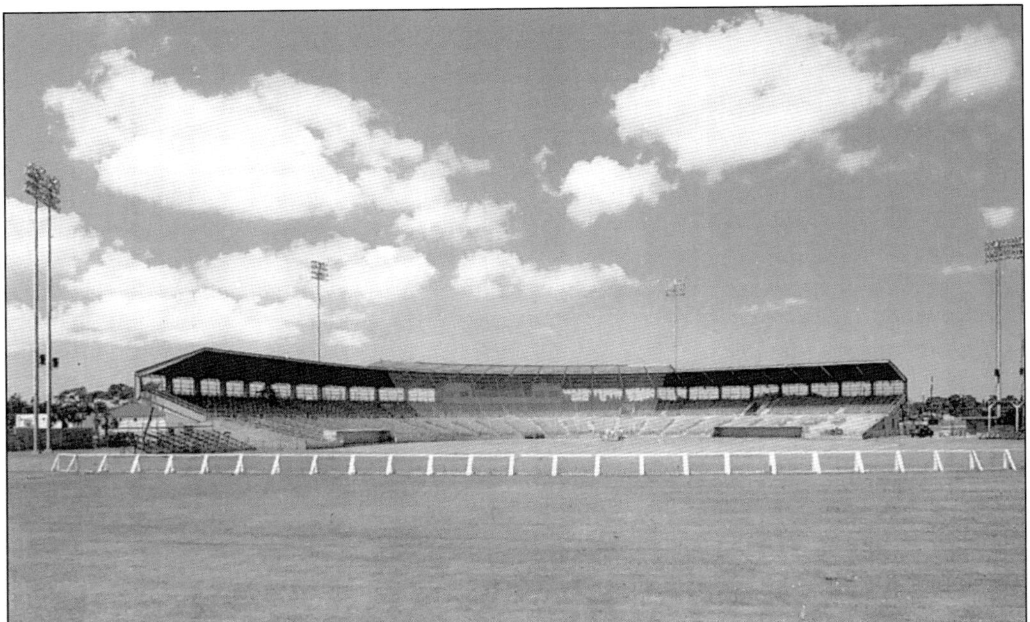

Jack Russell Stadium was later built to become the Clearwater home of the champion Bomber softball team and the spring training headquarters for the Philadelphia Phillies, c. 1960s. (Courtesy of ADEQ Historical Resources.)

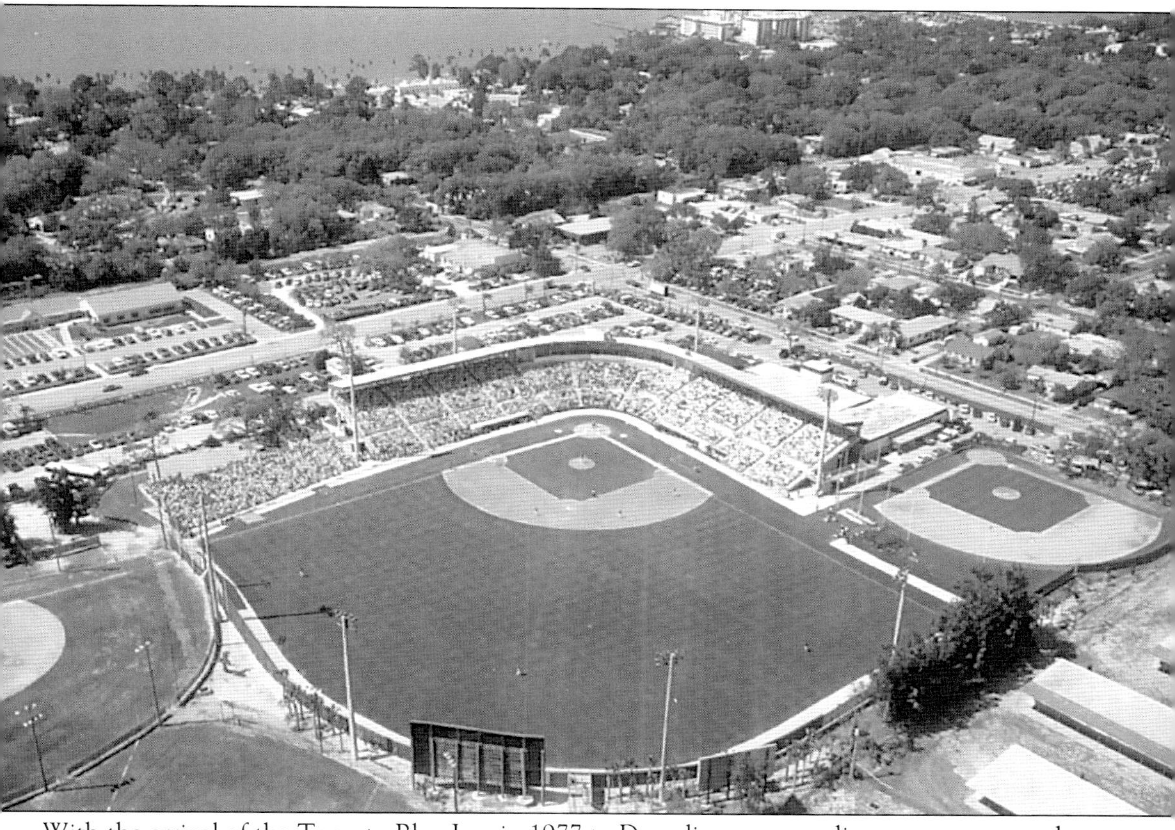

With the arrival of the Toronto Blue Jays in 1977 to Dunedin, a new stadium was constructed on old Grant Field to accommodate the team. The field is also home for the Dunedin Blue Jays, a Class A farm club. (Courtesy of ADEQ Historical Resources.)

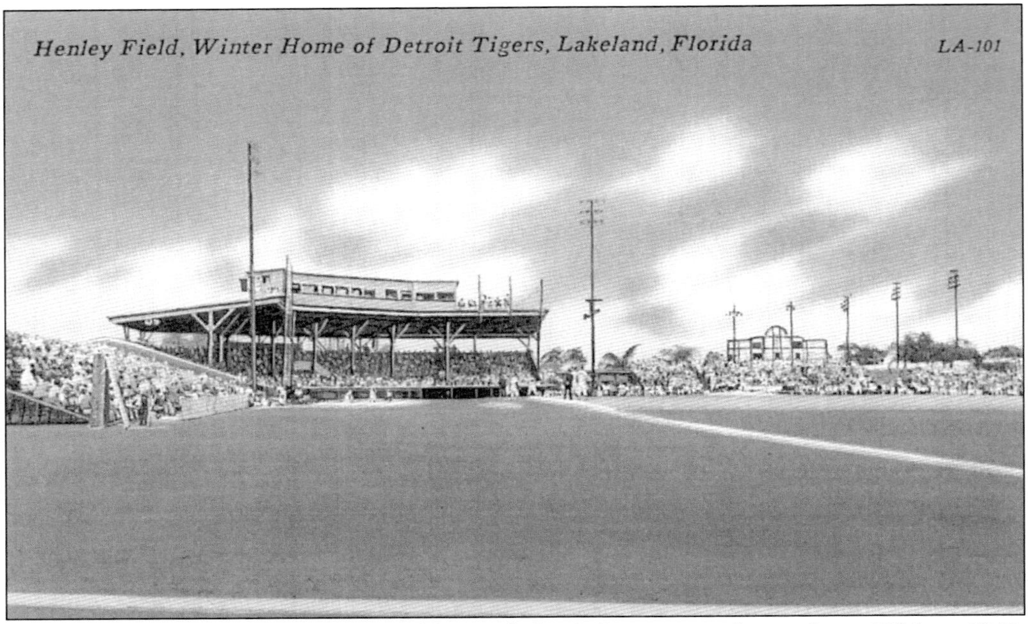

The Detroit Tigers made Henley Field in Lakeland their winter home from 1934 to 1942. (Courtesy of ADEQ Historical Resources.)

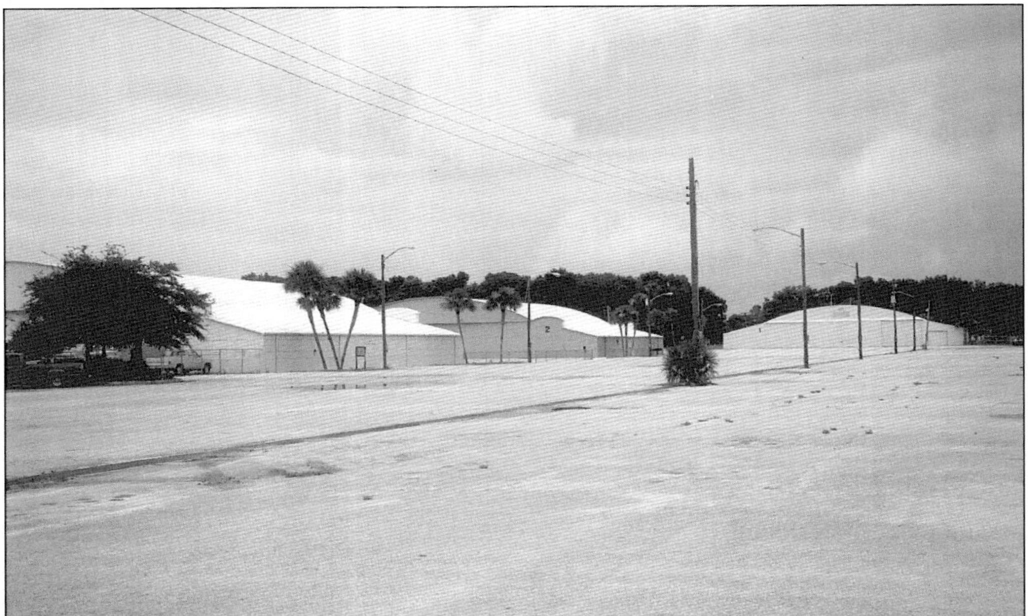

After World War II, the Tigers returned to Lakeland in 1946. The team moved in to an old airfield that was once the Lodwick School of Aeronautics. The school trained American and British airmen to fly during the days of the Second World War. On the corner of the field, the Tigers built a stadium. Seen here, in 1995, are some of the remaining hangars still being used by the Lakeland Parks and Recreation Department for exhibition or club events. (Photo by the author.)

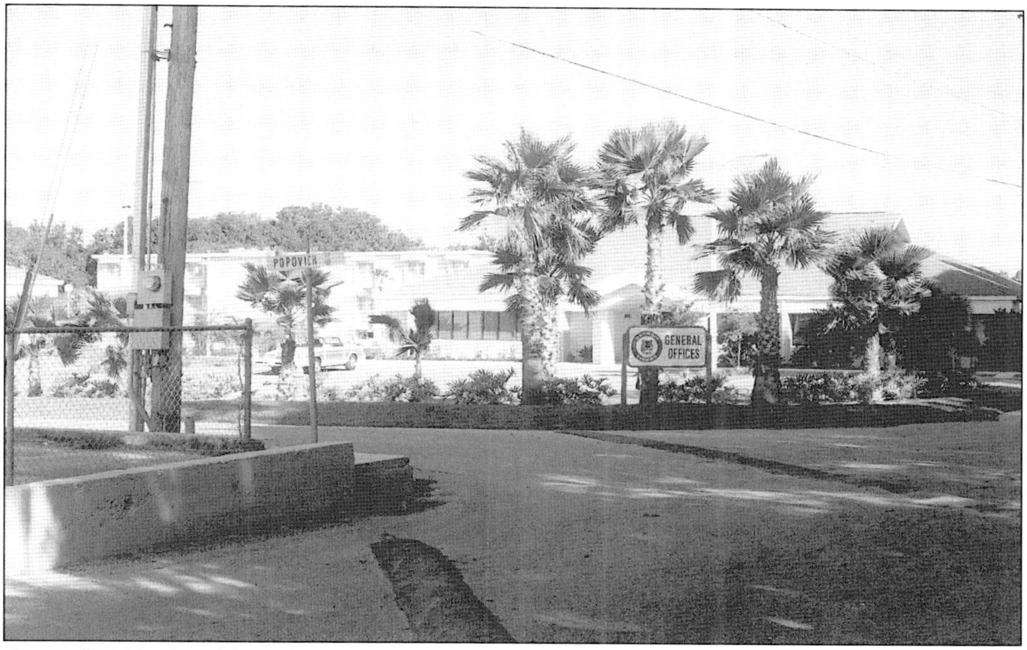

Around 1993, the old art deco-style mess hall of Lodwick Field was torn down to make way for the new general offices of the Detroit Tigers. The baseball team shares the site with the city of Lakeland. (Photo by the author.)

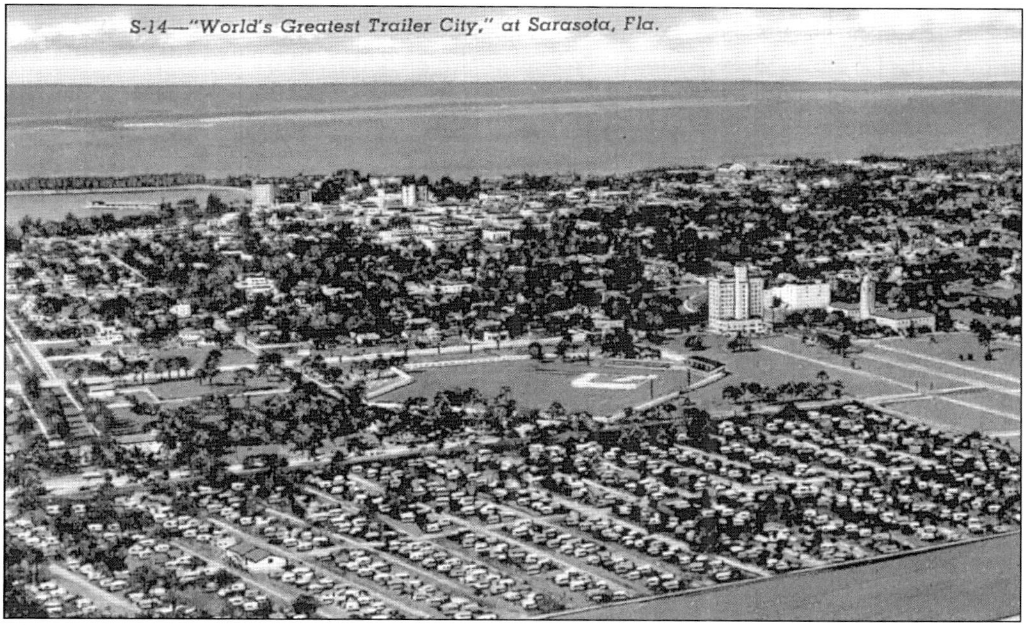

This aerial view of Payne Park in Sarasota shows the park as it appeared in the 1930s and 1940s. The Boston Red Sox made Sarasota their winter home from 1933 to 1942 and from 1946 to 1958. The Chicago White Sox came to the city in 1960 and still make an appearance there every season. Two other teams temporarily in town were the Giants (1924–1927) and the Orioles (1989–1993). (Courtesy of ADEQ Historical Resources.)

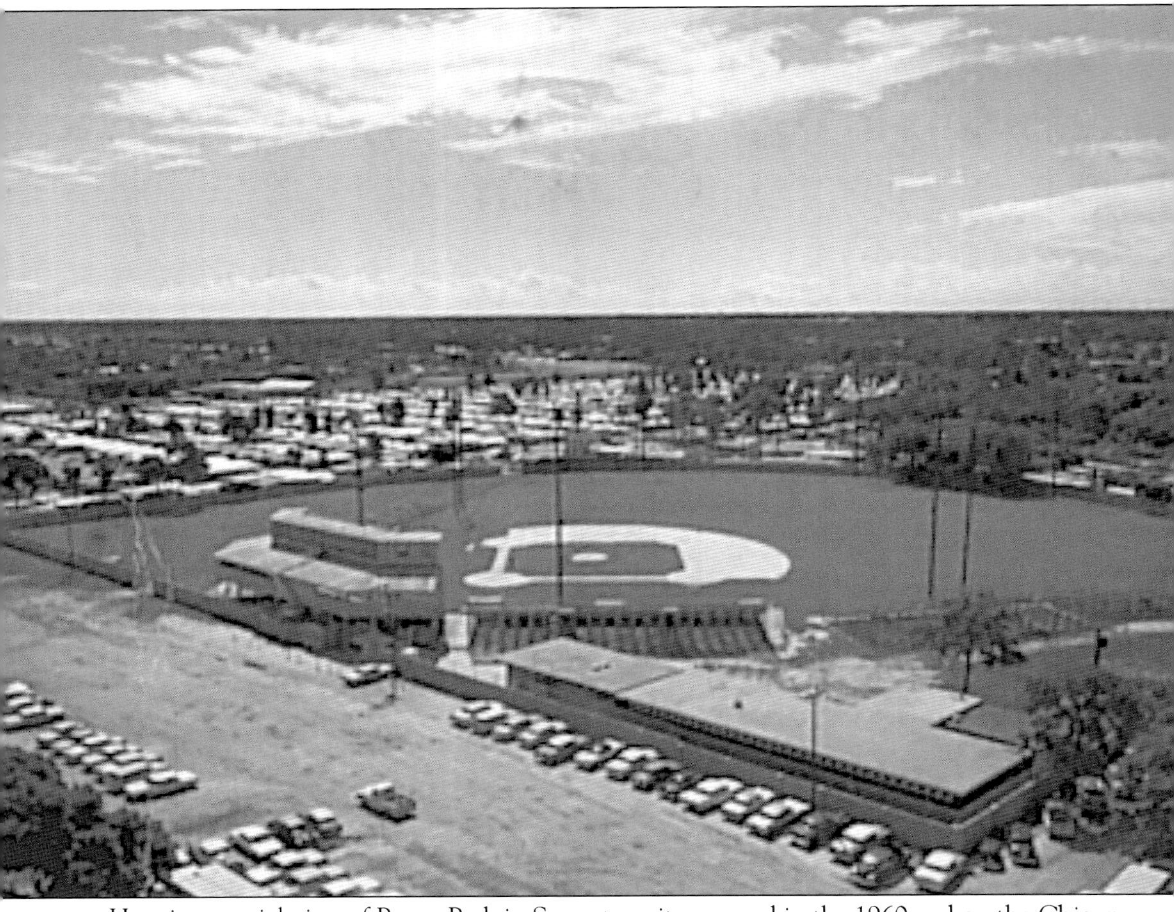

Here is an aerial view of Payne Park in Sarasota as it appeared in the 1960s, when the Chicago White Sox were training there. (Courtesy of ADEQ Historical Resources.)

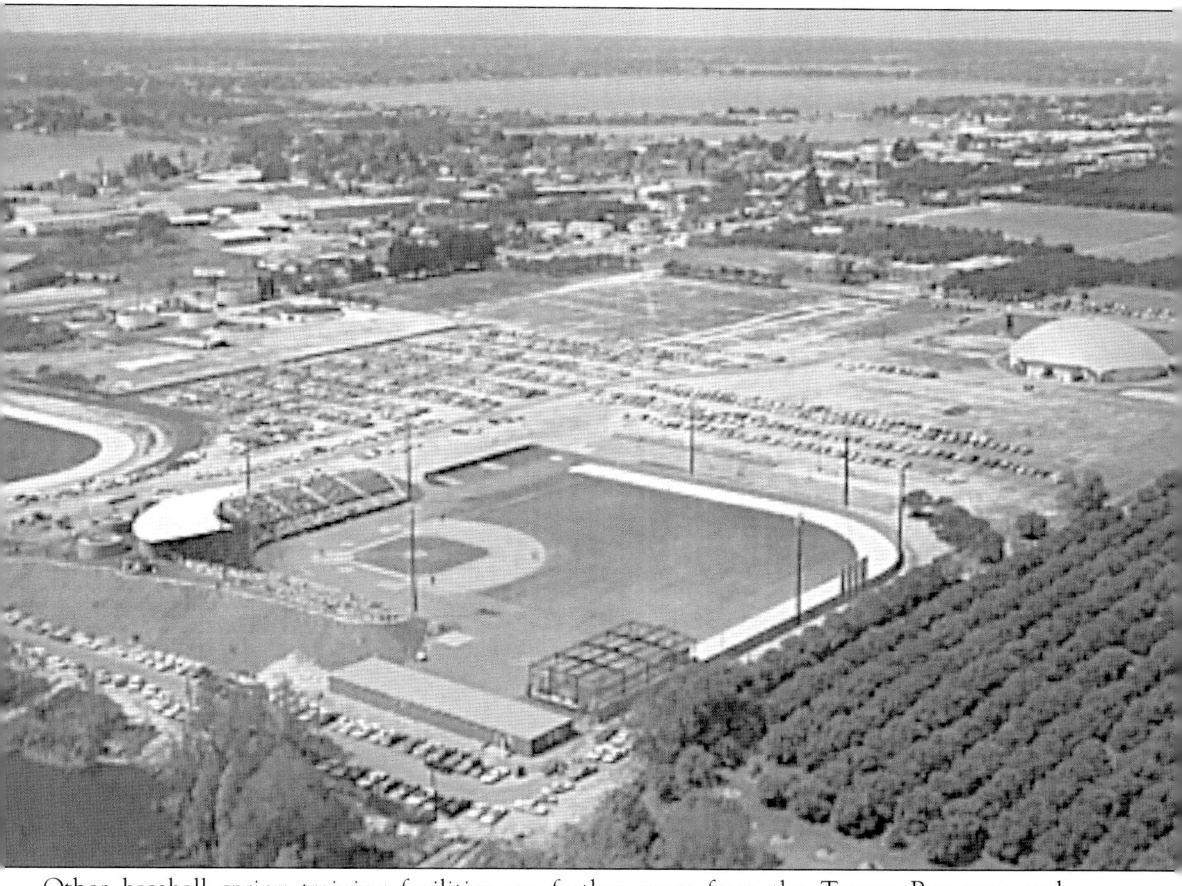

Other baseball spring training facilities are further away from the Tampa Bay area and are scattered from Cocoa Beach to West Palm Beach. Seen here is the Winter Haven training base for the Boston Red Sox, who trained there from 1966 to 1992. (Courtesy of ADEQ Historical Resources.)

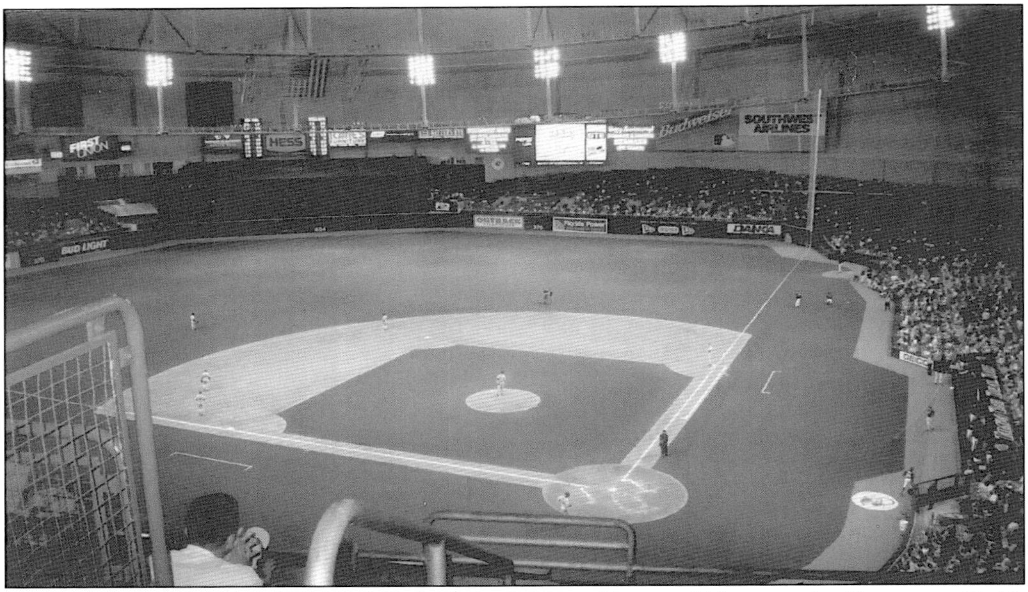

The gem of all baseball fields and stadiums in Tampa Bay would have to be Tropicana Field, formerly the Thunderdome, in St. Petersburg. The field caters to Tampa Bay's first major league team, the Tampa Bay Devil Rays. (Photo by the author.)

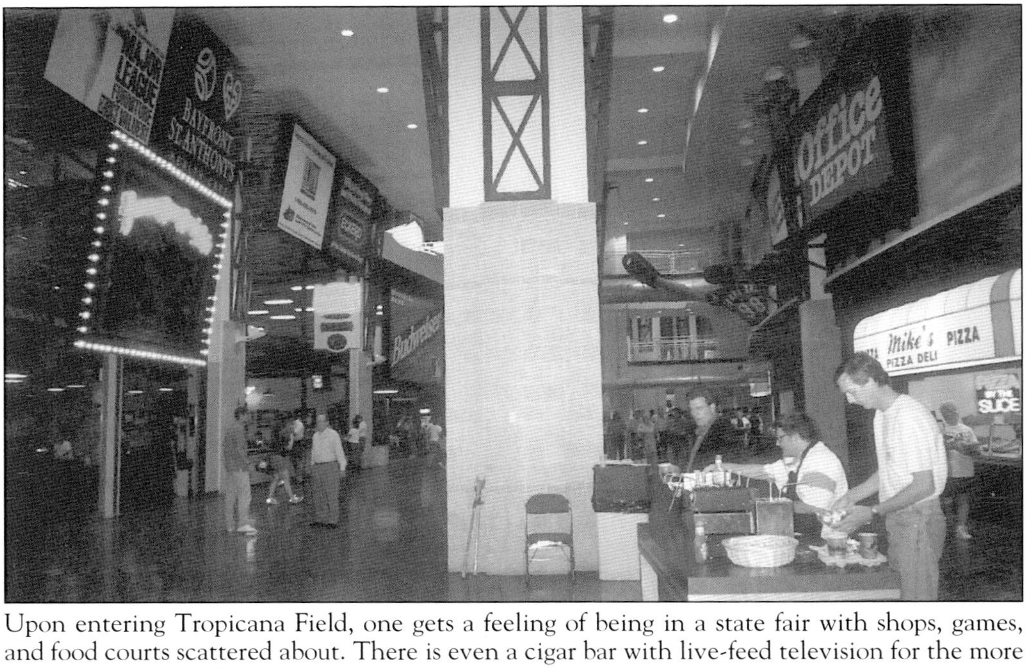

Upon entering Tropicana Field, one gets a feeling of being in a state fair with shops, games, and food courts scattered about. There is even a cigar bar with live-feed television for the more "sophisticated" baseball fan. After nearly a century of baseball history in the area, Tampa Bay finally made it to the big league! (Photo by the author.)